EVIL
Incarnate

DAVID FRANKFURTER

Rumors of

Demonic Conspiracy

and Ritual Abuse

in History

PRINCETON UNIVERSITY PRESS

PRINCETON AND OXFORD

Copyright © 2006 by Princeton University Press
Published by Princeton University Press, 41 William Street,
Princeton, New Jersey 08540
In the United Kingdom: Princeton University Press, 3 Market Place,
Woodstock, Oxfordshire OX20 1SY

Library of Congress Cataloging-in-Publication Data
Frankfurter, David, 1961–
Evil incarnate : rumors of demonic conspiracy and ritual abuse in history /
David Frankfurter.
p. cm.
Includes bibliographical references (p.   ) and index.
ISBN-13: 978-0-691-11350-0 (cloth : alk. paper)
ISBN-10: 0-691-11350-5 (cloth : alk. paper)
1. Demonology—Public opinion—History.   2. Conspiracies—Public
opinion—History.   3. Ritual abuse—Public opinion—History.   4. Good
and evil—Public opinion—History.   I. Title.
BF1543.F73 2006
133.4'2—dc22   2005044499

British Library Cataloging-in-Publication Data is available

This book has been composed in Goudy Olde Style Typeface
Printed on acid-free paper. ∞
pup.princeton.edu

Printed in the United States of America

10 9 8 7 6 5 4 3 2 1

For Raphael and Sariel

Contents

List of Illustrations

Preface

WHAT WOULD induce someone to spend more than a decade immersed in scenes of infant-cannibalism and Satan-worship? It was a 1987 *Village Voice* article by journalist Debbie Nathan that first alerted me to the sheer power of these scenes of evil, even when patently false. The article described how two women—day care workers—in El Paso, Texas, had just been sent to jail for over two hundred years each for child molestation.[1] What struck me at the time was the sentence, a kind of vengeance or permanent exile, and the evidence upon which the women were convicted: children's allegations of sexual perversions in fantastic scenarios of masks, airplanes, zoo animals, and Satanic cults. Here, I felt, was gross injustice, but paired with and apparently induced by images of absolutely terrifying evil. And if in 1987 this pairing might loosely harken back to witch-hunts of a truly bygone age—might suggest a momentary paroxysm of community cleansing that was at least comprehensible given the culture's new awareness of sexual abuse—by 1991 America was gripped by widespread panics about Satanic cults, which were allegedly abusing children in ever more day care centers, impregnating girls for infant sacrifice, brainwashing their adult victims with multiple personalities, and controlling the highest levels of government. Many more day care abuse trials followed—in California, North Carolina, New Jersey—with coerced confessions and sentences ever more cruel, while psychotherapists and law enforcement confronted this new conspiracy with ever more elaborate theories about why Satanic cults did what they did. Indeed, the panic hit close to me too, as friends and acquaintances came to believe that they too were victims of Satanic Ritual Abuse.

As I followed these events over the 1990s and the impressive scholarship that arose to make sense of it, my interest returned to those initial questions, where do these images of extreme evil come from? What is the relationship of such extreme images to the popular wish to expel it so violently from our midst? Why are people's larger anxieties and traumas expressed in these particular images, with rituals, perversions, cannibalism, and infant-sacrifices—how do these kinds of scenarios come to represent evil? And what is the nature of the resemblance between this Satanic Ritual Abuse (SRA) panic and those in history that alleged that Jews sought out Christian children for ritual sacrifice, that witches engaged in Sabbat atrocities, as well as with those I knew sprouted occasionally in the Roman Empire around Christians and other "ritual" subversives? Can one make cogent comparisons among these widely disparate cases while taking appropriate account of their very different historical contexts? This book represents an attempt to tackle these questions over the *longue durée*, folding the SRA panic, so closely monitored by journalists and social scientists, into a larger comparative discussion of incidences of terror of widespread evil and the purges that followed.

This book also represents an experiment in the use of multiple disciplines: not only history, anthropology, and religious studies but folklore and psychoanalytic theory as well. For in making sense of cultures' obsessive discussions of these images of organized, ritualized evil, often in quite pornographic form, I found myself confronting the strange allure of the perverse and repulsive—an allure to both groups and individuals. What theories and terminology have social scientists developed to describe this irresistible yet plainly disturbing fascination with grotesque and monstrous things that runs through all the historical examples of my topic? Only psychoanalytic theory—the early work of Sigmund Freud and Melanie Klein and their modern interpreters like Bruno Bettelheim and James Twitchell—offers a real sense of these dynamics. Of course, employing these psychoanalytic models to address the ambivalence of perverse imagery does not compel us to accept every tenet or technique of Freudian theory (some of which, in distorted form, ironically contributed to SRA allegations). Moreover, it is the understanding of the discourse of evil that religious studies provides that helps us to grasp the peculiar power of atrocities and rituals framed as Satanic: utterly repudiated, yet utterly gripping.

I also make continual use of anthropological models in this book, especially for the insight they provide into that deepest of cultural tendencies, the construction of the other—the foreigner, the neighbor, the distant savage—in terms alternately bestial, sexual, demonic, and amoral. Other such models help us to make social sense of those tableaux of polluting things that fill our various narratives of realms of evil: blood, feces, semen, corpses, incest. And both anthropological and sociological models inform my discussions of social dynamics in chapters 3 and 5, addressing the question, *who* are the players in these cultural dramas, wherein evil becomes not a speculative notion but a tangible, subversive reality? Through what social roles does evil become situated, even embodied, among us and so terrifying as to require our immediate mobilization?

History and ethnography, of course, provide the essential contexts for the multiple witch-cleansing movements and panicked mobilizations against Satanic evil, while literature, interpreted critically, provides the voices, the allegations, the confessions, the instructions, and the actual fears of people at different places and times of history. Indeed, a book like this one would simply not be feasible without the rich and insightful scholarship of the last forty years on European and African witch-cleansing movements, Jewish "blood libel" panics, and possession and exorcism in multiple contexts.

Ultimately, however, it is the field of religious studies that inspires my larger questions and the order of this book. For this young field, requiring rapid comparative shifting between particular context and broad humanistic questions about collective experience, has the unique capacity to grapple with the *conceptualization* of evil—as a device, a frame, a mythology, a realm, and a motivation for violent purge. Religious studies teaches us how to engage seriously with the often intense experience of supernatural forces even while *bracketing* (not explaining away) their metaphysical reality. Yet in the cases I address in the pages to follow, in which real people have been alleged to engage in ritual atrocities, I will begin and conclude with the unusually positivistic statement that those ritual atrocities, imagined as the very substance of evil, never took place. Only from this position can we ask how these images of evil can develop in the cultural imagination. If over history people keep conjuring horrific conspiracies at the hands of infanticidal, licentious, cannibalistic, evil-worshipping cults, what do we learn about the cultural construction of evil and the demonic—indeed, about the overlaps cultures experience between supernatural and interpersonal "evil"? These are the questions that led me to this book.

Acknowledgments

EVEN MORE than my previous books, this one has been an experiment in interdisciplinary scholarship that has required extensive consultation with—and encouragement from—specialists in areas far afield from my own native ground in the comparative study of ancient Mediterranean religions and early Christianity. I have also depended on the remarkably high levels of ongoing scholarship on early modern European witch-hunting, modern African witch-hunting, Jewish ritual murder claims, and the diverse sources of SRA rumors. If I pillage these fields to make my larger comparative observations, I do so out of admiration for, not dissatisfaction with, their nuance and sophistication.

Through the years that I have been conceptualizing this book, my most essential conversation partner has been my wife, Dr. Anath Golomb, from whose training in psychodynamic clinical psychology I have gained both a nuanced perspective on the genesis of Satanic abuse beliefs among therapists—including some in her own professional world—and an appreciation for psychoanalytic theory as a key to how these beliefs have served patients and therapists alike. Likewise, my conversations with David Finkelhor, UNH colleague and preeminent expert on child abuse, have contributed to my understanding of the world of child advocacy and of the realities of child sexual abuse. I have also valued correspondence with psychiatrists George A. Fraser and George K. Ganaway about their first-hand experiences with SRA patients.

But the scope of this book goes well beyond the growth of SRA claims. It has been my great privilege to have been working on the construction of images of evil at the same time as several distinguished scholars and friends, both in ancient religions and modern ones. David Brakke, Misty Bastian, Beryl Satter, Jean La Fontaine, Robin Sheriff, and especially Sarah Iles Johnston have been invaluable conversation partners, generous sharers of their own writings, incisive critics, and enthusiastic supporters of this enterprise. I am also indebted to Nicole Jacques-Lefèvre, Birgit Meyer, and Charles Stewart, who offered helpful suggestions on various chapters, and to Asbjørn Dyrendal, Bruce Lincoln, Kathryn McClymond, Karen Stroup, and Hugh Urban for essential discussion, criticism, and generosity with their own work at all stages of this project. History colleagues Charles Forcey, Eliga Gould, and Jan Golinski allowed these topics to dominate hours of mountain hikes and contributed much to my formulation of ideas. Of course I am particularly grateful to my editor, Brigitta van Rheinberg, for believing in the worth of "Evil Incarnate" as a topic.

Some of the ideas in this book originated in public lectures and papers. For comments on chapter 2, "An Architecture for Chaos," originally delivered at the 1991 Society for Biblical Literature Annual Meeting, I thank Roy Kotansky and Martin Schwartz. Lectures and seminars at Wellesley College (1997–1999), Wesleyan University (1999), Marlboro College (1999), and Ohio State University (2002) allowed me the opportunity to try out various approaches to the modern Satanic abuse panic in a religious context; and I am grateful to Joan Bamberger, Jeremy Zwelling, Jet Thomas, and Sarah Iles Johnston (respectively) for sponsoring these fora.

Completing this project while teaching classes (and maintaining a foothold in religions of antiquity) has depended on fellowship support; and this came at key points from the Faculty Scholars program and the Center for Humanities of the University of New Hampshire. The American Academy of Religion also provided an Individual Research Assistance Grant in 1999 to develop the article "Ritual as Accusation and Atrocity" (*History of Religions* 40 [2001]) on which chapter 4 is based.

I am also grateful to some extremely helpful archivists and librarians who made it possible for me to include the images I do: Martha Caspers of the Frankfurt Historical Museum, Gregory Finnegan of Harvard's Tozzer Library, Anja Sauter of the Berlin Jewish Museum, and Patrick Stevens of the Cornell University Rare Book Collection.

It had been my hope at the beginning of this project to develop an analysis of these myths of evil conspiracy that might actually serve a public function in inhibiting the conviction of people on such outrageous claims—that might bolster people's awareness that stories of

Satanic atrocities are perennial phenomena, not authentic criminal events. In the meantime, America's enemies have changed (even if the discourse has not), and my analysis turned to deeper goals. But I remain committed to my original purpose: creation of a greater awareness of the forms of demonological imagination that might contribute to justice. In dedicating this book to my children, who are already living up to their archangelic names, I look forward to the many ways they themselves will bring light against the darkness of these mythic fears.

1 Introduction

Basque villagers of the sixteenth century had always known that some people could be malevolent, dangerous; and they had long speculated on how such people perverted human custom and brought catastrophe down on their neighbors, how they got their powers to strike ill, what made them *different*. But as rumors filtered up the mountain valleys that French judges to the north were discovering organized *groups* of witches, and then when, around 1610, Franciscan friars arrived with the first, horrific details of a witches' *aquellare*, or Sabbat, with its orgies, feasts on infant flesh, desecration of Christian sacraments, and obscene contracts with the Devil, people grew anxious: malevolence was much bigger than anyone had thought—much worse than one or two village malcontents. It was coordinated by Satan himself, in the form of an anti-Church; and women were particularly bound to the sect through their sexual pleasure with demons. So when children began to let it be known that they had seen these *aquellares*, that they had been taken to them by strange means, and that they had seen people there—neighbors, playmates— panic swept the mountain villages. Lynch mobs formed to deal with those whom the children accused, to root out this Satanic conspiracy from their midst. Local judiciaries tortured those whom the mobs brought in, extracting some of the details of what was going on and how far the conspiracy reached.

By early 1611, responding to the mountain villages' appeal for official help against the witch conspiracy, a formal inquisition was established in a number of towns, using the most authoritative books on the witches' Sabbat. The Inquisition also drew on the best means of extracting testimony, so that the confessions demanded of each village suspect could be fit to a scenario of widespread Satanic conspiracy and witch-evil that had riveted ecclesiastical minds since the late fifteenth century. Hundreds in Basque country were tortured and burned to death as examples of the Inquisition's omnipotence in saving Christendom from Satanic corruption.[1]

The Basque case is but a microcosm of a much broader series of Satanic witchcraft panics that took place in many parts of Europe between the fifteenth and seventeenth centuries. Of course, there were no witches or Sabbats or Satanic conspiracies, just the typical village tensions and suspicions—that one person has the evil eye, another has the power to bless; that one has always borne a cloud of hostility, another enjoys mysterious fortune. How such rudimentary, even inchoate beliefs about evil people or people's consort with spirits could be transformed into the terrifying Satanic conspiracy epitomized in the Sabbat has been the subject of extensive historical analysis for each witchcraft panic. Historians have gone far to comprehend what intellectual, judicial, and political circumstances framed this kind of transformation and why other cultures (like early modern England) could be gripped with witch-fears without any rumors of the Sabbat to integrate them.[2]

But there have been other historical cases as well whose resemblance to these early modern witch-panics cannot but strike us: Roman rumors about Christians, that they engaged in infant-feasts and orgies and sought the collapse of the moral order, sparking lynchings and executions in the second and third centuries CE. Once again, there was no substance to these rumors in real Christian practice.[3] And in the early 1990s a region in southwest Kenya erupted in a witch-panic following an evangelical Christian preaching campaign that equated traditional witchcraft ideas with the Satanic power that Kenyans were increasingly perceiving around the government and new wealth. Witches abducted children, ate corpses, ran naked at night, killed, corrupted village life with their secret poisons, and—most frighteningly—were now in league with that new global power, Satan. At least sixty people died of burns as local youth, encouraged by other villagers, took the expulsion of Satanic power into their own hands, beating and incinerating those they believed to be Satanic witches.[4]

This book, however, stems not from these distant events but rather from some in the most recent decades of American history. Beginning in 1987, a series of television specials broadcast around the country the idea that a large and insidious network of Devil-worshippers were committing a range of atrocities—from cannibalism and human sacrifice to especially lurid forms of child sexual abuse. These cults, it was said, had enslaved thousands of women to breed babies for sacrifice, and they had insinuated themselves into the upper levels of government to conceal their crimes. Quickly this Satanic conspiracy was adopted as an explanation for the massive day care abuse panics in California, North Carolina, and elsewhere; and Satanic cult details came to figure prominently in the "memories" that a phalanx of psychotherapists were eliciting from patients across the country. These patients—now "Satanic Ritual Abuse survivors"—and the parents of children reporting weird Satanic rites in nursery schools, along with self-proclaimed ritual abuse experts and police cult experts, all began to troop across the nation's television screens, popular magazines, and instant paperback shelves. They even went on international tours, such that the United Kingdom itself succumbed to the SRA panic by the late 1980s. By the mid-1990s, one could buy Joan Baez's CD *Play Me Backwards*, with a song about recovering real SRA memories, and one could read articles and reviews in professional journals that premised SRA as a real "cult" scourge and source of trauma.[5] Meanwhile, charismatic Christian leaders, for whom the rise of Satanism signalled both the reality of Satan and the imminence of the Last Days, communicated the features of Satanic cult conspiracy even further abroad, such that Nigeria and Kenya absorbed rumors of Satanic cults even while the panic began to subside in the Anglophone West.[6]

This SRA panic repeated many of the ancient and early modern features of evil conspiracy panics, yet it erupted among—and was led by—*secular* groups like social workers, police, and psychotherapists; and in this way it confronts us with the real endurance and power of rumors of evil conspiracy, right down to the atrocities performed, its pseudo-religious cast, the wide reach of the conspirators' malicious deeds, the utter depravity and perversity of their habits and central rituals, and their basic opposition to everything moral and human. From rumors as far back as second-century BCE Rome concerning the atrocities of the Bacchanalia, through panics in medieval and early modern Europe about Jews' ritual murders of Christian children, to these recent SRA panics, it would seem that rumors about an evil conspiracy, especially of a pseudo-religious character, can take form in almost any ideological system, not simply a Christian one. Furthermore, it would

seem that such evil conspiracies can be extended to almost every aspect of experience, from child abduction to moral decline, from sick
livestock and storms in the sixteenth century to police departments
and day care centers in the late twentieth. All these realities become
tentacles of the conspiracy.

Such a conspiracy—of witches, Satanists, Jews, Christians, heretics,
or whatever—has never existed, even if (as chapter 7 will discuss further) violent, even homicidal, rituals have certainly been recorded.
(Such rituals, it must be said, have been recorded most vividly and extensively in *public religious circumstances* and by those *purging* evil
rather than celebrating it). So is there something common to all these
incidents of conspiracy rumors and panics, a *myth* of evil conspiracy
that, if not transcending history, kicks into action under certain circumstances? How do we explain the similarities across cultures and
time periods? And what exactly *is* similar: the beliefs? The social dynamics of conspiracy panic? Are we "hardwired" to believe in monsters
or demonic enemies? Or do the patterns we observe across history and
cultures come down simply to influences—books and ideas passed
across territories and down through centuries?

Sorting Out Resemblances

Fundamentally, each incident must first reflect a particular
situation, an historical and social context, before it can be said to be an
example of a pattern. Rumors about early Christians as orgiastic cannibals in the Roman Empire of the second and third centuries CE, for example, clearly reflect Roman traditions of imagining foreign cults as
antithetical to Roman morality.[7] The representation of witches in 1692
Salem and the ensuing community panic about diabolical witchcraft
must certainly be understood in relationship to the region's experiences
of the Indian wars, social tensions in the community, and the lives of
the "afflicted" women.[8] Witch panics in contemporary Africa cannot
be understood apart from individual regions' particular encounters with
modernity, with global economies, and with the new notions of power
and exploitation that these forces present to ordinary Africans.[9] A
modern American community's inclination to embrace the Satanic

cult conspiracy—in a day care center or local families—depends on the books and television shows in circulation and the theories (and even conference attendance) of local detectives and social workers.[10] No myth of evil conspiracy arises apart from distinct historical stresses.

But do these immediate contexts exhaust our understanding of the events or the rumors—the very images of demonic corruption and demonic rituals? How far do they go to explain the passions involved in the panics: the *terror* communities experienced by facing unseen conspiratorial forces, or the *fascination* with which people who are beset by these panics bring to contemplating "ritual" perversions and atrocities they believe to take place at the center of conspiracy? We know that the great early modern European witch-panics, for example, arose not simply because of ecclesiastical politics or village tensions but, perhaps most centrally, because of the stark power of the witches' Sabbat, a picture of Satanic conspiracy broadcast through much of Europe through popular preaching and torture. The Sabbat image had a curious hold on audiences, as have Satanic conspiracies in modern America and Kenya, and others before.

So rather than attributing every incident to its particular social, political, and intellectual context, this study suggests that there are meaningful patterns across them: "something" about abducted and abused or sacrificed children, "something" about a secret counter-religion bent on corruption and atrocity, "something" about people whose inclinations and habits show them to be not quite people, and "something" about the authoritative way these stories are presented. There exists, in some sense, a *myth of evil conspiracy*—using "myth" in the sense of master narrative rather than false belief. The problem is how to explain this myth and its patterns with due regard to their contexts: not as timeless, omnipotent archetypes but—as I will argue—ways of thinking about Otherness, of imagining an upside-down world that inverts our own, of encountering local malevolence suddenly in universal scope, and of sensing the collapse of vital boundaries between "us" and those monstrous "others."

There is, furthermore, a depth to these ways of thinking and imagining. The universality of a child-eating, backwards-walking, misshapen witch, the anthropologist Rodney Needham points out, cannot be explained simply through influences or historical circumstances. The consistency of such witch-figures across time and space, from ancient Mesopotamia and traditional Asia through early modern Europe and modern Africa, bespeaks some kind of "psychic constant," he concludes, some "autonomous image to which the human mind is naturally predisposed." Witches represent the cross-cultural tendency to construct images of *inversion*—the opposite of what "we" do and are—for diverse social purposes. The historian Norman Cohn, in the first edition of his magisterial study of the roots of the witches' Sabbat, *Europe's Inner Demons*, proposed some tentative links between the relentless perversity of the Sabbat, so gripping to judges and inquisitors, and the preoccupations with cannibalism and inverse sexuality in the Grimms' tales and children's fantasy. Witches and the fascinated horror that surrounds them seem to correspond to what psychoanalysts call "primary process" thinking.[11] When we describe cross-cultural and transhistorical patterns of a myth of evil conspiracy, we must be as open to this kind of depth as to the immediate contexts. We must also frame the patterns not as immutable archetypes but as *clusters of related images or social dynamics*, comparing (for example) various images of perversion and savagery, or comparing various forms of charismatic expertise in identifying evil, rather than *the* child-eating myth or *the* witch-hunter. (The night-witch, on the other hand, is cross-culturally so consistent an image of predatory monstrosity that we can speak of this image in more monolithic terms). Defining patterns in this way allows us to compare and contrast the discrete historical occurrences—ancient Christians and early modern Jews, putative Nigerian Satanic cults and South African sorcery cults—more productively than simple *impressions* of resemblance would allow. This book, then, is about the patterns that frame the differences. For we will always understand better the meaning of cultural and historical differences, especially among such conspiracy panics, when we have some framework by which to compare them.

Circumstances for Imagining Evil

Obviously much about these historical occurrences will *not* subscribe to patterns. Why one culture can hold myths of evil conspiracy

as latent assumptions about reality for decades without acting to expel it, while another will become so gripped with fear that it launches
full-scale exterminations, are questions that come down to many social and historical factors. The latent patterns that this book addresses, however, do seem to be activated—to shift from legend to
preoccupation—in the encounter between local religious worlds and
larger, totalizing, often global systems. In those local worlds, experiences of misfortune and dangerous people are negotiated through customs and landscape, often (as we will see in chapter 2) in improvised,
situationally specific ways rather than by handbooks or institutionally established procedures. When such worlds come into contact
with some larger ideology, like the centralizing Church of fifteenth-
century European heresy-hunts or the global capitalist discourse of
twentieth-century colonial powers in Africa, several shifts in worldview take place. First, that global or totalizing ideology is granted the
authority to define what is sacred, what is prestigious, and often what
is subversive or evil—in the sense of counterhuman. Secondly, as a
consequence of this authority, those in local worlds begin to think in
terms of that global ideology, to appropriate its symbols and terms
and even accoutrements (like books or medical instruments, for example) in order to reframe the misfortunes and pollutions of the local
world.

By assuming to itself what we may call the "totalizing discourse" of
that global ideology, the local world comes to recast the bad or suspicious people in their midst. Their *tools* for harm, for example, come to
resemble the tools of the global system: they are *like* the Church's
sacraments, they are *like* computers or radios, and they are the more insidious for their modernity. The *celebrations* of evil people sound like
perversions of what the global authorities enjoy. They participate in a
global organization, with links to foreign countries.[12] They are *organized* in just the kind of hierarchies that integrate the global system. Indeed, this encounter of worlds and their worldviews produces notions
of *conspiracy*—of a quintessentially "modern," hierarchical kind of
subversion—where beforehand there was seldom more than individual
maliciousness and capricious spirits to mobilize communities. What
produces panics and mass purges, then, is thinking about familiar

anxieties—witches, foreigners, immorality, even economic inequality—in newly ramified terms, and especially (although not exclusively) in the radically polarized Christian terms of Satanic evil.

In some of these encounters, such as those in colonial Africa, local worlds confronted with a global system of modernity and capitalism readily appropriated that totalizing discourse, producing the distinctive witch-cleansing movements of the later twentieth century, in which wealth, exploitation, commodities, and often the Devil were prominent features of the feared witchcraft power.[13] In other cases—those of early modern Europe and the Roman Empire, for example—the sheer might behind the totalizing, transnational (if not actually global) system simply forced that worldview and its sense of conspiracy into local worlds. But synthesis would follow enforcement, such that one eventually finds, in many places, local authorities trying witches (or *magoi* in the Roman world) as cosmic enemies—that is, in the ramified terminology of the totalizing system. And in still other cases, such as the modern United States and United Kingdom, the very erosion of the local world as a real social entity capable of maintaining traditions for the resolution of misfortune—indeed, an anxious tendency to frame every misfortune or deviant behavior in global terms—led communities to seek ever new totalizing frameworks for local crises. Conspiracies, as we well know, have historically figured large in this regard.[14]

And in these encounters—these representations of local crisis and anxiety in totalized, cosmic terms—monstrous images rise from the depths of the cultural imagination, from story and fantasy, to become organizing devices—the faces of evil. Evil itself becomes a context, a theater, for individuals to simultaneously, project and repudiate, uncomfortable spectacles of immoral, perverse behavior (cannibalism, incest) and everyday pollutions (menstrual blood, death, sexuality). But the terror of evil seeks some kind of *organization*, albeit inverted or distorted from familiar institutions like the Church, to make the "worst thing" somehow comprehensible. Organized conspiracies always have a peculiar reassurance, for they suggest that not just misfortune but *evil* exists and has its own horrific intentions. Indeed, it is by our discovery of organized evil that we can obliterate it—at least through the bodies of those who manifest it.

Evil in the Perspective of This Book

The chapters that follow work comparatively across the various historical incidents of a myth of evil conspiracy, from Roman fears of subversive cults up to the Satanic Abuse panic of the early 1990s, laying out some clear patterns through which terror expresses itself in notions of organized, pseudo-religious evil. Beginning with the historical and social origins of demonology itself, the very idea that misfortune can be understood through a hierarchy or geography of demons (chapter 2), I focus in chapter 3 on the role of independent professionals in the identification of evil in broadcasting notions of organized, widespread evil. Whether for the sake of some new religion or merely by their own convictions, these figures lead audiences first to see the same widespread demonic conspiracy that they themselves do, and then to enter states of anxiety about organized evil—the only solution to which anxiety is public expurgation in the form of exorcisms, witch-hunts, or other forms of purification. Chapters 4 and 5 shift to those core atrocities of Satanic conspiracy myths that the professionals in evil lead audiences to contemplate: first, *rituals* that celebrate evil, especially in blood-sacrifice; and secondly, *perversions* like cannibalism, infant-murder, orgy, and the whole panoply of inverse habits imputed to the truly monstrous.

In chapter 6, I look at how these wild ideas about evil conspiracy become real, as it were, through individuals who act "as if" a Satanic or witch-conspiracy and its core atrocities were actively tangible. This is an important feature in the vitality of these myths of organized evil, for people's very experience of—not to speak of credulity in—the myths inevitably comes down to such allegedly direct testimony. Because this phenomenon has not before been addressed comparatively, I offer a classification for comparing the different ways that individuals and groups "perform evil," either *directly*, as confessing witches or demons in the process of exorcism, or *indirectly*, as (alleged) victims or witnesses of Satanic atrocity. I describe their functions in "realizing" and situating evil as types of *mimetic performance*. Never have these performances constituted reliable proof for the historical or forensic reality of Satanic conspiracy—witch-cults, Satanic cults, Jewish ritual murderers. They have only been performances: sincere ones, we can be confident, arising from complex social and psychological backgrounds, to be sure, but performances nonetheless.

This book emerges at a time when documentation of violent sorcery practices cross-culturally, ritualized slaughter and cannibalism by militias, and extreme forms of child abuse committed under religious auspices have saturated both scholarly literature and popular media. Because contemporary theorists of a Satanic cult conspiracy have often cited such cases to lend plausibility to secret Satanic atrocities otherwise lacking documentation, it is important to clarify the significant differences between, on the one hand, these documented atrocities and their occasional, complicated ritual contexts, and, on the other hand, those ritual atrocities alleged to take place at the center of the various evil-conspiracy panics discussed in this book. I address these differences in chapter 7, drawing on a wide range of documented atrocities and with attention to the meaning of "ritual" in each case.

Evil in this book, then, is not something out there, organized and corrupting, but something constructed and acted out—a myth that can take on a life of its own, gripping us with terror and fascination, impelling us to purge it from our midst. This book examines the forms and the allures of that myth as it has played out in history. It takes seriously, too, the rationality of these images of organized evil, offering the reader a generalized sense of how they are experienced, what types of fantasies and fears give shape to them, and how, as extreme as the stories might be, they gain a kind of presence in the world through the gestures and voices of real people. Indeed, to express the worldview of those consumed by the myth of evil conspiracy, I will occasionally move into the first-person "we"—not to endow this worldview with credibility but rather to suspend the judgment, the incredulity, that comes from distanced description, to allow some temporary participation in the encounter with organized evil: to experience it as a mode of human religious experience rather than a bizarre form of collective delusion. It is, in the words of William Ian Miller, "an invitational we . . . the voice of attempted sympathy and imagination"—even in such disturbing encounters as this book demands.[15]

Of course, there might be some irony in trying to explain, even to imagine sympathetically, a conviction in evil forces during a time when our own culture is preoccupied with the evils of terrorism. Indeed, we ourselves very much crave a rhetoric of evil—and the certainty that follows the deployment of a word like "evil," signifying what is absolutely inhuman, beyond the pale of comprehensible behavior, and of a nature that transcends the individual atrocity. We feel a comfort in the clarity the word offers: that the mother who kills her children, the commander of genocide, the unrepentant mass murderer need not be "understood" but be called for what he or she is; and it seems like we are always encountering these personifications of evil in the news. The contemporary evangelical Christian rhetoric of our leaders, commentary on our television and radio shows, the bestselling *Left Behind* book series—all of these strong voices encourage us to see evil "for what it is" and to feel comfortable applying the term. It is a familiar, useful word, "evil," so is it not obvious what it means? Is it not obvious what it describes?[16]

Yet this book rests on the fundamental humanistic stance that evil is a *discourse*, a way of representing things and shaping our experience of things, not some force in itself. The most horrible atrocities—and those of us who have studied religion under the shadow of Auschwitz, Jedwabne, Srbenica, and Kigali can hardly ignore their significance—can and must be rendered sensible as human actions with proper contexts. The application of the term "evil" to some horrible act or event renders it *outside* the realm of human comprehension and identification—in many ways "safely" outside that realm, where we no longer need to contemplate our own inclinations to such acts or to understand events as part of some cycle of misfortune (as in recent tragic cases of mothers who killed their children). This observation, that applying the word "evil" amounts to a strategy for setting things apart from comprehension, is not in any way original. Dividing deviant acts between human and monstrous—setting an implicit boundary beyond which acts are no longer worthy of context or empathy—is a common phenomenon of cultures. The word "evil" may have a distinctly modern absoluteness but such moral divisions, such zones beyond which is only monstrosity, are the habits of national leaders and small groups equally. Still, I start this book from the position that for the interpreter of cultures, the critic, or historian, or social scientist, the use of the term "evil" amounts to intellectual laziness, shutting off inquiry and the proper search for context. Indeed, the gravity of the panics discussed in this book suggests that the discourse of evil inevitably takes on a life of its own, shifting into large-scale myths of evil conspiracy and Satanic rituals, and almost never with any forensic basis at all. Perhaps for that reason alone, evil should be scrutinized as a way of thinking rather than held up as a reality for our time.[17]

If there is irony, then it lies not in my having to describe the experience of evil in its extreme but rather in the fact that, in every one of the historical cases I address, it was the myth of evil conspiracy that mobilized people in large numbers to astounding acts of brutality against accused conspirators. That is, the real atrocities of history seem to take place *not* in the perverse ceremonies of some evil cult but rather in the course of *purging* such cults from the world. Real evil happens when people speak of evil.

2 An Architecture for Chaos

THE NATURE AND

FUNCTION OF DEMONOLOGY

Thinking with Demons

AN EMINENT HISTORIAN of religions once posed the question, "Why is it that the demonic, associated with the marginal, the liminal, the chaotic, the protean, the unstructured appears cross-culturally as so rigidly organized a realm?"[1] It is an intriguing paradox: the precise hierarchies that religious institutions construct, with their ranks and titles and weaponry, that consist of half-animal, perverse beings bent on wreaking havoc in the world. And yet in the local landscapes where people really tangle with demons, in which demons are believed to pose concrete threats to health and social welfare, there is actually little to no organization or system to these beliefs. Even while demons—malign supernatural beings—are a quite real part of local experience, the understanding of how they operate in both the immediate and the broader universe of beings remains fluid and unsystematized. Moreover, demons in the local environment are not evil in a uniform sense, polarized against a realm of beneficial spirits, the way that Christian cultures have been accustomed to define the "demonic." Rather, they comprise a diverse realm of ghosts, night-witches, capricious minor deities, ambiguous major deities in local form, and easily angered spirits of the landscape.[2] And as in modern local religion, so in the village worlds of antiquity: the "demonic" is less a ⟨category⟩ of supernatural being than a collective reflection on unfortunate occurrences, on the ambivalence of deities, on tensions surrounding social and sexual roles, and on the cultural dangers that arise from liminal or incomprehensible people, places, and activities.[3]

Indeed, the most basic form by which this flexible notion of the de-monic is systematized—to become a "demonology"—is in the informal or traditional mapping of misfortune onto the environment. A group of villagers agrees after much debate that the death of five cows should be attributed to their grazing by a particular tree where a particular spirit is known to dwell; that spirit's anger must have been kindled recently— or long ago? Is it the spirit's habitually ornery nature, or is it the herder's negligence in not propitiating the spirit? The local landscape—with its points of mystery (crags, corries), danger (ponds), expanse (fields), se-crecy (caves), and ancient associations (anthropomorphic boulders)— becomes thus a topography of catastrophe, as place and passage become correlated to misfortune through the stories of local demons. Conse-quently, avoidance of misfortune is expressed through the conscious avoidance or ritual attention to places in the landscape.[4]

Animals also serve a purpose for conceptualizing demonic power. In ancient religions particularly, fauna are the very image of demonic powers and so serve an additional means for cultures to map their sense of malign powers. Public protective rites in ancient Greece in-volved the repelling of lions, wolves, bears, and insects, and in ancient Egypt antelopes, scorpions, and serpents—as manifestations of cosmic power rather than simple pests or wildlife, while even private rites of protection might adjure demons exclusively as "wolves" or "dogs."[5] Goats and jackals represented demonic powers in ancient Israel and certain cats "witchcraft" to the Azande.[6] The demonic is often imag-ined not only in terms of animals but also as having an intrinsic affiliation with the animal world, often manifest in the polymorphic appearances attributed to demons: monstrous combinations of woman and horse, ass-legs and human body, wolf's head and man's torso. While presenting a horrible picture of the monstrous—the marginal, the unclassifiable, the perverse—these demons are at the same time fixed and located by reference to particular animals and therefore, ten-tatively, organized into the comprehensible world.[7]

Demons also gain specific characters through being attached to weather, to stars, to sins and impurities (like lust or menstruation), to parts of the body, and to specific maladies. But rather than demons' personifying misfortunes in these domains, one might say that *misfor-tune itself* is classified and (therefore) controlled by reference to these basic cultural systems of classification: the body, moral codes, observable features of the environment. Through an eternally fluctuating context of traditional lore, public discussion, and appeal to local authorities, misfortune and danger become no longer ambiguous and chaotic but located, as a rudimentary system of demons that might be identified, discussed, and ritually averted. To paraphrase Claude Lévi-Strauss, animals, bodies, and landscapes are "good to think with" when a community is confronted with things inchoate.[8]

But all this rudimentary systematizing of demons belongs to the oral, interactive domain of popular discussion, legend-telling, and the recommendation (or composition) of protective spells. It is in conversation that one identifies a demon, draws out its history and tendencies, and proposes a resolution to its afflictions. Demon-belief in this case is *context-specific*—to a certain affliction, to a certain group of participants in conversation—and it is ad hoc. It is neither relevant nor conceivable to contemplate the entire range of potentially malign spirits or to integrate them with the formal theology of the dominant religious institution.[9] Demonology of this sort, involving the collection, classification, and integration of demons out of their immediate social contexts, arises as a function of religious centralization: sometimes in the oral teachings of prophets, preserved over time in formulas and poetry, but more often as a function of writing itself. In either case, the essential stage in drawing demons out of their particular "lived" situations and oral discussion into a speculative system involves the *list*.[10]

Demonology, Lists, and Temples

Religious centers claim authority for themselves in the landscape not only architecturally—with imposing temples and splendid iconography—but also through appropriating and recasting local religious beliefs so as to make the temple priests and their rituals indispensible to public religious life. To be sure, this may involve the revaluation of local gods (from familiar gods to hostile demons), but our interest lies in the treatment of local malign spirits—which often shade over into the image of malign people. Studies of ancient Babylonian

exorcistic rites, for example, have shown how, in the process of posi-
tioning the temple priest-exorcist as the quintessential regional authority over demonic powers—as indeed the one whose rituals protect the
very cosmos—the ritual scribes enhanced various local Babylonian
concepts of "witch" to create a single, cosmic purveyor of evil. The
witch becomes, in fact, the very antithesis or inversion of the priest-
exorcist himself. This evil archenemy becomes thus the dramatic object
of extensive incantations, as the witch is cursed and expelled.[11]

The broad demonology of ancient Zoroastrianism also drew upon
and recast local demonic beings as well as older gods with ambiguous
status. In its origins, this religion was maintained orally, its centralizing
character a matter of priests with their rites of purification and exorcism, their ritual centers, and—most interestingly for the history of
demonology—an ideology of cosmic dualism that they passed down in
poetic formulations. Two categories of supernatural beings inherited
from even more ancient Indo-Iranian traditions, *devas* ("gods") and
ahuras ("lords," eventually in India with the sense of "demons")
evolved in Zoroastrianism to signify, respectively, demons and (beneficial) gods; and by the time of the great Persian and Hellenistic empires
(ca. 500 BCE and on) these two categories, of demons and gods, incorporated all known great and local gods, spirits, and malign forces, classified under one or the other category and aligned against each other
in battle as two cosmic hosts.[12]

Not only was their perpetual opposition an important framework for
priestly ritual and authority, but their characters were rendered ethi-
cal, not simply hostile. Demons were evil, impure, and associated with
cosmic disorder; *ahuras* were pure, associated with cosmic order, and
instruments of the great god *Ahura Mazda*. The local supernatural universe, under this system, no longer involved ambiguous deities and
spirits who might bring fortune (or leave in peace) if propitiated but
rather "teem[ed] with countless invisible malignant forces at all times
threatening one's crops, livestock, family, body, and mental and moral
well-being"; and it was to repel this inevitable host of evil that Zoroastrian priests promoted cults to *ahuras* and their own rites of purification and exorcism.[13] Ritual texts like the *Vendidad* show a predilection
for naming demons, drawing them from various archaic and foreign
deities of originally ambiguous, but now uniformly dangerous, character,

combining them with abstract negative qualities like envy or lust, and arranging them in lists:

I drive away Ishire, I drive away Aghuire, I drive away Aghra, I drive away Ughra; I drive away sickness, I drive away death, I drive away pain and fever; I drive away Sarana, I drive away Sarasti, I drive away Azana, I drive away Azahva, I drive away Kurugha, I drive away Azivaka, I drive away Duruka, I drive away Astairya; I drive away the disease, rottenness, and infection which Angra Mainyu has created by his witchcraft against the bodies of mortals. I drive away all manner of diseases and deaths, all the Yatus and Pairikas, and all the wicked Gainis.[14]

Performed as protective incantation by a priest, such lists would function as declarations of power over the demonic and of the expulsion of evil. As the Babylonian priest verbally raises the specter of evil witch before juxtaposing himself to her and declaring her vanquished, so the opposition of a list of *daevas* to the power of priestly ritual—or to a list of *ahuras*—would both intensify the cosmic opposition in the participants' experience and effect verbally its resolution. *Daevas* are conquered by *ahuras*, one by one, in the very cosmic combat intoned by the priest.[15]

By the Greco-Roman period [ca. 300 BCE–200 CE), this magical arrangement of demons against their angelic destroyers appears in a more speculative context, eschatology. At the end of the world, following the purification of mankind, "Vahman will seize Akoman, Ardvahisht Indar, Shahrevar Savol, Spendarmad . . . Nanhaith, Hordad and Amurdad Turiz and Zairiz, Truthful Utterance Lying Utterance, and the just Srosh Eshm of the bloody club."[16] All *daevas* and *ahuras* would be matched along an infinite battle line. But despite the list of names, this demonology of the end-times conjures more of a faceless horde of demonic millions than a sense of individual character or local origins. Eschatology demands a spectacularly cosmic demonology whose spirits have departed their complex local functions to assume uniform position in the final battle.[17]

In the Zoroastrian example, then, the list of demons represents both an abstraction of local supernatural beings—from their immediate environments and associations to a speculative arrangement: class *daeva*—and a method of centralized ritual control. That is, the priest claiming the authority to expel and protect pronounces the names of

multiple spirits, ambiguous and malign, not to be exhaustive but in order to demonstrate total power against the demonic in a ritual performance. And given the formulaic and frequently archaic features of
such exorcistic listing, they also would present a sense of tradition:
spells that have been passed down through an authoritative institution, with proper priests, and therefore possess efficacy.[18] But when
such lists were written down as part of the rite, they could maintain
their efficacy against hostile forces beyond the particular space and time
of the ritual performance. Thus we find, in a species of Egyptian temple oracle, decrees from the temple god to protect the client from all
manner of environmental threats, arranged in a list format that seems
to recall local schemes of demonic classification: *topological*—"We
shall keep [the client] safe from demons of a canal, from a demon of a
well, from a demon of a river, from a demon of a lake"; *ethnic*—"I shall
keep [the client] safe from the magic of the Syrians, from the magic of
the Ethiopians, . . . from the magic of the Libyans"; *zoological*—"We
shall keep [the client] safe from the bite of a crocodile, from the bite of
a serpent, from a scorpion, from the bite of every snake, every reptile,
and every ophidian, . . ."; and even *theological*:

> We shall keep her safe from the manifestations of Amun, Mut, Khons,
> Amenemope, Mont and Maet. We shall keep her safe from a harsh oracle
> and a harsh word. We shall keep her safe from the gods who seize someone
> in flight, from the gods who seize someone by capture, from the gods who
> find someone in the country and kill him in the town or *vice versa*. We
> shall keep her safe from every god and every goddess who assume manifes-
> tations when they are not appeased.[19]

The resulting text, delivered to the client, would be rolled up and
carried in a small tube around the neck, as an amulet.[20] The amulet
was *apotropaic*—that is, it would "ward away" hostile powers. So in this
case, rather than abstracting a separate demonic class like *daeva*, the
scribes who prepared these amulets gathered the habitats and characteristics of dangerous spirits (or, in the case of gods, beings that *could*
be dangerous) as these spirits would have been typically conceived in
local culture. It was a practical form of folklore-collecting. Now, this
kind of extraction of demons from their local contexts and their
replacement in apotropaic lists certainly took place in the oral priestly

culture of ancient Zoroastrian priests, too. But here in Egypt the writing of such lists was critical to their purpose, for it allowed a visual and permanent collection of many different types of anxiety about supernatural attack, it allowed the preparation of an amulet that would control the entire array beyond the protective rite, and it maintained physically a connection to a temple and its god.

Indeed, the temple is particularly important as a backdrop to these amulets and their power, for the written list itself and the priestly rites that produced it, and even the claim to repel such a wide swath of the supernatural all represent the temple's authority in matters of coping with the spirits of the landscape. We might well imagine, as in the Babylonian and Zoroastrian cases above, that a variety of local exorcists and wise women also existed in these cultures who could diagnose and recommend solutions for local crises with supernatural beings. But it is in the nature of centralizing religious institutions to claim *greater* authority over spirits and even to demonize those local experts, as in the Babylonian rites discussed above.[21] In this process, demons get collected from their local domains and ambiguous intentions, abstracted in lists, polarized as uniformly hostile, and speculatively combined with opposing gods or angels.

Beyond the Temple: Demonology among Scribes and Ritual Experts

A diversification of centers in the Greco-Roman Mediterranean world—the culture in which Judaism, Christianity, and many other religions grew—forms the context of demonology's efflorescence, with combinations of local beliefs and names that would directly influence the culture of demon-speculation in subsequent Judaism and Christianity. But now the temple-cults' claims to authority over spiritual forces of malevolence were rivalled by mere individuals with shrines, by itinerant literati and prophets, and by esoteric scribal groups with an interest in assembling all sorts of cosmological lists—all of whom had clienteles who credited these new centers with great authority.

Although itinerant exorcists were hardly a new phenomenon in the ancient world, their contributions to the development of a Mediterranean market for exorcism emerge most prominently in the early Roman era, and indeed are often taken as the primary context for the spread of Christianity.[22] The role of the exorcist, as I discuss further in chapter 3, requires his compelling authority as discerner of demons in an ambiguous situation of misfortune. That situation—illness, infertility, catastrophe, impurity—does not imply demonic presence in any intrinsic way and may often be more customarily addressed in a village through other ritual or medical means.[23] It is up to the exorcist, or the prophet, or the ritual expert claiming the capacity to exorcise demons, first to interpret demonic presence, then to project a general expertise in demons, perhaps to set this innovative demonology within a wider cosmic framework (such as the End of the World), and finally to stage an effective ritual for the demon's expulsion—all tasks requiring the full involvement of audiences. While texts—lists, manuals, amulets—will inevitably *aid* claims to expertise, the overall process obviously revolves around dramatic performance.

Hence in antiquity it is important to note that even those figures whom ancient writers describe as claiming power over demons exclusively through oral performance—*without* devices such as lists and texts—still present to their audiences a creative understanding of demons, where demons change from local and capricious to evil and cosmic. One ancient writer of the second century CE caricatures a species of marketplace wizard who claimed affiliation with Egyptian temples and promoted his demonology as a "sacred lore"—that is, as a system brought from afar to interpret the strange malign forces that plagued clients.[24] A curious teaching attributed to Jesus of Nazareth (and probably deriving from oral tradition) holds that a demon expelled by lesser exorcists will "wander through arid regions seeking rest without finding it" and then try to return to its human host. Repelled once, the demon "brings seven other spirits more wicked than itself, and they go in and settle there."[25] Demons are thus anonymous and peripatetic beings, allied with each other, rather than the capricious spirits located in a desert or on a hilltop. It is a demonology developed to frame exorcistic ritual and its results, not local religious experience.

But it is writing, as a technology allowing both abstraction from local experience and the magical force of the inscribed name, that contributed the most over time and space to conceptions of a class or host of spirits bent on affliction. Here we look at two types of text from the Greco-Roman period in which demons were gathered in lists: protective amulets from the late antique (second through seventh centuries CE) Mediterranean world and Jewish apocalyptic texts.

The wording of the protective amulets shows that they often followed exorcistic rituals as a kind of seal to the utterances and gestures, much like the Egyptian oracular decrees discussed earlier. But these were rituals that sought to label affliction as much as to remove it; and it is probably not surprising, given the ambiguity of spirits in the bearers' environments—for after all, *anything* might strike and any misfortune *might* be demonic—that the identity of the supernatural beings repelled could be quite vague. The ambiguity of classes of afflicting spirit as well as the slippage between demon and animal are reflected in an amulet found in a child's grave in Crimea: ". . . that every spirit and every apparition and every beast be gone from the soul of this woman." A Jewish amulet from Sicily demands that the local deity Artemis "flee from Judah [the wearer] along with all evil", while a curse text—seeking a spirit's malign services—appeals to the "demon menacing here [i.e., in the particular place where the text was deposited, to] menace on my behalf . . . Julia Cyrilla."[26] Such texts show the local character of demons as we saw earlier: ambiguous and unidentifiable, or else associated with animal, place, or archaic deity.

To this unsystematic spectrum of dangers, demon-lists contributed the pretense of certainty, control, and ritual tradition. Thus an exorcist's spell from Lebanon recalls the Egyptian oracular decrees' lists of places and modes of demonic attack in declaring the impotence of "all male <demons?> and frightening demons and all binding-spells" from the client "lest you harm or defile her, or use magic potions on her, . . . either in bed or intercourse, either by the evil eye or a piece of clothing."[27] An Aramaic spell from early Roman Palestine lists "[all who en]ter the body, the male Wasting-demon and the female Wasting-demon . . . the male shrine-spirit and the female shrine-spirit, breacher-demons . . . ," combining the supernatural denizens of illegitimate holy places ("shrine-spirit") with spirits of illness.[28] Another Hebrew protective spell of much later composition (though based on earlier models) protects its bearer, a pregnant woman, from

[A]ll kinds of demons and demonesses, *lilis* and *liliths*, evil diseases, harmful male spirits and harmful female spirits, and evil spirits, male and female; and every sort of fear and trembling, faintheartedness and feebleness of the heart, and heart seizure, and any kind of pain in her limbs or her sinews . . . [as well as] any of the seven spirits which enter the wombs of women and deform their offspring.[29]

Demons and the illnesses they cause are not clearly distinguished, reflecting an ambiguity characteristic of popular discussions of misfortune and supernatural attack. Yet the list means to capture and categorize malign effects and perpetrators in order to project control.[30]

In some parts of the ancient Mediterranean world these vague demonological classes are sharpened to suggest a crude hierarchy of evil spirits. Thus, amuletic bowls used in the homes of Babylonian Jews in late antiquity might be expected to repel "devils, demons, spells, sorcery, all the messengers of idolatry, all troops, charms, goddesses, all the mighty devils, all the mighty satans, all the mighty liliths," or even, as in the following spell, the ancient Persian demon-category *daeva*: "Bound are the demons, sealed are the dēvs, bound are the idol-spirits, sealed are the evil liliths, male and female."[31] These spells develop and expand specific categories of demon, like *dev*, *satan*, *shed*, and even *lilith*—the ancient child-killing night-witch, here transformed into a type of demon.[32] This development of demonic categories reflects scribes or ritual experts' deliberate cultivation of demonological systems that could be projected onto clients' experience of misfortune and supernatural attack. It is probably not a coincidence that two religious ideologies that in principle opposed themselves to local spirits, Judaism and Zoroastrianism, are here combined in a list to create a practical demonology.[33]

All these materials come from literate scribes, sometimes demonstrably affiiliated with religious institutions; and they betray those scribes' endeavor to claim authority: sometimes by imitating the cadences of ancient liturgies, more often by simply listing names and repeating formulae to project a sense of tradition, wisdom, and broad coverage.[34] But in religious milieux more focused on speculation, such as the Jewish apocalyptic and Gnostic movements of the Greco-Roman period, similar lists were composed to organize and juxtapose sins, virtues, and the very components of the universe, as the products of demons and angels. In the *Testament of Reuben*, "seven spirits of deceit" are the minions of the arch-demon Beliar, mapped onto the body and mingled with the spirits lent by God at human creation:

> The first, that of impurity, is seated in the nature and the senses. The second, the spirit of insatiate desire, in the belly. The third, the spirit of fighting, in the liver and the gall. The fourth, (is) the spirit of flattery and trickery, . . . The fifth (is) the spirit of arrogance, . . . The sixth (is) the spirit of lying in destruction and jealousy, . . . The seventh (is) the spirit of unrighteousness, . . . For unrighteousness works together with the other spirits through the receiving of bribes. Besides all these, the spirit of sleep, the eighth spirit, is connected with deceit and fantasy.[35]

In the Dead Sea Scrolls, a similar matched list of good and evil spirits was developed into a great battle-array of the End Times, much as in the Zoroastrian materials. This demonology alternates between a list of demonic principles under Beliar's power—irreverence, deceit, trickery, blasphemy—and a broad eschatological army of demons, arrayed against the "Sons of Light" and utterly lacking individual character or names.[36] Another text from a similar apocalyptic Jewish religious environment, the *Book of the Watchers* (second century BCE), specifies the individual natures of malevolent spirits in two lists of angels who had fallen in the time before the Flood. One list consists simply of names; the second associates each name not with a habitat or some type of affliction but rather with the illicit teachings that these demonic angels had handed down to mankind before the Flood:

> Semyaza, who was their leader, Urakiba, Ramiel, Kokabiel, Tamiel, Ramiel, Daniel, Ezeqiel, Baraqiel, Asael, Armaros, Batriel, Ananel, Zaqiel, Samsiel, Sartael, . . . Turiel, Yomiel, Araziel. These are the leaders of the two hundred angels, and of all the others with them. [*1 Enoch* 6.7–8]

> And Azazel taught men to make swords, . . . bracelets, and ornaments, and the art of making up the eyes and of beautifying the eyelids, . . . Amezarak taught all those who cast spells and cut roots, Armaros the release of spells, and Baraqiel astrologers, and Kokabel portents, and Tamiel taught astrology, and Asradel taught the path of the moon. [*1 Enoch* 8.1–3][37]

In these last cases, the list form serves to pluck social or cultural threats from their immediate circumstances of experience (a local ritual expert or a cosmetics seller at the market), to personify them as demons with a mythology, and to arrange them with other threats of the same class for further speculation: where did they come from? To what powers are they beholden? How are they opposed? What will happen to them? As the list form in exorcistic spells functions to exert control—verbally, then through the power of the written word—so in these apocalyptic demonologies the list defines and controls the experience of the demonic.

These rudimentary demonological lists show, on the one hand, a continuing endeavor on the part of scribes to abstract and list negative experiences as a form of control, and, on the other hand, the beginnings of a real demonological literature—a sort of canon, to which both amulets and later demonologies might refer. "Demonology" emerges in these texts as a literary-theological pursuit basically divorced from the local experience of spirits, yet it pretends to embrace and define that local experience. We must be extraordinarily careful not to infer from these texts and their descendants a uniform Jewish or Christian demonology, for in village culture misfortune would continue to be mapped according to landscape, fauna, time, and quite particular demonic personalities. On the other hand, as the *Book of the Watchers* and its teachings were taken up repeatedly in later Jewish, Christian, and Manichaean literature as a framework for history and religious tensions, its abstracted lists of fallen angels assumed a special authority in literate society and scribal subcultures. "To the Christians of the second and third centuries," one historian has observed, "this story of the mating of the angels with the daughters of men and of its dire consequences for the peace of society was not a distant myth: it was a map on which they plotted the disruptions and tensions around them."[38] We are then at the very beginnings of demonology as a learned scribal effort to collect, speculate on, and control the cosmic sources of misfortune.

It is with the *Testament of Solomon* (ca. first–third century CE) that such literary demonology takes on a real importance in religious cultures, both as a frame of reference sensitive to local realities and as a radical expansion of the list format. This text combines an extensive catalogue of demon names with the more cosmological interests evident in the Jewish apocalyptic literature just discussed. The bulk of this document conforms to a simple narrative formula: each demon is trotted out to reveal its habitat, the misfortune it causes, and its opposing angel and/or protective rites. These details are fit into a larger frame-narrative describing Solomon's use of demons to construct his temple in Jerusalem (an expansion of 1 Kings 6–7); and it is likely that behind the *Testament of Solomon* lay some sort of prior demonological collections such as might have been compiled for the purpose of exorcisms. Indeed, given the considerable variations among the ancient manuscripts of the *Testament of Solomon*, one can suppose that the text served as a kind of looseleaf compendium of ongoing demonological lore for much of late antiquity.[39]

Although woven into a dramatic narrative, the demons of the *Testament of Solomon* have the kinds of natures typical of local demon notions: classified by place or form of affliction or relationship to animals. Thus the demon Onoskelis, with female torso and mule's legs, inhabits cliffs, caves, and ravines (chap. 4). A nameless, headless demon and another named Obyzouth attack newborn babies, knowing the precise times that women give birth (chaps. 9, 13). Kunopegos ("dog-flow"?) sinks ships with giant waves (16); while a variety of demons of illness and strife are linked to the thirty-six heavenly bodies: for example, Sphandor, who weakens shoulders, numbs hands, and paralyzes limbs (13.11). In these ways, the *Testament of Solomon* reflects its collectors' sensitivity to the real worlds of demon-concern and protection rather than a tendency to speculation out of whole cloth, to organize ranks of *satans* or *devs*. Furthermore, the practical benefit of this text—indeed, what led it to influence exorcism and amulet-manufacture around the Mediterranean world—lay in its simple matching of demon with apotropaic or exorcistic ritual: holy names to be uttered, angels to be invoked, gestures to be made, amulets to be blessed. Thus the text lies quite close to the simple lists of demons that underlay so many protective spells.[40]

However, like any classification system, the *Testament of Solomon* offers the potential of control over its subjects.[41] And toward this function of control the frame-story of the text serves a curious purpose. By describing how Solomon coerced the demons of the world to build the various sections of his temple (and then how he imprisoned them there), the text effectively reassigns demons from their initial realms in dangerously marginal habitats—in chaos—to specific sections of the Temple. The true significance of these reassignments only appears when one considers what the Jerusalem Temple's walls, corridors, and courts actually meant to Jews and Christians in Roman antiquity, and even after its destruction in 70 CE: the heavenly archetype of order, precision, and purity, certainly the opposite of the various habitats and activities of demons that the *Testament of Solomon* describes. In this way the *story* of Solomon's coercion of demons to build the temple carries a *declarative* function typical to any demonology (especially the spell-lists): to control demons by locating them, fixing them in a structure of classification. Yet it is an unusual one, wrestling demons out of their habitats, replacing them in the mythical Temple of God.[42]

The *Testament of Solomon* was certainly intended to serve as a basis for exorcistic and protective rituals. Its speculative interests consist in the frame-story of Solomon's temple building and in establishing—via the list—the symbols, angels, and invocations for each demon's expulsion. There were other, more abstract attempts in late antiquity to assemble a demonic hierarchy and integrate it with a monotheistic or polytheistic cosmos. But in its proximity to local understandings of supernatural dangers in the landscape, the *Testament of Solomon* underlines the significance and efficacy of listing as a basic form of demonology—a preliminary attempt to move from a world of inchoate danger, ambiguous places, and ambivalent spirits to a sense of demons that could be repelled. The text also demonstrates the fundamental utility of such an exhaustive demonology, for it not only offers the potential for comprehending misfortune; its structure virtually demands application or ritual performance "in the world."

Conclusions

We stop before the full efflorescence of demonological speculation in Byzantine and medieval ecclesiastical works, yet the patterns and nature of literary demonology have become clear. Demonologies seek to control—through order, through writing, through the ritual power of declaration—a chaotic world of misfortune, temptation, religious conflict, and spiritual ambiguity. The landscape or bestiary of misfortune for villages *cannot* be grasped in such demonologies, nor the capriciousness of ancestral pool- and tree-spirits, nor can the lewd dreams and emotional tempers of monks in the desert.[43] The truth or heresy of some new teaching or some sect does not immediately or obviously reflect the deceptions of the demon Azazel (as Church leaders were wont to accuse rivals of demonic inspiration). Demonology collects from and attends to these various domains of apparent demonic action, yet its interest lies in grasping totality, simplifying and abstracting immediate experience for the sake of cosmic structures. Thus, in the tradition of the *Book of the Watchers*, the *Testament of Reuben*, and the *Testament of Solomon*, synthetic works on demons in Byzantine and Western medieval Christian worlds returned continually to the list format: demons of the days and hours, of weather, of sexual sins, all exhaustively arranged by name. To be sure, some of these demonic names and activities corresponded to those discussed in village environments, although even in these environments a demon like Lilith or Stoicheios would have a far richer folklore and set of associations than in the speculative list.[44] Other names were simply passed down from list to list, culminating in the learned charts that Church investigators brought to cases of demonic possession and witchcraft in early modern Europe. In 1634 Loudun, France, such experts brought to their investigation of some twenty-seven possessed Ursuline nuns a rich catalogue of demonological lore, which might (they believed) bear on the women's strange behavior and afflicted bodies. Indeed, their demonology was so elaborate by this time that it allowed the experts to locate in each victim the names and classes of each demon possessing her, the demonic realms from which they came, and the parts of the body in which they were lodged. As the historian Michel de Certeau observed,

> The "girls" belonged to "houses" in a hierarchy of families; in their bodies, "residences" belong to these fallen angels, whose hierarchy again is determined by their rank of birth. Between houses and residences, between social-upgrading and diabolical grottoes, the lists posit series of "proportions," of which the body is the table. As demons are both possessors and properties, both signs of dependence and of rank, more of them—and posher ones—are associated with the superior [of the convent], a relative of [Cardinal] Richelieu, or the daughter of a marquis. The "residence" of the devils in the forehead, the stomach, or "below the navel," indicates not only their character (described at length, for there are the haughty, the choleric, the talkative, the obscene, and so forth), but also recondite

correspondences between their celestial functions and the body's physiological ones. An entire network of relationships sustains the coherence of this *locus communis*, this common place.[45]

In this way, the disturbing portent of a convent possessed, spiritually afflicted, is interpreted as a kind of demonological displacement—from cosmic positions to the bodies in the convent. Moreover, the very credibility of such demonological speculation would be borne out in the nuns' very fits—a quality of possession I will develop further in chapter 6.

Even today, "Deliverance Ministries" and exorcistic cults cleave closely to demonic lists and hierarchies. This is partly in order to gain a sense of control over possession performances that could be quite disruptive. But exhaustive demonologies also provide those in the process of embracing the role of demon-possessed with a cast of characters and a script for behavior (a topic I will also address in chapter 6).[46] As one of the most popular deliverance manuals instructs:

> Demons that manifest themselves in these ways through the hands are usually demons of *lust, suicide,* or *murder*. Other types of evil spirits, especially those associated with wrong use of the hands, may also manifest themselves in this way. Sometimes it is helpful for the person to shake the hands vigorously in order to dislodge the spirits.
>
> *Arthritic* spirits often manifest themselves in the hands. The hands will become very stiff and the fingers gnarled. This may happen in the hands of teenagers and young persons who as yet have no visible indications of arthritis, yet the demon of arthritis is already at work on a long range plan.[47]

From such discussions of manifestations, the manual proceeds to order individual demons into a hierarchical list of "demonic groupings," each with its own "'strong man' or ruling spirit":[48]

COMMON DEMON GROUPINGS

1. BITTERNESS	Retaliation	Antisubmis-
Resentment	Murder	siveness
Hatred		
Unforgiveness	2. REBELLION	3. STRIFE
Violence	Self-will	Contention
Temper	Stubbornness	Bickering
Anger	Disobedience	Argument

Quarrelling
Fighting

4. CONTROL
Possessiveness
Dominance
Witchcraft

. . . . .

21. PARANOIA
Jealousy
Envy
Suspicion
Distrust
Persecution
Fears
Confrontation

. . . . .

27. MIND IDOLATRY
Intellectualism
Rationalization
Pride
Ego

. . . . .

30. PRIDE
Ego
Vanity
Self-righteous-
ness
Haughtiness

Importance
Arrogance

31. AFFECTATION
Theatrics
Play-acting
Sophistication
Pretension

. . . . .

43. CURSING
Blasphemy
Course jesting
Gossip
Criticism
Backbiting
Mockery
Belittling
Railing

44. ADDICTIVE AND
COMPULSIVE
Nicotine
Alcohol
Drugs
Medications
Caffeine
Gluttony

. . . . .

48. SEXUAL IMPURITY
Lust
Fantasy lust

Masturbation
Homosexuality
Lesbianism
Fornication
Incest
Harlotry
Rape
Exposure
Frigidity

. . . . .

50. OCCULT
Ouija board
Palmistry
Handwriting
analysis
Automatic
handwriting
ESP
Hypnotism
Horoscope
Astrology
Levitation

. . . . .

51. FALSE RELIGIONS
Buddhism
Taoism
Hinduism
Islam
Shintoism
Confucianism,
etc.

This contemporary demonological scheme focuses not on places or times of demonic attack but on the ambiguities of psychological and emotional experience. Feelings and thoughts are themselves fixed in a classification system and labelled as demons much in the way that the early demonologies abstracted and listed a great variety of ambiguous spirits in the village world. Those spirits had likewise represented a classification of fear and misfortune according to some rudimentary system involving places or animals. In exorcistic missionary cults outside the West, what gets classified and controlled as demonic is the ambiguous power of spirits familiar to traditional culture but peripheral (even hostile) to Catholic teaching.[49] To whatever degree listing and classifying are natural to written culture, demonology represents their frontier, gathering, organizing, and *hopefully* controlling the most inchoate and unfortunate of human experiences.

In general, we have seen that the identification of demons and their appearance as beings with origin, character, and modes of avoidance are communal activities that merge real experience and real people with tradition and with various local systems of classification. The demonic emerges as a concept in conversation; collectively, people come to imagine the demonic in landscape features, immoral behaviors, parts of the body or afflictions, and animal attributes. Popular demonological thinking is situation-specific, embedded in the world—part of the larger endeavor of an individual, family, or community to negotiate the immediate environment and its margins.

To turn this ad hoc sense of demons into demonology proper, self-defined experts and institutions have taken to lists, plucking local spirits from their embedded natures and combining them as members of a class, "demon." This activity, we have seen, was once typical of priesthoods claiming exorcistic authority, if not advocating a general division of spirits (for example, clean and unclean), and it came about especially through the technology of writing. The enumeration of demons not only rendered ambivalent spirits demonic; it also claimed power over them—what is listed is thereby repelled. Moreover, the lists evolved, creating new categories of demons (*satans*, *devas*, sins) simply out of the list's generic penchant for categories, or filling out the categories with narrative (demons' origins, tales of demons, demons' ultimate end).

The materials examined here from early Zoroastrianism and Judaism not only serve as examples of stages in a process of conceptualizing a demonic host in the landscape; they also stand at the historical genesis of demonological speculation in the West. So also with the cases that follow in this book. Primarily they will contribute to the understanding of further patterns in the image of the demonic. But they also in many ways follow historically from these early ways of controlling the ambiguous forces of misfortune, now imagining those forces' organization in a myth of evil conspiracy.[50]

3 Experts in the Identification of Evil

CHAPTER 2 exposed the difference between local understandings of ambiguously dangerous forces and the *demonologies*—
systems—developed by religious experts: priests, exorcists,
scribes, ritual specialists. Demonologies can be heady things,
but we must understand them first as the innovations of certain self-
defined experts, and also as the weapons of institutions. In this chapter
we look at the expert in the discernment of evil, sometimes in cooperation with an institution, as a central force in transforming those
unsystematic local understandings of capricious spirits and malevolent
neighbors into an elaborate and coordinated assault on all aspects of
life by a conspiracy of evil: demons, witches, Devil-worshippers, subversive cults, or the like. It is a radical shift in both perspective and social
experience, when the hierarchy of demons becomes frighteningly tangible through—or even replaced by—their human acolytes walking
among us and preying on us. But this shift must be understood in
comparison with more restricted demonological transformations of the
local religious cosmology, when the categories of Devil and evil are insinuated into or cast over traditional spirits. These situations allow us
to ask, what is the *appeal* of thinking about evil? What inspires people
to *accept* a prophet or religious system that casts the world in such
starkly polarized terms, if until now they have understood misfortune
and malevolent power simply through the range of capricious spirits,
jealous neighbors, and ambiguous ritual specialists and sorcerers in the
immediate area?

Sometimes, it appears, local communities' experience of modernity
and a wider world comes with the sense that new, hostile spirits are
afoot that seem to belong not to "our" landscape but to the periphery—
some savage outside world. Perhaps individuals are claiming affliction
by such spirits—a truly disruptive and frightening experience, even for
cultures familiar with spirit-possession. The supernatural world may

then already be somewhat polarized between familiar-capricious and alien-hostile spirits, and some prophet or new religious system that can expel such hostile spirits will have the upper hand, even if it defines as "hostile" or "demonic" spirits with which the community is familiar. Christianization in many parts of Africa, for example, redefined the traditional local gods and spirits into the ranks of the demonic, juxtaposing them to the all-powerful Christ. Christ (and his missionaries) seemed the perfect evil-expelling power for the modern age, and the evil he expelled—in the form of the Devil—was strikingly reminiscent of traditional witchcraft fears. So also the various spirits that missionaries redefined as demonic—as instruments of the Devil—maintained a certain familiarity for people, anchoring this new religious system of evil and expulsion of evil in the traditional world, even the very landscape.[1]

But in every historical case where communities undergo such shifts in worldview—from a map of relatively hostile spirits and people to a battle against absolutely evil spirits and people—the appeal, the power, and the clever nuances of the new worldview depend ultimately on the missionary, the expert. It is he who articulates the uniform, coordinated threat posed by demons and the Devil—a threat corresponding to the power he himself brings against it. Thus what interests me in this chapter is the "charisma" gained by this expert, who enters a community from the outside and addresses quotidian misfortune or inchoate anxieties with the specter of a far-reaching, pervasive evil. I argue that a person's ability to see the activity of evil behind misfortune, or to articulate anxiety in terms of evil, has a reciprocal effect on that person's authority. Perceiving what others cannot, he becomes an "expert in evil," and his clairvoyance becomes essential for people in their anxiety to avert misfortune. In his ability to show the evil system behind inchoate misfortune, he offers his audiences the tangible hope of purging it. And in conjuring a counterrealm of demons, witches, or subversives (whose activities only he can identify), the expert in evil grows into a heroic, solitary warrior against evil. As he lays out the nomenclature and intentions of the demonic, as he projects order onto incomprehensible current events, he himself gains a preternatural power.

*Prophets, Exorcists, and the Popular Reception of
Demonology*

"Prophet" is the general term for the historical figures associated with bringing this kind of worldview to small-scale, transitional
societies—in Africa, the Pacific Islands, and Native America, for example. Prophets have always brought to their cultures some condemnation of an evil in the world: a lapse in proper religion, perhaps, or
some kind of witchcraft or sorcery, or some kind of harmful spirit, the
existence of which, the prophet asserts, has caused havoc and pollution in society and cosmos. Indeed, what makes the prophet compelling to the culture, even while he might appear as an outsider with
destructive notions of cultural renewal, is his depiction of this evil as a
system and a threat to society: demons and their nature, perhaps their
relationship to Satan, witches and how they operate, and the signs by
which we might know them. Even more importantly, the prophet
demonstrates *how* evil might be located and then purged, offering dramatic illustrations like exorcism or the identification of witches. In the
end, if he is successful, audiences feel a confidence that the prophet
has understood local cultural realities within a credible larger system—
demonology or conspiracy—and that his means of purifying the culture are powerful and effective. Indeed, in embracing the prophet's
ideology and submitting to his rituals of healing and purification, audiences allow a new dispensation—a demon- or witch- or illness-free
culture—to take place among them.[2] Thus, for example, in mid-
twentieth-century Sudan, the Nuer prophet Ngundeng "waged a consistent campaign against magicians, insisting that they bury their
magic in [his specially-constructed shrine]. He denounced magicians
in his songs and accused some pretended prophets of conjuring." The
early-nineteenth-century American Seneca prophet Handsome Lake
railed against witches as the primary threat to community health and
welfare, but he predicted they would soon defer to his revelation and
confess their sins. A Melanesian prophetess of the 1950s, whose
charisma revolved around her possession by a local goddess, warned
devotees of the particular danger of sorcery, inspiring anxious hunts for

sorcerers as communities sought to follow the goddess's instructions to purify the landscape.[3] In these particular cases, the evil indicated by the prophets rests not in hostile spirits but rather in a kind of false ritual: sorcery or witchcraft and their shadowy experts. Sorcery serves as the foil, the converse, to the newly established prophet, his charisma and ritual innovations. While he brings beneficial magic and ceremony, his—and by extension his audiences'—opponents practice all sorts of malicious, disgusting ceremonies and cause danger.

The scheme, we shall see, is not unlike witch-finding movements in Europe, in that evil comes from dangerous people, their ceremonies and conspiracies, but it is only one type of evil on which prophets have depended to establish charisma. In other cases, as we saw in chapter 2, it has been the identification and elaboration of demons and their expulsion through exorcism that has brought authority to prophet figures. At the very origins of Christianity, so the Gospels of Mark and Luke and the apocryphal *Acts of Paul* and *Andrew* portray, the formative heroes of the new religion are aligned against a uniform onslaught of demons and depict these figures' "ministries" as primarily exorcistic. Indeed, these texts already display different attitudes toward exorcism: was it simply a form of innovative healing in a world plagued by malicious spirits, or did it function as a kind of apocalyptic combat against Satan's empire? This starker and more dualistic worldview would have transformed the exorcist from expert in demonological hierarchies, as chapter 2 described, into the heroic opponent of Satan himself.[4]

The same alternation between exorcism as dramatic healing, based on the expert's knowledge of demons, and exorcism as apocalyptic combat with a Satanic host continued through the literature of the evangelists and saints, types of prophets, who set themselves up in countrysides, villages, and towns throughout the eastern Roman Empire as divinely inspired mediators—and, indeed, local interpreters—of the new religious order, Christianity. Egyptian monks in particular were remembered as discerners and dispellers of the demonic. In some cases these holy men demonized old gods of the Egyptian landscape; in other cases they invented new classes of demons to oppose; and in still other cases the demonic forces from which they rid villagers and townspeople were personifications of misfortune itself.[5] But the saints' abilities to identify and purge the demonic seem to have been a prominent expression of their charisma (and Christianity's authority) as they spread the religion into further regions. The saints appeared like gladiators against a demonic host of which people had only recently become aware. As a hymn from the period describes,

> The fearsomeness of demons
> and their many delusions
> always war
> with our fathers in the desert.
> Jesus brings them to naught,
> gives strength to his saints,
> through the lifting up of their hands,
> as they pray to his goodness.[6]

These saints' charisma presupposed that audiences bought into a dualistic, Christ-versus-Satan worldview in which the monk was the central *dramatiste*. In this respect we can understand these early Christian exorcist-saints as types of prophet, for they define a new dispensation (Christianity), they envision a pervasive evil that threatens that dispensation, and they create the ritual means (spell, prayer, gesture, substance) for averting that evil. Their Christianity was a Christianity of exorcism: "By the life of the religion," promises the hero in one Egyptian Christian legend, "you will drive away the demons."[7]

It is important to recognize *what* is demonized in these demonological scenarios: not only the malicious and capricious spirits that inhabit the landscape and strike the unwary but *all* the spirits and gods traditionally revered, protective and procreative as well. In this way, as we saw in modern cases, the depiction of a pervasive demonic threat does not *reflect* the experience of misfortune but, rather, *changes* it; it is *prescriptive* rather than *descriptive*. Indeed, it takes the resolution of misfortune beyond the capabilities of the local community, forcing people's dependence on the prophet. The prophet becomes the arbiter of the entire supernatural world.[8]

And the effects of assimilating these new, radical demonological schemes can be quite dramatic, as people flock to the prophet for his unique and essential exorcistic services or, in many cases, crusading out with cleansing zeal against the newly demonized "idols" or even traditional healers and elders.[9] In modern Sri Lanka the enthusiasm for the demonologically polarized worldview promoted by one Catholic priest centers around the shrine where he performs his mass exorcisms. As the anthropologist R. L. Stirrat describes it,

> [T]he regular attenders at shrines such as Kudagama were and are fascinated by the demonic. At Kudagama, demons have a very real existence, as real an existence as people or animals or objects. The nature of the demonic is a continual topic of conversation at the shrine. Newcomers . . . who arrive knowing little or nothing about the demons quickly learn their names and habits. Furthermore, during the fits and trances of the possessed, more knowledge is generated. The world of demons is continually being reshaped and reformed in its details. New demons are discovered; new aspects of their being are made plain. Yet at an overall level certain contours of the cosmos remain constant, in particular the essentially dualistic framework of the Catholic tradition which is made manifest in the continual cosmic battle between the forces of good and evil.[10]

Of course, as I have suggested, this view of the world of spirits would lie in some tension with the traditional village worldview, with its much more fluid pantheon of ghosts and harmful spirits. Indeed, the village Buddhisms that surround Kudagama embrace capricious, often angry gods, monstrous gods of protection, and major Hindu deities.[11] But at Kudagama, Stirrat observes, a simpler and starker cosmology is revealed: "In general, all evil beings are described as *yaka*, 'demons.' The aim of this demonic pantheon is to attack the teachings of Christ and to entice humanity away from God's path. They do this by causing suffering, which lessens people's faith in god, or by encouraging them to commit evil."[12]

And it is the exorcisms themselves that give this polarized worldview, with its overwhelming sense of evil, a tangibility—a reality—among devotees. For in these dramatic ritual performances devotees translate their own local experiences of misfortune and supernatural affliction into the language and gestures of the Kudagama exorcistic cult. Before coming to Kudagama, one of Stirrat's informants claims, she had

> no idea that her problems were demonically inspired. It was only after she had come to Kudagama and seen others rolling in the mud, with demons screaming abuse through their victims, that she began to suspect her own

possession before receiving proof of it. Furthermore, what started out as one form of suffering—in her case arthritis, but it could have been any illness or misfortune—was widened to include all those other incidents and experiences, not only her own but those of her family, which involved various degrees of suffering. . . .

Each time a person is exorcised at Kudagama, the truth of the dualistic version of the cosmos is once more shown to be true. Exorcism provides proof not only of the claims made for the shrine but also of a particular view of the cosmos.[13]

What we find at Kudagama, then, is not only an articulated sense of evil typical of Christian missions (and many prophet movements more generally), but also a *ritual process* by which that demonological worldview, defined by the missionary or prophet, comes to be accepted among audience members and participants. People come to the prophet with particular experiences of misfortune, of the supernatural world, and of modernity and its anxieties. Through participating in his dramatic gestures, commands, and teachings, people reinterpret the experiences within the prophet's radical scheme of evil and purification. Possession performances and legends of demonic combat contribute to the dramatic realization of the evil forces so essential to this scheme. Overall, we might say, the success of such a charismatic figure depends on his own innovation in casting a radical scheme of evil and purification in terms and ritual forms that are acceptable within a culture that previously held much more complex, fluid notions of misfortune. At the same time, we see how a sense of predatory evil in the world— demons for Kudagama, witchcraft with other movements—arises through the instruction and innovative rituals of a prophet or missionary, a charismatic leader, to whom has been attributed the gift of discerning and expelling such evil.

Witch-Finders: Charisma in the Discernment of Evil

From dramatic bodily display to acts of destruction, the new dualistic worldview that the prophet brings demands ritual expression: some act the performance of which or participation in which demonstrates that demons are real, harmful, and in imminent retreat at his command. Whether the evil the prophet identifies is demonic or some sort of polluting ritual (like sorcery or witchcraft) or some combination of these two spheres (like Devil-worshipping witches), the audience's ability to perceive this evil, to accept it as a real threat, depends on the prophet's charisma—his appearance of having inner power and "gifts." And this charisma is in turn a function of his unique expertise in discerning evil, along with his innovation of rituals to expel evil. What distinguishes such evil-discerning prophets, observes the anthropologist Jean Comaroff, "is that they *experiment* with ideas and images; that they try to make universal signs and forces, money and markets, books and bureaucracy, electricity and automobiles responsive to local realities and moral panics."[14]

Indeed, African witch-cleansing movements seem to represent, not a throwback to primitive times, but a distinctly modern phenomenon, often reflecting aspects of colonial experience like economic inequity and the allure of commodities. If people traditionally resolved tensions and competition with neighbors, or dealt with those neighbors' malicious powers, through negotiation and avoidance (with the occasional purge, as instructed by an oracle), now in witch-panics these forms of resolution are replaced with an anxiety to purge completely all powers of human malice. At the same time, the community's problem is no longer one malevolent individual and his secret sorcery, but a far more terrifying specter: a *cult* of witches actively kidnapping children, causing havoc, and gaining powers to control society. To engage such an enemy the witch-finder—in a pattern repeated throughout sub-Saharan Africa since at least the early twentieth century—would need to construct himself as a new kind of ritual expert in the religious environment. The results often constitute a sort of "theater of authority." A team of acolytes may herald his arrival and aid in the discovery of witches. The witch-finder will present villages with a new theory of witchcraft signs and activities, a hybrid of local witch beliefs and innovations: witches' own special coins or bottles, or dances, or markings by their navels. He will draw on various colonial accoutrements to present his authority over witchcraft: a uniform, a book, a mirror or medical equipment, and his rituals of investigation and ordeal, structurally based on traditional divination, will now have the appearance of

Western scientific authority, with stethoscopes or syringes or medical bottles. Most of all, he and his acolytes will bring with them an intensity of purpose in finding witches that inevitably sweeps up villages and regions. Local villagers and their headmen alternate between anxiety about witchcraft in their midst and fear that not inviting the witch-finder would cast suspicion upon them. The witch-finder's crusade thus creates a wave, not of popular fanaticism but of increasing deference toward his clairvoyant powers and increasing fear of the witches he alone can uncover in one's village.[15] A Zambian witch-finder in the late 1980s, according to the anthropologist Mark Auslander,

> was spoken of as an unstoppable force making its way across the landscape, bringing a temporary reign of terror and social disruption until moving on to another village, all the time drawing ever nearer. Young male friends and informants assured me that a cleansed village "looked different" after a witchfinding and that they could more easily traverse its environs now that its huts, fields, and pathways were free of noxious witchcraft substances. A once-familiar landscape, it appeared, was being subtly altered.[16]

The pervasive evil projected by the witch-finder combines all the local fears, rivalries, suspicions, and hostile spirits. It is bigger and more urgent than these familiar causes of misfortune. Indeed, as we saw prophets and missionaries often laying a radically polarized demonology over a complex landscape of local spirits, so also the witch-finding expert transforms a complex environment of supernatural beings and people with potential hostility into one harboring a uniform evil—an evil that, conveniently, can be only be purged through his rituals.

Anthropologists have typically analyzed these witch-finding movements both for their use of indigenous witch-beliefs and for their reflection of modernity—that is, how witch-fears come to reflect predatory features of the state or economic power. These cultural factors explain why the evil projected by witch-finders is a *familiar* evil, and why his instruments and rituals to expel it strike audiences as full of authority.[17] Yet, as the Zambian movement described above makes clear, there is also a sense of terror that surrounds these movements—that leads people to incinerate relatives or convinces elders to sponsor the visits of notoriously brutal witch-finders—transcending immediate responses to modernity. Witch-finders articulate a scheme of evil in society that demands action in identifying culprits and purifying the community. They stand in the middle of the drama, mediating village social tensions with broader anxieties, traditional witch-beliefs with larger moral suspicions, the local authority of a village ritual expert with the exotic authority of the politician. He is a hybrid leader, and thus his vision of evil and purification rites have the ring of authenticity.

If it is difficult in modern Africa to locate accusations of witchcraft apart from these dramatic displays of expertise, village-cleansing, and their distinctively modern idioms, in early modern Europe expertise in witch-finding represented a social role even at the village level.[18] The cunning man or wise woman, as this expert was often called, held a relatively peripheral status in a region, combining divination and healing with the investigation of misfortunes. "It was the function of the cunning man" in early modern England, the historian Keith Thomas has pointed out, "to make the victim face up to the suspicions he had already formed, to strengthen them by the addition of a magical *imprimatur*, and thus to create the circumstances necessary for converting a mere suspicion into a positive accusation."[19] This accusation system worked when other sources of supernatural malfeasance— fairies, dissatisfied saints and Virgins, vampires, and ghosts—might not have been regarded as threats equivalent to the malevolence imputed to neighbors. Often, too, the resolving of misfortune through discovery and punitive action in one's own village might seem to people preferable to more mysterious negotiations with spirits and saints. Thus, in the wry words of a seventeenth-century English Protestant, "every new disease, notable accident, miracle of nature, rarity of art, nay and strange work or just judgment of God, is by [the witch-finders] accounted for no other, but an act or effect of witchcraft."[20]

As in the African movements, experts dominated the process of identifying witches in Europe, gaining authority for their unique gifts and ingenuity in discerning evil in village society: an eleven-year-old boy "exhibited from town to town in Lancashire [1612] as a great wonder and witch-detector"; a monk and several clairvoyant women identifying witches and healing their afflictions in late-sixteenth-century Lorraine; and two teenage boys in early seventeenth century Basque country, who claimed to be able to discern witches simply by looking at them.[21] In the public square of 1427 Siena, Italy, the maverick

Franciscan friar Bernardino described the pyres of witches he had personally oversaw in Rome:

> What was done to [those witches in Rome] should be done wherever one of them is found. And therefore I would give you this caution and warn you that wherever one may be, and whoever may know him or her, in any place whatsoever inside or outside the city, straightaway accuse her before the Inquisitor. Whether within the city or outside its walls, accuse her— every witch, every wizard, every sorcerer or sorceress, or worker of charms and spells. . . . And I tell you another thing: if any man or woman shall be accused of such things and if any person shall go to their aid, the curse of God will light upon his house and he will suffer for it in his goods and in his body, and afterwards also in his soul. Oh! Answer me: does it really seem to you that someone who has killed twenty or thirty little children in such a way has done so well that when finally they are accused before the *Signoria* you should go to their aid and beg mercy for them? If it had happened that she killed one of your little children, what would you think about the matter then?[22]

In this case, ironically, the expert's call to cleansing evil aroused little interest in Siena beyond the burning of "magical" objects and books. Bernardino did have an effect, though, in Rome, Todi, and Arezzo. Across Europe, in both maverick and institutional guises, expert witch-cleansers could instigate murderous panics. Such "witch-busters," as the folklorist Jacqueline Simpson has called them, "were not admirable people; they had a vested interest in keeping the [witchcraft] belief alive, and, by encouraging rumour and suspicion, they brought suffering to many."[23] At the local level, the cunning man's witch-finding services often shaded into his other abilities—divination, for example, or mediation with spirits and saints, or healing. His image of the witch was in many ways an inverse projection of his own charisma: the witch was the malicious competitor, the foil to his ritual expertise. Although these kinds of witch-finders could cause considerable panic, their sense of witch-evil was idiosyncratic and usually worked only in a circumscribed social environment, a particular region, where the cunning man or wise woman could carry on a diversified craft credibly, where she was known and revered.[24] When witch-finders came from the outside, and when regions were already in some state of anxiety, their arrival could spark witch-hunts on a large scale, akin to those in modern Africa; and these panics often created additional "markets" for local witch-identifiers from among the socially marginal, like children and possessed women. Yet when official inquisitions were established in places like the Basque country and Switzerland to combat Satanic witchcraft on the broadest scale, these same local witch-finders were often rounded up as witches themselves.[25]

The theories of witch-evil promulgated by these local and regional witch-finders reflected two basic considerations: on the one hand, the various misfortunes befallen in the social orbit of the accused witch, and on the other, the personal or genealogical constitution of the ac-cused witch—that is, her social status, reputation, behavior, and fam-ily background. Rarely, it seems, did regional witch-finders (at least in England and in Europe before the late fifteenth century) assimilate the accused to some larger witch-cult or realm, even as stories and experi-ences of such a realm—of fairies, the dead, or demons—began to per-vade European folk-culture.[26]

To extend these village-based, socially embedded concepts of witches and witchcraft to the enormous dimensions of evil envisioned in the large-scale witch-hunts of the sixteenth and seventeenth centuries thus required two key historical developments: first, the establishment of centralized and coordinated methods for identifying witches; and sec-ond, the exportation, from central religious institutions out to these local worlds of witch-finding, of much broader concepts of human maleficence: witchcraft as a Satanic evil.[27] These concepts, as Norman Cohn has described, had percolated in Church and monastic milieux since late antiquity, as ecclesiastical officials speculated on the relation-ship between demonology and religious heresy and impelled civil au-thorities to exterminate heretics as so many Satanic infections. By the fifteenth century the Church's endeavor to centralize and control reli-gious practice across enormous territories brought ancient notions of heresy, its perverse practices and Satanic motivations, into contact with far-flung local beliefs in witchcraft and the ambiguous powers of cun-ning folk.[28] Indeed, these efforts were now facilitated by witch-hunting manuals—the *Errores Gazariorum*, Johannes Nider's *Formicarius*, and others—produced during witch-trials in the Swiss Alps, which con-structed a diabolical world of witches, infanticide, and terrible unguents, followed by Henry Institoris's radical and quickly influential tract *Malleus Maleficarum* (1486). Thereafter, through the seventeenth century, witch-finding officials from both in and outside the Church continued to issue a stream of learned tracts that explained, in alarmist and pornographic detail, the conspiratorial links between local witches and Satan himself. Indeed, they provided literary and even legal authority for a myth of pervasive witch-evil that could be sown broadly through Europe, and, significantly, for the means of its discovery and purging from one's midst.[29]

From a comparative perspective, this scenario, whereby a central institution claims authority over the definition of supernatural attack and its repelling, resembles the efforts of ancient temple priests. As we saw in chapter 2, temples had sought similarly to centralize religion and thus produced demonologies that reconfigured the nature and resolution of supernatural attack, from a locally embedded problem to enmity against the temple god. The prosecution of witches was, to be sure, a different sort of projected evil, and it was prosecuted at a much greater scale. Yet the motivation for establishing the new conception of evil in each case stems from religious centralization. It is the representatives of the Church or the judiciary, with their systematic manuals that produce and guarantee the new demonology of Satanic witchcraft; and that demonology is credible not only for its intrinsic details (like infanticide and Sabbat perversions), but also for the fact that it comes from the "center"—with all the ecclesiastical, literary, and judicial trappings of the center. The participation of an accused witch in the atrocities of the Sabbat is not secured by the unique clairvoyance of a maverick witch-finder. A shift in authority takes place with these kinds of accusations, as the historian Christina Larner explains: "The power of the local witch was [now] heavily reinforced by the conviction of the authorities that her power was real and to be feared. At the same time, the capacity to punish her was intensified by the codification of laws against witchcraft both in canon law and later in the statute law of Protestant countries."[30] Institutions and institutional process served as the principal authority behind the promulgation of the Sabbat idea. And to the extent that officials imagined witchcraft as subversive to civil and Church authority itself, they prosecuted it with an energy and mobility impossible for independent witch-finders.

The witch-finding manual lent an authority to the elaboration of lo-cal witch-beliefs as Satanic and conspiratorial on a broad scale. Such manuals presented themselves as works of case study, citation, and cross-reference, as well as logical deduction. The *Malleus Maleficarum* worked closely with local witch-beliefs, drawing familiar folk legends into a learned demonological matrix. Consequently, the trials of ac-cused witches proceeded through harangue and torture with the spe-cific aim of getting individual testimony to conform to scenarios depicted in the manuals, like copulation with demons or magical uses of baby parts. The manuals established a mythological context—an evil realm, a Satanic conspiracy—by means of which an inquisitor could cast an accused witch as servant of Satan and himself as Satan's heroic opponent, as unveiler of his conspiracy, and as advocate of Christ.[31]

The spread of the European witch-hunts reflected and even aided the authority of books and official institutions, but these "centralizing" factors did not preclude certain personalities from also gaining charisma through prosecuting Satanic witchcraft. The semiliterate no-bleman or civic official gained political attention or ecclesiastical ap-proval through pursuing the Church's spiritual war and cleansing his region of witches. The Protestant evangelist, whose fiery preaching of a new spiritual dispensation required the extirpation of witches wherever he travelled, could also gain charisma as witch-finder. The ecclesiasti-cal witch-expert who could disclose the particular dangers that witch-craft held for civic officials appeared indispensible to social and political stability.[32] Friars, priests, and lawyers all versed in the literature of the Sabbat led efforts to convince villages to give up their witches or aided them in investigating the extent of local witch-conspiracies. Like local witch-finders they had the ability to communicate with traditional witch-notions—mysterious powers, the ability to fly, malevolence—but as envoys of the center they held great authority.

In the sixteenth-century Basque region, towns anxious about the di-abolical witchcraft reportedly pervading the land would have to call in an ecclesiastical inquisitor—a professional witch-hunter—to discern the nature and extent of the plague. Such inquisitors, like Avellaneda and Pedro de Valencia, were steeped in the burgeoning witch-finding literature and had particular interests in extending the official image of witches' Sabbats through their own investigations—even through writing their own manuals. Their claims to have been victims to Satanic onslaught themselves could not but have strengthened their authority in these matters.[33] In the mid-seventeenth-century Jura region it was a Father Symard who, with the cooperation of civil authorities, instigated a witchcraft panic, discovering witches in the thousands through a network of deputies, such that he had to request new prisons be constructed to hold all the accused.[34]

The forensic-literary culture spawned by the Swiss manuals and the *Malleus Maleficarum* produced secular experts as well. In Scotland, James the First imported European concepts of a diabolical witchcraft conspiracy and, by 1590, was enthusiastically promoting witchcraft prosecutions in Scotland. The promulgation of a Satanic conspiracy allied against him "became an integral part of the myth of kingship which James was using to glamourise his personality."[35] In the French Basque region, Pierre de Lancre, an early seventeenth-century lawyer, was obsessed with both witch-finding and the elaboration of the Sabbat's perversities. For de Lancre, a witch-cleansing based in secular jurisprudence and a secular assessment of Satanic conspiracy would demonstrate the superiority of the secular institution in protecting society from subversion. His crusade resulted in the trials of three thousand alleged witches in the area of Labourd. These successes, combined with his thorough reading of prior witch-finding manuals, resulted in his *Tableau de l'inconstance des mauvais anges et démons* (1610), the most elaborate depiction of the Sabbat and Satanic conspiracy in the history of the literature.[36]

One also occasionally finds maverick witch-finders and experts without the badges of either the Church or jurisprudence alongside the offical inquisitors. In the western Pyrenees of the mid-fifteenth century a Master Jehan was active, "saying that he could easily recognize those people who involved themselves with sorcery." According to a legal record, "He did much abuse, under the guise of medicine and divination, throughout the territory."[37] Pierre de Lancre himself mentions a Don Pedro who was discovering witches in 1610 Pamplona, and in the Basque region he was aided by a surgeon who claimed expertise in finding the Devil's mark on accused witches.[38] While in England the Sabbat myth was not a prominent feature of witch-hunts, the region of Essex suffered an especially determined witch-finder:

Over the winter of 1644–5 Matthew Hopkins, an obscure petty gentleman living in Manningtree in north-east Essex, became worried about witches in his neighborhood. His worries bore fruit in the prosecution of thirty-six witches, of whom perhaps nineteen were executed, at the summer 1645 assizes in Essex. Accusations spread rapidly over the Suffolk border, and we know of 117 witches who were examined or tried in that county. . . . Altogether we have references to some 240 alleged witches who came before the authorities during this episode, over 200 of them between July and December 1645.[39]

In the frontispiece of his self-promotional tract *Discoverie of Witches* (1647), written under considerable skeptical scrutiny, Hopkins presents himself as "witch-finder Generall," overseeing two women's calm revelations of their animal assistants. (See figure 1.) He is clearly the means by which such grotesque truths become apparent to society.[40]

As in Africa, then, witch-finding and -cleansing movements in early modern Europe quite often devolved upon particular personalities; and it was their discovery of pervasive witch-evil—often culminating in a new text with new literary elaborations of witchcraft's perversity and danger—that contributed to their own charismatic authority as experts in evil. The apocalyptic overtones in witch-finding and -cleansing—that an apparent rise of subversive evil heralded the era of the Antichrist—often gave these experts the appearance of establishing a new order, much like African witch-finders, who often figure as veritable prophets of the last days. One witness to the Hopkins crusade complained that "the Cuntrey People talke already, and that more frequently, more affectedly, of the infallible and wonderfull power of the Witchfinders; then they doe of God, or Christ, or the Gospell preached."[41]

In the largest witch-hunts and inquisitions, of course, it was not imminent apocalyptic purification that was promised but a protracted holy war against an invisible enemy on many fronts. A faceless institution engaged in witch-cleansing, whether Church, royalty, or secular jurisprudence, would offer villages and cityfolk a sense of security and moral protection—that the king himself can identify and repel what ails society. Here in the broadest, "macrocosmic" dimension, then, is one of the chief features of the witch-finder's charisma: the ability to

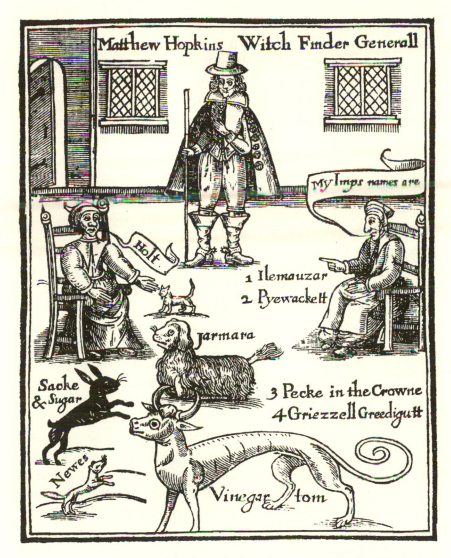

FIGURE I   Frontispiece to Matthew Hopkins, *Discoverie of Witchcraft* (London, 1647). From reprint by H. W. Hunt, 1931. Hopkins is depicted as the orchestrator of witches' confessions, presiding over their revelations of animal assistants.

save society through identifying, explaining, and annihilating evil. And it is notable that in the mid-1990s, this same shift from microcosmic witch-finding complex to macrocosmic—in this case, national—battle against evil occurred explicitly in Kenya under President Daniel Arap Moi. In the early 1990s, having been accused of sorcery himself, the president launched a highly publicized inquiry into "Devil-worship" in Kenyan society, to which was attributed everything from train disasters to moral decline among youth. The resulting report, to be discussed in greater detail in chapter 4, was assembled partly from Western evangelical Christian anticult literature, partly from traditional notions of witches, and it received the endorsement of major ecclesiastical bodies in Kenya. As in early modern Europe, here the state took up the role of discerner of Satanic evil and protector of society from Satan's minions.[42]

From modern African examples through large-scale European crusades against Satanic witch-cults, then, the dynamics of identifying evil and mobilizing its "solution" have revolved around individual witch-finders. These may be relatively familiar figures, as we see in parts of Africa and Europe—individuals distinguished by their clairvoyance or ritual techniques; or they may be distant figures, representatives of the state like James the First of Scotland or Daniel Arap Moi of Kenya or Pierre de Lancre of France; or they may be agents of the Church, carrying out to the hillsides and villages literary and theological constructions of evil that could be forced into relevance to village witchcraft beliefs. Witch-finders construct a picture of evil conspiracy in familiar terms, using traditional notions of witchcraft or malevolent powers, traditional landscapes and images of moral inversion (as chapters 4 and 5 will discuss), as well as new concepts of pervasive threat, coordinated conspiracy, even secret institutions, all of which ramify the horror people feel about malevolence around them. Compelled by the scope of such evil, people consequently depend on the techniques and purifying rituals offered by the witch-finder to root out evil and cleanse it from society. The witch-finder gains charisma by becoming increasingly indispensible as expert and innovator.

The Possessed as Discerners of Evil

There is another type of expert in evil who figured prominently in European and Anglo-American witch-hunts: that is, possessed women and children. In seventeenth-century Switzerland, Sweden, and Normandy, for example, such individuals consistently stood at the origin of witch-hunts, being the first to accuse others and serving indispensibly, as I will discuss further in chapter 6, to dramatize the evil said to pervade the landscape. In certain cultures, of course, spirit-possession has often served as a kind of behavioral idiom, especially for women, the disenfranchised, and in periods of crisis, children as well. When they speak as spirits, saints, or demons, or if they convey dramatic affliction from a demon's violent whims (or a witch's spectral control), women and children have often gained charisma in their communities. In such roles subordinate members of society can participate actively in the dramatic expression of religious belief. But in times of witchcraft anxiety or apocalyptic fervor the range of meanings that spirit-possession typically assumes often extends to clairvoyance: the identification of the witches who are attacking the possessed.[43]

In early modern Europe, the historian Stuart Clark has shown, that the possessed represented veritable portents of the End-Times, battlegrounds between Christ and Satan or Antichrist, but in this capacity they required interpreters: the exorcists and experts in evil with which the Church was brimming in the sixteenth and seventeenth centuries.[44] The possessed's status as herself a discerner of evil arose in close connection with some institutional professional (a priest or judge) who might bring to bear on her experience of possession the highly eroticized Sabbat legends and the latest theories of how witches attack the vulnerable. Professional exorcists like the Puritan John Darrell made a specialty of turning exorcisms into opportunities to finger witches.[45] But it could be a dangerous role: as much as possession had the potential to insulate one from suspicion of witchcraft, some particularly dramatic cases in seventeenth-century France resulted in the execution of the possessed as witches as well as their alleged afflicters.[46]

The Salem, Massachussetts, witch-panic of 1692 provides a signal example of the possessed as witch-indicators. Here the possession performances of young teenaged girls (and, in one notable case, the mother of one girl) served as the essential proof to judges, Church figures, and the populace that witchcraft was real and pervasive.[47] In Salem (as in other cases of child witch-indicators) possession behavior described by observers as "fits" became gradually articulated as affliction, induced by hostile spirits that were observable only to the girls. Thus the girls became virtual windows into a pervasive world of angry ghosts and the malicious acts of neighbors, who otherwise struck everyone as harmless. Cotton Mather, the preeminent ecclesiastical systematizer of witch beliefs at the time, saw them not as victims but as "visionary girls," for they "saw all that was done."[48] In one of the best-known trial scenes (of March 21, 1692), three girls, joined by seven older women, claimed in their possessions to see the accused, Martha Corey, *at that very moment* "bringing a Book for them to sign; . . . and that she had a Yellow Bird, that did use to suck between her Fingers, and that the said Bird did suck now in the Assembly." Indeed,

> when the Accused had any motion of their Body, Hands or Mouth, the Accusers would cry out, as when she bit her Lip, they would cry out of being bitten, if she grasped one hand with the other, they would cry out of being Pinched by her, and would produce marks, so of the other motions of her Body, as complaining of being Prest, when she lean'd to the seat next her, if she stirred her Feet, they would stamp and cry out of Pain there.[49]

The effect on the audience and magistrates was electric: they demanded to know why Mrs. Corey was afflicting the girls, and when Mrs. Corey suggested the girls may be deluded, the magistrates insisted they could only be victims of witchcraft.

In another case (May 24, 1692), Nathaniel Cary and his wife, who had been implicated by the Salem girls, travelled from their home in Charlestown to verify the accusation. In the Meetinghouse, Cary describes, they encountered "two Girls of about Ten Years old, and about two or three others, of about eighteen; one of the girls [Abigail Williams, one of the initial instigators] talked most, and could discern more than the rest."[50] The girls launched their fits whenever Mrs. Cary looked at them, so the judges required she face toward the bench. Subsequently, they ordered that the girls be carried over to Mrs. Cary to be touched by her as a cure. Later, Mr. and Mrs. Cary were brought together with Abigail Williams in a tavern, but then, Mr. Cary describes, "instead of one Accuser, they all came in, who began to tumble down like Swine, and then three Women were called in to attend them. We in the Room were all at a stand, to see who they would cry out of; but in a short time they cried out, Cary; and immediately after a Warrant was sent from the Justices to bring my Wife before them, who were sitting in a Chamber near by, waiting for this."[51]

The girls' roles as witch-indicators involved both their physical demonstration of the witches' powers and their clairvoyance into an unseen world of specters. In several cases they "saw" murders and the ghosts of victims of murders that the accused had allegedly committed.[52] In this way the girls rendered themselves indispensable to the community—judges, ministers, and populace combined—for transmitting and articulating that unseen world of evil.

Indeed, so indispensable did they become for the discernment of witchcraft and the resolution of accusations that in the months following the cessation of the Salem witch-trials the same girls were brought to other towns in the region for their "spectral sight." In Andover their effect was terrifying:

> When these [girls] came into any place where such were, usually they fell into a Fit; after which being asked who it was that afflicted the person, they would, for the most part, name one whom they said sat on the head, and another that sat on the lower parts of the afflicted. Soon after [Joseph Ballard of Andover sent for the girls to discern whether his wife's illness was witchcraft,] . . . more than Fifty of the People of Andover were complained of, for afflicting their Neighbours. Here it was that many accused themselves, of Riding upon Poles through the Air; Many Parents believing their Children to be Witches, and many Husbands their Wives, etc. When these Accusers came to the House of any upon such account, it was ordinary for other young people to be taken in Fits, and to have the same Spectral sight.[53]

However, when in November the girls were travelling to a case of suspected witchcraft and were "passing over Ipswich-bridge, they met with an old Woman, and instantly fell into their Fits: But by this time the validity of such Accusations being much questioned, they found not that Encouragement they had done elsewhere, and soon withdrew."[54]

These examples—in one case mass hysteria, in the other skepticism—show in particular detail the subtle cooperation that had to occur between the possessed girls and their audiences. It was a dialectic requiring intense anxiety on the audience's part and insightful performance on the girls' part—to know the circumstances most conducive to success-ful witch-identification.[55]

What the girls had to gain from these performances and to what de-gree their performances were deliberate has been a subject of specula-tion since the time of their first critic, Robert Calef, but it is not as important for this study as the role they assumed as principal *drama-tistes* of the 1692 witch-hunt. As clairvoyants they served as windows into a supernatural world that, they revealed, was pervaded by evil and subversion. As ecstatics they served as somatic proof of the malefi-cence brought on by that world. The girls brought witchcraft to life, not unlike the Central Asian shamans who climb or call or descend or fly or wrestle through the worlds of the spirits. As accusers the girls seem to have given vent to social tensions and sentiments for which there were no expressive forms equivalent—or quite so dire. And as children, they represented the communities' principal concern, their afflictions seeming to be of catastrophic emergency. It was impossible (at first) for their families and communities not to believe them.[56]

And it is perhaps partly because of this latter social status that the girls' pretenses to see into a demonic world—even to be invited to "sign" Satanic books there—gained their audiences' concern rather than condemnation as witchcraft. For as children they required adult concern—and adult aid in shaping their possessions and accusations.[57]

Those who present themselves as possessed by spirits may experi-ence that possession as a form of affliction, an attack by hostile spirits rather than an "incorporation" by familiar spirits. Many factors con-tribute to these varying interpretations of possession, as I. M. Lewis outlines in his classic study, *Ecstatic Religion*, but cultural traumas (in Salem's case, recent Indian massacres) and the pressures of powerful outside ideologies on local moral worldviews can both trigger these negative possessions.[58] It is then up to regional experts, like the witch-finders discussed in the last section or the demonological experts dis-cussed in chapter 2, to nuance the affliction as the work of this demon or that witch, or as indicating the onset of the Last Days. The pos-sessed thereby becomes a manifestation of the evil that the witch-finder is identifying and that his audiences have begun to sense around them. As chapter 6 will explore further, the possessed "performs" the very conspiracy of evil that has been hitherto but an idea, a framework for understanding reality. But she also may serve as a discerner herself—an acolyte of the witch-finder or an independent charismatic figure—with the capacity to see directly into a malevolent, conspiratorial world that others cannot. The Salem trials provide us with an especially detailed illustration of this social role, although it is certainly not unique, as European and African witch-finding movements are replete with examples of the possessed as discerners of evil.

Contemporary Forms of Expertise in the Discernment of Evil: Secular and Religious

The witch-finder role is no longer identifiable in the West, and even in postcolonial cultures witch-finders have a protean character, establishing their own authority and the nature of supernatural threat according to modern crises and idioms: Satan, vampires, television, paper money, body parts. But the absence of clear roles for discerning and expelling evil in society has not in any way meant that Western cultures have grown beyond the need for such roles. Indeed, as Andrew Delbanco has argued, the late twentieth century saw a growing fascination with evil—evident in films, television, and popular books—that sometimes captured new cultural anxieties like child-safety or technology and sometimes veered off into fantasies of monsters and demons. Much of the media supporting this popularization of evil as a cultural discourse (such as the apocalyptic writings of Hal Lindsey and Tim LaHaye) came explicitly from evangelical Christian quarters.[59] Much as early modern expertise in witch-finding sometimes arose from prior social offices, like priest, friar, jurist, king, or even local cunning man, so in America and the United Kingdom in the mid-1980s expertise in the discernment of Satanic cults became a hybrid role that extended from, most often, social service positions: social workers and child-protection advocates, psychotherapists and psychiatrists, police officers, and of course Christian ministers. In situations of moral anxiety, we might say, new organizational and clairvoyant roles for the discernment of evil open up, and anyone with some sort of recognizable authority and conviction in her own abilities can fill them.

And indeed, by the mid-1980s, two ideological movements had emerged to frame moral anxiety in the United States and United Kingdom, each with strongly articulated concepts of evil and each with multiple roles for leadership as moral crusaders.

One such movement was evangelical Christianity and its counterpart, the Catholic charismatic movement, both of which were promoting the idea that Satan, Satanic conspiracy, and demonic attack were cosmic realities that lay ultimately behind most social problems, that signalled the onset of the Last Days, and whose repulsion could only take place through rebirth in Christ and spiritual warfare. Among the Satanic evils identified in this ideology were "cults," the new alternative religions that had flourished since the 1960s and had taken on an insidious character to many in society because of well-publicized atrocities like the Manson murders and the Jonestown suicides. For evangelicals, cults were not just seductive lifestyle choices but Satan-inspired deceptions that inevitably maintained slavery or human-sacrifice practices on the inside.

As part of the later twentieth-century interest in self-fulfillment and spirituality, evangelical culture had also cultivated popular interest in what the anthropologist Tanya Luhrmann has called "trance states"—that is, a special attentiveness during prayer and ceremony to thoughts and feelings that seem to come from outside the body, and even an effort to cultivate those thoughts and feelings through certain ritual techniques.[60] Out of these new interests and the proliferation of "ministries" that encouraged them came a renewed attention to *demonic* possession—the particular trances that demons rather than the Holy Spirit might bring—as well as a related, if secularized, belief in various evil or evil-traumatized "personalities." Both forms of affliction could be healed through ritual or therapeutic procedures based in the recognition of evil as a real force.

Demon possession itself, as we saw at the end of chapter 2, could be elaborated to cause all manner of social and psychological ills. "Deliverance Ministries" thus grew around individuals who claimed the divine gift to "discern" demons by means of smell, sight, and intuition. These generally lay (and usually female) ministers would often work in combination with an exorcist, a minister or priest credited with the power of word, gesture, and resilience in the face of Satan to cast out demons, sometimes from audiences of hundreds.[61]

Several roles in the discernment and elaboration of evil thus arose in the evangelical and charismatic culture: on the one hand, ministers and priests variously preoccupied with the demonic; and on the other, lay experts in discernment, including "cult-experts"—moral entrepreneurs of a Christian cast, many of whom were members of police departments. Such "cult cops" became popular speakers at schools, youth groups, and other organizations subject to moral crusades.[62]

The other ideological movement with a strongly articulated concept of evil that spawned experts in the discernment of evil was child-protection advocacy, including social workers, psychotherapists, and, increasingly, feminists. In both the United States and United Kingdom, anxieties about child safety began to shift in the early 1980s from lone predators lurking on the periphery, as it were, to dangers within the domestic sphere—child abuse and incest—and that modern extension of the domestic sphere, the day care center. In the United States, ambivalence over the importance of day care and the status of the day care provider—family member or civil servant? Suspicious functionary or neighborhood caregiver?—contributed to a popular anxiety about children's vulnerability in society.[63] At the same time, documentaries and television dramas, organizations and telephone hotlines, and new psychotherapy specialties all began to address incest as a terrifying new— that is, hitherto suppressed—evil in society. For some feminist groups, father-daughter incest (and maternal denial) epitomized the trangenerational terror that patriarchy wreaked on women. The family was reconstructed in this ideology as a potential—for some advocates, probable—microcosm of rape culture and male sexual domination.[64]

Whereas the ideology of evil in evangelical Christian culture concerned the reality of Satan, Satanism, and demonic powers, and the efficacy of the Christ-endowed exorcist, that of secular child-advocacy culture had the character of a moral crusade. Emerging leaders asserted the widespread reality and importance of child sexual abuse, first as a domestic or child-care phenomenon, and eventually as an organized conspiracy behind these spheres. They cultivated techniques for determining incidents of child sexual abuse that assumed the total credibility of alleged victims—that no one would make up such claims. And certain professionals were elevated as masters of these techniques, as experts in the detection of evil. The field of experts grew and diversified: a new professional corps of social workers and police, claiming unique abilities to discern the nature and pervasiveness of the conspiracy (which was now linked to the "cults") and to extract evidence for it from ostensibly afflicted children and adults. They also claimed authority to determine social and criminal policies with the potential of purging the threat.[65]

Both ideologies began to merge and feed on each other by the end of the 1980s on both sides of the Atlantic. Evangelical notions of organized evil gave shape to the horrors of abuse conspiracies formulated by psychotherapists and child-advocacy groups, such that a secular SRA expert in the United Kingdom could declare in 1991 that "a member of the *church* can reassure the victim by presenting the possibility of a *countervailing power*, a source of energy to combat the feelings of helplessness that engulf children who have been brainwashed in the ways of evil."[66] At the same time, the evil of domestic sexual abuse, its allegedly organized character, and its psychotherapeutic recovery offered a powerful focus for evangelical Christian demonology and for new methods of deliverance, which involved the repudiation of one's past. As Lurhmann has argued, the new professional interest in multiple personalities seems to have reflected closely the evangelical scrutiny of trance states and the different personalities—evil, afflicted, innocent—to which these states could give rise.[67] Indeed, the full merger of these ideologies was encouraged by the book *Michelle Remembers* (1980), coauthored by a Canadian psychiatrist and his female patient, who came to "remember" through therapy sessions multiple personalities stemming from child sexual abuse at the hands of a highly organized Satanic cult practicing cannibalism, infanticide, and all the perverse atrocities inherited from depictions of witches' Sabbats.[68] The book was extremely influential among child-advocacy and psychotherapy professional communities in both the United States and United Kingdom as the first systematic revelation of SRA as an organized conspiracy manifesting itself in homes. Henceforth, SRA became the combined focus of evangelical Christian leaders, cult cops, child-welfare advocates, social workers, psychotherapists, and psychiatrists, all of whom served as professionals in the identification and expulsion of evil.

We will here look at some of the major types of professionals in the cultivation of the Satanic cult abuse panic: first from the secular world of child advocacy and psychotherapy, and then from the evangelical Christian world.

SATANIC RITUAL ABUSE: SECULAR DISCERNERS

Social crises often precipitate a shifting and expansion of social roles, as familiar, established forms of professional authority become virtual staging grounds for new "gifts" and new "callings." In the later 1980s, individuals trained in mental health and children's services sought authority in areas of social control—in defining criminality in prosecution, and most generally in defining social evil. "Never before," the sociologist Jeffrey Victor has written, "had a new form of secretly organized criminal activity been discovered by mental health experts. In this way, they functioned as agents of social control more than as scientists or therapists."[69]

The social worker Kee MacFarlane exemplifies this construction of a new expertise. In 1982 MacFarlane joined a network of Los Angeles area child-protection workers after losing a job at the National Center for Child Abuse and Neglect to budget cuts. MacFarlane developed new ways of interviewing children suspected of abuse using hand puppets, dolls, and playful interview techniques. When investigations into possible large-scale, "organized" sexual abuse at the McMartin preschool in California began in 1983, MacFarlane took the opportunity to apply these techniques to some four hundred children, and through protracted sessions and leading questions she diagnosed sexual abuse in virtually every child.[70] But this was not the child sexual abuse typically documented by social scientists and police (i.e., intrafamilial). MacFarlane was discovering group perversions, organized child pornography, and—as she warned a congressional committee at the end of 1984—"bizarre rituals involving violence to animals, scatological behavior and what they perceived as magic, and children threatened into silence with the use of weapons, threats of harm and death to family members, and observing the slaughter of animals."[71]

MacFarlane presented herself to the government as a lone expert coping with an "avalanche" of child abuse revelations—a disaster, she insisted, on the scale of any earthquake or fire, and equally deserving of the full benefits of disaster relief. She offered herself as the voice for "three hundred or four hundred small friends under the age of five," fighting in the front line with only a small staff against an enormous network of evil. And organized it was:

> I think you need to know that I believe we are dealing with no less than conspiracies in these cases, organized operations of child predators, whose operation is designed to prevent detection, and is well insulated against legal intervention.
>
> Preschools in this country in some instances I think we must realize have become a ruse of larger unthinkable networks of crimes against children. . . . [M]any of the cases I am aware of under investigation, and most of the alleged abuse that I described, could only have existed under such conspiratorial circumstances.[72]

Convinced by MacFarlane's grandiose scenario, Congress doubled its budget for child-protection programs. Thus a minor social worker specializing in child sexual abuse emerged as one of the primary experts in pervasive evil, transforming several complex community scandals in California into manifestations of a horrible conspiracy against children. Much as in the cases of witch-finders whose demonstrations of elaborate witchcraft conspiracies serve to establish their own indispensability, MacFarlane shot to charismatic prominence as a hybrid discerner of evil and moral crusader. With little to work with besides their own interview techniques, deeply malleable preschool children, and, most of all, their complete conviction in the techniques' efficacy to procure truths from the children's mouths, MacFarlane and other social workers began to weave the conspiracy and its organizational character from what they "discovered" in interviews—and their own imaginations—during the early 1980s.

The conspiracy, we see in MacFarlane's testimony, initially echoed legends of pornographic rings, the mafia, and child predators—a horrific counterworld to the secular child-protection worker who had turned crusader. It was a conspiracy based on oral reports and familiar cultural narratives of subversion rather than texts. And yet "bizarre rituals," as MacFarlane proclaimed, were among the most frightening parts of the children's revelations. The explanation of these revelations, which gave a new "cultic" cast to the child sexual abuse conspiracy, became the preoccupation of a psychiatrist, Roland Summit, and Brad and Carol Darling, respectively a police lieutenant and a social worker.[73]

Summit came to the day care abuse panics as a self-defined theorist of incest mentality, linking fathers' incestuous wishes to their wives' career ambitions. But in the series of professional symposia that took place in the wake of the McMartin preschool panic, Summit was particularly captivated by the allegations "that children are forced to eat feces and drink blood and participate in blood sacrifices and in sexual ceremonies with robed figures and people in costume," as he told a conference of child abuse professionals that met in Washington D.C. in October 1984.[74] Two years later he was offering "expert" comments at another conference (in Santa Clara, California) on child sexual abuse at which Brad Darling also lectured, in which Summit referred to the writings of British "Satanist" Aleister Crowley and suggested that anyone now skeptical of widespread SRA might be "reflecting an obligation to the other side or are agents in some ways controlled by the other side."[75] Emergence as Satanic cult expert required for Summit, as for MacFarlane, the depiction of the conspiracy as actively seditious.

The Darlings, each deeply involved in sexual abuse investigations from the early 1980s onward, also began to promote the notion of subversive Satanic cults. Carol Darling, the sexual abuse coordinator for Kern County, California, had been involved in a prior abuse-ring investigation in southern California that had produced allegations of "ritual abuse" even before the McMartin panic. By 1986 she was arguing before a grand jury that the Satanic conspiracy had permeated local government, including Child Protective Services and the Sheriff's office.[76]

In this perception of a broad Satanic threat Carol Darling was joined by her husband, who had been promoted to lieutenant in 1986, following his lurid syntheses of "cult" and ritual themes in the sexual abuse cases he had been pursuing as sergeant. In his new role as Satanic cult abuse expert and seasoned police officer, he had become leader of a police investigative team and promoted the Satanic cult conspiracy in connection with the various day care abuse panics before the media, sexual abuse conferences, and grand juries. Drawing on children's coerced testimony and a random collection of Satanic books and symbols, Brad Darling portrayed Satanic cults to various audiences as a conspiracy of great antiquity, now permeating American communities. They were sacrificing thousands of babies, drinking blood, engaging in perverse sexual acts, and using bodily wastes to defile children's innocence.[77]

Each arising from more prosaic (if quite diverse) careers and roles, MacFarlane, Summit, the Darlings, and other maverick experts in child sexual abuse in the early 1980s developed an obsessiveness in their investigations and revelations that struck many observers at the time. In their zeal to extract children's testimony, to recite pornographic scenes of ritual abuse to any audience, and to exhort the public and district attorneys' offices to prosecute and convict on little evidence, their expertise turned into a crusade: to rescue children and purify society from evil. This pattern, from social worker to zealous moral crusader and discerner of evil, occurred throughout the United States well into the 1990s.[78]

Indeed, the very zeal with which these experts sought to inform their colleagues of Satanic cult abuse led to the exportation of the Satanic cult abuse panic to the United Kingdom.[79] Not only were American Satanism experts from both evangelical and secular camps feeding Satanic cult signs and symptom lists to their anxious British counterparts, but from the middle of the 1980s several American experts were invited to lecture around England on Satanic cults and abuse: in particular, the social worker Pamela Klein and Sandi Gallant, who had the distinctive credibility of a woman police officer.[80] The American-formulated Satanic conspiracy had a compelling coherence to social workers in a country already beset by child-safety anxieties; and thus new experts in evil arose in the United Kingdom itself. Through the late 1980s, Dianne Core, an English social worker and organizer of the advocacy group Childwatch, was drawing on American SRA materials to prove that abusive Satanic cults were pervading English society at every level. By the early 1990s Core had become one of the most prominent Satanic cult experts in the United Kingdom, organizing television appearances of converted Satanic "baby-breeders" while claiming herself to "live with the threat of being imprisoned if she revealed all she knows about Satanism."[81] Here again, charisma and authority increased according to the degree of threat the expert could claim to be personally suffering in her role as crusader. Other experts followed: the evangelical Christian Maureen Davies and the psychiatrist Joan Coleman, both of whom directed prominent organizations combatting Satanic cults.[82]

As the panic about abusive Satanic cults spread over the course of the 1980s, the identification of its child "victims" came to include adults who claimed in psychotherapy to have experienced similar kinds of ritual abuse. The direct appearance of posttraumatic stress that these adults presented lent them greater credibility on Satanic cult abuse than small children, whose testimony had obviously been the subject of interpretation and synthesis by interviewers like Mac-Farlane. A good number of psychotherapists thus also rose quickly to the status of experts, but now in the identification and treatment of SRA among adults. More importantly, they also began to contribute to the elaboration of the Satanic cult threat as a conspiracy worthy of public attention.[83]

One of the first SRA experts from the field of psychotherapy was the psychiatrist Lawrence Pazder, coauthor of *Michelle Remembers*, who presented himself as having uncovered a Satanic cult conspiracy over the course of therapy with "Michelle." Michelle, whom Pazder later married, claimed to remember a series of lurid scenes of sexual and physical abuse whose character appeared to Pazder quite similar to what he had read and heard about as a Catholic medical missionary in Africa. "I've been thinking about it for some time," Pazder recalls his answer to Michelle's question about the nature of her abusers,

They seem more complex than ordinary cults or secret societies. Their rituals are very formal and established. When you stepped out of line and got your mother's dress dirty, they were furious. Nothing really spontaneous is allowed to happen, you know? All that makes me think this group has a long history. . . . The only group I know that fits your description is the Church of Satan. . . . There's a lot in the psychiatric literature about them. Most people think they're strictly Dark Ages, but the fact is, the Church of Satan is a worldwide organization. It's actually older than the Christian Church. And one of the areas where they're known to be active is the pacific Northwest.[84]

In the book's dramatic unveiling, over months of psychotherapy sessions, of an ancient conspiracy to rape and terrorize children for Satan, *Michelle Remembers* became the primary manifesto on SRA, invoked in numerous investigations of day care abuse. Pazder himself flew to Los Angeles in 1984 to meet with the panicked parents of McMartin Preschool children and the various therapists already involved, to propose that the sexual atrocities had occurred as part of an international Satanic cult conspiracy.[85] Subsequently, Pazder appeared on a television documentary alongside two cult-cops and a Christian evangelist to elaborate his SRA theories.

The entry of Satanic cult conspiracy ideas into the field of psychotherapy now led to the rise of a new network of experts in the discernment of evil, who saw such a conspiracy as a terrifying vindication of their particular therapy interests. Therapists interested, for example, in the ambiguous diagnostic category Multiple Personality Disorder, like psychiatrist Bennett Braun of Chicago's Rush-Presbyterian Hospital, concluded that Satanic cult abuse must lie behind the lurid traumas their severely dissociated patients reported. Braun initiated a special research unit in his hospital for curing Satanic cult-induced trauma.[86] Therapists interested in the potentiality of hypnotism to "unlock" traumatic memories that had been hidden away in the psyche, and unversed in the situational suggestibility of hypnotized subjects, were astounded to find lurid scenarios of cult ceremonies and atrocities flowing out of their patients' mouths.[87] Some feminist therapists saw Satanic cult abuse as the very epitome of the evil that was sexual abuse itself.[88] And a new field, evangelical Christian psychotherapy, which often reconfigured therapy as a context for spiritual warfare, spawned experts like James Friesen, for whom abusive Satanic cults represented the very Satanic opposition he had seen already in Christian therapy sessions.[89]

Psychotherapy—its meetings, continuing education seminars, and journals—became a crucible for the interpenetration of the diverse ideologies of evil discussed earlier.[90] Furthermore, as I will describe in chapter 6, psychotherapists in the late 1980s, overwhelmed with their encounters with real sexual abuse cases, were acutely receptive to a myth of evil conspiracy such as SRA offered. But here our interest lies in the emergence—from this social world, awash with notions of evil—of experts: that is, individuals claiming a particular clairvoyance into the activities of Satanic cults, or revealing particularly elaborate scenarios of Satanic conspiracy. One self-declared SRA therapist, Catherine Gould, revealed a nationwide Satanic plot to brainwash hundreds of thousands of victims through their rituals:

> Survivors of ritual abuse whom I have treated, or on whose cases I have consulted, have also discovered that they have worked for the cult/perpe-trator group as bookkeepers and money launderers, as drug dealers and couriers, as pornography subjects, as programmers/torturers of children, as computer programmers, as investment specialists, as legal advisers, and even as government agents, always outside the conscious awareness of their core personalities. . . . Most often as the survivor accesses the memories that are buried under countless layers of torture trauma, she has to contend not only with the rude awakening that since birth she has lived a life of un-speakable pain and horror outside her conscious awareness, but also that she has been literally enslaved to a perpetrator group. . . .
>
> . . . While ritual abuse is certainly an integral part of some kinds of sa-tanism, it is most likely that the deeper reason for the prevalence of ritual abuse is that, simply put, it reliably creates a group of people who function as unpaid slaves to the perpetrator group. Because their core personalities are amnestic to their cult activities, these ritual abuse victims pose little threat to their controllers.
>
> . . . It is by definition difficult to know who belongs to groups whose membership is highly secretive, especially when many of the membership themselves are amnestic to their involvement. Therefore, it is difficult to assess the degree to which members of these groups *influence media ac-*counts of ritual abuse, *derail ritual abuse investigations* by law enforcement, are instrumental in getting children complaining of intrafamilial ritual abuse sent back to an abusing parent, or *hire officials to make public state-ments* on behalf of a national law enforcement bureau to the effect that no substantial evidence of ritual abuse exists.[91]

Other therapists proposed, on the basis of cursory research in old books on Devil-worship and human sacrifice, the continuation of ancient secret societies, or deviants on the periphery of normal religion who pervert their sacred teachings, or mutations of primitive shaman-ism, or even the "cultic" enactment of some primitive urge to sacrifice

children for ritual power.[92] These far-reaching, pseudohistorical rationales for Satanic abuse claimed to link individual psychotherapists'
experiences with patients, day care "cults," group-atrocities of recent
decades like Manson and Jonestown, and anthropological accounts of
child sacrifice and cannibalism both illusory and reliable, all within a
larger perception of the decline of morality. The individual patient's
experience became but the tip of the iceberg, while the therapists
emerged as valiant revealers and opponents of a horrible underworld.

Indeed, as we have seen, the most prominent experts in detecting
SRA claimed to be victims of that Satanic underworld conspiracy
themselves. A general paranoia pervaded therapists, social workers,
and treatment centers claiming to take SRA seriously, and therapists
began to feel themselves subject to covert threats and harrassment.
Such paranoia seemed to validate their acknowledgment of Satanic
cult abuse and patients' stories, and for some SRA therapists fear became a badge of authority. Psychologist Cory Hammond, delivering a
major conference lecture (1992) on the revelations of Satanic abuse
that he had uncovered through hypnotism, announced to lengthy ap-
plause that, "I've finally decided—to hell with it, if the cults are going
to kill me, then they are going to kill me."[93]

Expertise in the discernment of Satanic evil was expressed most directly in the techniques that therapists advocated for unveiling patients' "memories" of Satanic cult victimization. Hypnotism, drugs, and
coercive visualization practices were justified on the basis of the conspiracy's real existence and the clever "brainwashing" to which the Satanists had subjected the patients.[94] Satanic abuse "indicator lists," such
as those circulating between the United States and United Kingdom
during the late 1980s, were developed not only to translate patients'
immediate problems into symptoms of SRA, but also to interpret every
ambiguous experience in the ongoing life of now-traumatized patients
as cult messages. Signs and clues were perceived in the patient's clothing, in the phone calls she receives and remarks she overhears; messages appear on her car. Psychiatrist Bennett Braun gave a 1992 lecture
at a conference on child sexual abuse in which he showed slides of
greeting cards and mentioned the flower arrangements through which
(he assured his audience) a Satanic cult had tried to contact his

patient: "Pink flowers mean suicide, red means cutting. . . . Red roses or white baby's breath means bloody suicide. Pink roses mean hanging. Blue is death by suffocation. Yellow is silence or fire. Green means go ahead and do something. If the card is signed 'Love you,' then that is a danger signal."[95]

By such confident means of interpretation, adult psychotherapists, like child advocates and social workers, expanded their professional roles from healing specialists, trained in the focused and self-critical resolution of individual cases, to moral crusaders and experts in the detection of evil. This transformation certainly involved, on the one hand, personal convictions and predilections to authority on the part of these emergent experts, and on the other hand, a context of new social crises and panics that required new leadership roles. Yet my interest here has been in the construction of the expert discerner of evil: her innovative techniques, her articulation of conspiracy, her sense of embattlement by a powerful adversary, her tireless crusade in multiple fora and media, and—a key feature in the "performance" of expertise in this panic—her identification with, even embodiment of, the victim, such that audiences would see not a crusader or fanatic but a heroic and passionate revealer of conspiracy.

It is in this social context that an ancient, ultimately theological concept of evil threat, carried in ecclesiastical tracts on heresy (and then revitalized in popular form in movies like *The Exorcist* [1973] and *The Devil's Rain* [1975]), came to dominate secular professional worlds. And yet, as we have seen, this reappearance of Sabbat-type images of Satanic perversion did not represent a shift from evangelical Christian ideology but rather its increasing influence on American and British popular and professional cultures during the 1980s. Indeed, evangelical Christian leaders and authors continued to play important roles in promulgating the image of Satanic cult abuse and conspiracy.[96]

SATANIC RITUAL ABUSE: EVANGELICAL CHRISTIAN DISCERNERS

For many evangelical leaders and authors, the prospect of healing those with prior lives in Satanism (even as victims of Satanism) simply brought a starker clarity to the traditional evangelical emphasis on rebirth through Christ and the cleansing of all that preceded.[97] Indeed, one of the most influential exposés of a Satanic underworld, preceding the revelations of Satanic cult abuse, came from an evangelist who claimed to have been a Satanic high priest before his conversion: Mike Warnke, author of *The Satan Seller* (1972). Warnke was a prominent speaker and consultant on Satanic cults throughout the 1980s, advising law enforcement and child abuse professionals on the hierarchy of the Satanic world from which he claimed to have been delivered. His authority as *ex*-Satanist and his charisma as born-again evangelist bolstered each other—made his ministry that much more focused and combative, for he had been (he claimed) on the other side. The effect on audiences of such passionate warning was clear: in July 1988, after Larry Nelson from Mike Warnke Ministries gave a two-day seminar at a church in Steubenville, Ohio, "Many parents kept their children home, due to fear that they might be kidnapped and sacrificed by the 'cult.' At a press conference, [the] County Sheriff announces that a dozen teenagers are involved in Satanism and two are getting therapy."[98]

But the evangelical investment in SRA also brought to the broader cultural stage the reality of Satan and demons. The evangelical ministers' discernment and elaboration of the Satanic conspiracy, using the overt language of warfare, expressed their conviction that these were the End-Times: that in the era of the Antichrist's appearance Satanic worship would become ever more prominent. Evangelists and evangelicals with deliverance ministries thus saw themselves in a front line against Satan and sought out battles everywhere possible.[99]

"For our struggle is not against enemies of blood and flesh, but against the rulers, against the authorities, against the cosmic powers of this present darkness, against the spiritual forces of evil in the heavenly places. Therefore take up the whole armor of God, so that you may be able to withstand on that evil day, and having done everything, to stand firm" (Eph. 6:12, NRSV). Thus reads one of the central scriptural mottoes of spiritual warfare, in which individual laity, not just ministers, would engage against the demonic in everyday life and popular culture. In its rise during the 1980s, spiritual warfare represented a popularization in the engagement with evil: not just experts but *everybody* might have the capacity to perceive and "take up arms against" the demonic. Yet spiritual warfare ideology also created multiple new charismatic roles for those laity especially gifted—in their own and others' eyes—in the so-called "discernment" of evil beings. Those with the gift of discernment would work independently at Christian events or alongside exorcistic ministers in teams, claiming preternatural bodily responses that indicated the presence of demons.[100] Such discernment often assumed a psychotherapeutic character: demons of sin, of obsession, and of hidden or suppressed occult pasts, all of whom might be addressed verbally and even traced back to original entry points in patients' early lives, much like the "multiple personalities" of dissociative patients—and evangelical therapists made much of the resemblance. The new field of evangelical Christian psychotherapy thus adopted demonic discernment and spiritual warfare models for working with individual patients of the most extreme sort in a religious mode.[101] Mirroring evangelical Christianity's attention to various trance states, the SRA model offered a convincing synthesis of demonic symptoms, prior sins, and the omnipresent threat of a Satanic realm. The result was a phalanx of experts in discerning evil, some freelance laity and some with psychological training, all absolutely convinced of their own divine talents, who would appear in evangelical or charismatic Christian settings, confront people, and detect SRA in their pasts.[102] The journalist Lawrence Wright recounts the following example from 1988 in Olympia, Washington—the prelude to a massive SRA investigation:

[Karla] Franko is a charismatic Christian who believes she has been given the biblical gifts of healing and spiritual discernment. Before going to Bible college, she had been a dancer and stand-up comic as well as an actress, and had parts in several sitcoms and TV commercials, which added a note of celebrity in the minds of the young girls in the audience. Often in speaking to youth groups such as this one, Franko would feel herself filled with the Holy Spirit and would make pronouncements that the Spirit urged upon her. Many extraordinary events took place at the 1988 retreat [at a Christian youth camp]. At one point, Franko told the mesmerized group that she had a mental picture of a little girl hiding in a coat closet, and saw a crack of light under the door. Footsteps were approaching. There was the sound of a key locking the door. At that, a girl in the audience stood up, heaving with sobs, and cried out that she had been that little girl. Franko then had another vision. She said that someone in the audience had been molested as a young girl by a relative. Suddenly, a deaf girl rushed out of the room. A woman named Paula Davis, who, along with Ericka [the girl who would ultimately claim SRA], was interpreting for the deaf campers, went after the girl and found her in the bathroom with her head in the toilet, trying to drown herself. In this charged atmosphere, a number of girls came forward to say that they, too, had been abused. The counselors had their hands full.[103]

Within five months of this event, a confluence of experts and their SRA manuals had revealed that a Satanic cult was pervading Olympia and its police department. The charisma of experts like Franko derives from their convincing presentation of pervasive evil as something that can be "spiritually perceived" in another person's past. The campers clearly invested her with full clairvoyant authority.

The evangelical Christian ideology of deliverance thus spawned a plethora of roles, from full-fledged "ministries" (including highly charismatic exorcist-preachers) to individuals with various "gifts." In these roles people would claim the ability to discern the demonic in others and then to help them be rid of demonic affliction through private and publicly staged exorcisms. If this movement's most dramatic expressions occurred with demonic possession and the gifts of the Holy Spirit, the early 1980s saw a turn in the focus of discernment—especially among the new ranks of Christian psychotherapists—to sensing SRA in clients' backgrounds and aiding those clients to acknowledge it in connection with embracing Christ's salvation. This new turn in discernment and exorcism involved a combination of at least four successive lines of thought within evangelical Christian culture: first, 1970s beliefs in an *organized Satanism* as a cultural threat; second, traditional evangelical constructions of *presalvation sinfulness*—that the authenticity and power of one's rebirth in Christ required the starkest possible polarization to one's prior lifestyle, including Satanic office; third, an interest in the *discernment* of trance states and inner feelings that come from God or Satan, leading to the cultivation of the latter and the deliverance from the former; and fourth, new (1980s) notions that *demons might enter through past sins or traumas*, especially of a sexual nature. The resulting construction of a client's past abuse by Satanic cults would depend as much on the client's response and manifestation as on the discerner. As chapter 6 will describe, the so-inclined client or "victim" had an essential role in emphasizing Satanic cult activities, the presence of demons, or sexual perversion. Thus by the late 1980s, a discerner's or therapist's recognition of SRA could lead to a variety of resolutions, from Christian psychotherapy to the exorcism of demons associated with the occult, incest, or multiple personalities—and even to the development of highly separatist groups of "survivors" identifying themselves as anti-Satanic warriors.

Conclusions: Expertise and the Depiction of Satanic Conspiracy

The sociologist David Bromley has proposed that any conspiracy theory, but particularly those envisioning witches or Satanists—some flagrant evil—involves several key dimensions: a "history" in which the evil has an origin and has since operated covertly; a "space" or realm in which evil forces dwell separately from our own (or in the very interstices of our own); and a "counter-*culture*" of values, goals, and relationships that are invariably the inverse of our own in the treatment of children, corpses, blood, and sexual relations. To render this picture of evil conspiracy into a warrant for action, however, there must also be an equally detailed picture of evil "agency"—the multifarious ways that the conspiracy attacks our world and its hitherto secure institutions.[104] Evil agency, as it is imagined in ancient demonologies, witch-finding tracts, and modern pictures of Satanic cults, ranges from public catastrophes to the covert stealing of babies, seduction of youth, and brainwashing of adults.

The focus of this chapter has been the expert in evil who in fact develops these scenarios, assembling and promoting them, as well as urging their resolution through crusade and purge. Through this anxious projection of a conspiracy and its hierarchy, the expert also gains charisma—that is, power in the estimation of others, and authority in dictating action. The greater the threat he portrays—and the more anxious the audience becomes in consequence—the more important becomes the expert as discerner of evil, and the more indispensable he becomes as its expunger.

In the beginning of this chapter we saw how simply setting local misfortunes and malevolence in some larger, cosmic context—some "master" demonology—brought authority to temple or exorcist. Ancient demonologies and their temples and experts gained authority because of their pretense to control and avert powers popularly deemed ambivalent and chaotic. In contemporary society, those who label complex, sometimes imaginary acts of harm or cruelty "evil" and then systematize the concept have a similar effect on those in a state of anxiety or confusion over the nature of misfortune, for they transform the experience of misfortune from some inexplicable disaster or some uniquely horrible crime to an organized and subversive assault by an evil conspiracy.[105] Our more extreme examples of this process of articulating evil have included exorcistic movements like that of Kudagama, Sri Lanka, where specialists oppose the evil they have projected in the landscape, as well as those individuals who discover evil where others had not imagined it (witch-finders, SRA experts) and then mobilize audiences to prosecute. The leader who reinterprets negative, or simply ambiguous, experience within a framework of evil and subversion thereby makes himself indispensable to the resolution—the cleansing—of that evil.

Beyond the reciprocal charisma gained in discerning evil, however, we have seen a range of different roles—performances—for expertise. Most self-professed experts in evil have developed the role out of some prior status of authority: priest or friar, evangelist or prophet, police officer, judge, or minor civic roles like social worker or psychiatrist. In all these cases, experts bring the badges and idioms of their institutions, both to to define their own distinctive abilities to discern evil ("As a police officer, I know . . .") and to elaborate the evil itself ("They are organized like one of our churches, except . . ."). Thus modern evangelical ministers brought their churches' conviction in the reality of Satan and the Last Days to nuance Satanic cult abuse. Royal and juridical witch-finders in early modern Europe emphasized the witch-conspiracy's opposition to all branches of the social order. Social workers and psychotherapists presented themselves as singularly attentive to the "evidence" coming from children and adult patients of SRA, and in this way they lent the Satanic conspiracy the stamp of scientific legitimacy endowed by their professions.

Experts with these kinds of prior authority could also present themselves as agents of larger institutions for the cleansing of evil: the Church as protector of society in the case of early modern witchhunts; the mental health and social service fields as agencies of moral reform and forensic science in the case of Satanic abuse panics. What the African witch-finder brings, in contrast, is not an official institution but the renown and efficacy of his own movement and his own singular ability to encapsulate modern experience, elements of traditional thought, and current anxieties in an integrated picture of evil.

Among the most important influences on the development of elaborate demonologies and Satanic conspiracies is the book. If the earliest systematic demonologies, as we saw in chapter 2, could be preserved and interpreted in either oral or literary cultures (in either of which priests could construct lists of local demons for protective rites), the development of a *learned* demonology depended on the capacity of writing to organize demonological lore from local settings and to project a sense of order. Witch-finding from the fifteenth century onward likewise depended on books to guide the inquisitions' torture, to link the local incident of witchcraft to broad conspiracies, to link multiple cases of witchcraft, and to defend the ecclesiastical picture of witchcraft. Textuality became, indeed, a mode of the witch-finder's authority, as De Lancre and others published manuals that demonstrated their logic, familiarity with previous literature, adherence to ecclesiastical teaching, and preternatural cleverness in discovering witches. Books had only slightly less importance in the modern Satanic cult panic, for television and seminars also provided ways for experts to gain immediate publicity. Yet by the end of the 1990s the self-defined expert in Satanic evil—psychotherapist, charismatic Christian discerner, or cult cop—might refer to Larry Kahaner's *Cults That Kill* (1988), Michael Langone and Linda Blood's *Satanism and Occult-Related Violence: What You Should Know* (1990), David Sakheim and Susan Devine's *Out of Darkness: Exploring Satanism and Ritual Abuse* (1992), Daniel Ryder's *Breaking the Circle of Satanic Ritual Abuse* (1992), and James Noblitt and Pamela Perskin's *Cult and Ritual Abuse* (2000).

All these patterns, from the expansion of roles to the construction of threat to the use of texts, help to answer the questions: What is the role of leadership in the spread of a myth of evil conspiracy? Who is it who discerns evil among us? What constitutes his expertise, and how is it that such a figure can convince us that we must recognize and purge evil at any cost?

4 *Rites of Evil*

CONSTRUCTIONS OF MALEFICENT

RELIGION AND RITUAL

IN THE LAST CHAPTER we saw the indispensability of the expert in evil for assembling and laying out evil conspiracies and for demonstrating the tangibility of evil in the immediate world of audiences. In early modern Europe, as in modern Africa, myths of evil conspiracy have to a great extent come down to the activities of such experts.

In this chapter we shift from the social world of experts and their audiences to the stories they convey: tableaux of the most monstrous behavior, condensations of absolute evil. To some degree these evils will reflect discrete cultural values; and yet much is repeated across time and place: cannibalism, sexual perversion, abuse and eating of children, the desecration of sacred things, and—the subject of this chapter—the notion that some ceremony, some ritual, in particular a bloody sacrifice, organizes all the evil. The rites might be imagined along familiar lines, like an inverted Catholic mass, or as something entirely foreign yet recognizable as ritual, like a human sacrifice performed to loud drums. Here, for example, are allegations against Christians from the second century CE (reported, ironically, by a Christian), followed by a portrait of the Basque witches' Sabbat by the early seventeenth-century witchfinder De Lancre, and then a patient's "memory" of evil rites as reported by her therapists:

[The Christians, it is said,] actually reverence the genitalia of their director and high priest, and adore his organs as parent of their being. . . . Details of the initiation of neophytes are as revolting as they are notorious. An infant, cased in dough to deceive the unsuspecting, is placed beside the person to be initiated. The novice is thereupon induced to inflict what seem to be harmless blows upon the dough, and unintentionally the infant is killed by his unsuspecting blows; the blood—oh, horrible—they lap up greedily; the limbs they tear to pieces eagerly; and over the victim they make league and covenant, and by complicity in guilt pledge themselves to mutual silence. Such sacred rites are more foul than any sacrilege.[1]

After [the priest of the witches' Sabbat] has renounced his Creator, after having denied Him and having watched a host of others follow his example, after having frolicked, dancing obscenely and impudently, after having eaten at their festivities the heart of some unbaptised baby stewed in violence, after a hundred thousand impudent, sodomitic, and devilish copulations, . . . after having flayed a mass of toads to make and sell poison and infected powders to destroy both men and harvests, he then added as the final act of abomination the mockery of the most revered and precious Sacrament that God gave to men to gain salvation.[2]

The ceremonies had a congregation area facing a stage with an altar. There was a procession down the main aisle from the back of the arena to the stage area. This procession included the leaders of the cult, several adult women and children all dressed in a variety of robes depending on their level of command. Once all were on stage, the ceremony began. There was a service with chanting, the playing of drums in a beat of changing rhythms, and the chief leader speaking and chanting. There was a door on the back right side of the stone structure where children entered the stage. During the ceremony children were to drink a drug-induced [sic] liquid from a large cup as part of the service. The service continued to increase in intensity always resulting in the sexual molestation of children on the altar and during some ceremonies the killing of those children. . . . During the services that were held outdoors in isolated mountain camps the cult used torches and large bonfires to light the area. Fire was considered a special expression of their religion and used to frighten the children by human sacrifices, burning adults and children on large crosses.[3]

These depictions of horrific rituals occurring at the center of groups that are altogether evil, and somehow grounding all the harmful acts afflicting "us," suggest that the perpetrators, the participants, are not simply random criminals or psychopaths but a *cult* of evil-doers, who

wreak havoc out of some kind of religious devotion and actually celebrate their crimes in some covert ritual. The criminal or witch *we* see
is only one of a kingdom of devotees. These devotees engage in a religion of sorts—and in that way seem to resemble us—but it is a religion
of evil in every respect: sacrifices of babies, sacraments of blood or
feces, orgies, lewd parodies, liminal places and times. These religions
are not concocted as pretend worlds or fodder for stories, but as real
underworlds among us, whose proof and elaboration might guide
witch-trials or ritual murder investigations. "After three gruesome days
of torture," R. Po-Chia Hsia summarizes the 1470 ritual-murder trial of
Mercklin, a Jewish citizen of Endingen, Germany, "the climax of the
investigation was not the admission of murder by Mercklin but the
confession of motive: that Jews killed the children for the healing and
salutary power of Christian blood."[4]

The growing, panicked belief in a society devoted to child-sacrifice
and perversions, which preys on us out of allegiance to Satan or some
other dire system, has long inflamed communities and their professionals to find signs of that society in the village environment and its minions among our neighbors. The ritual focus has been central to the
construction of Satanic cult conspiracies in modern America, Africa,
and the United Kingdom. Encroaching evil and the corruption of society is configured not as some abstract moral decline but as spreading
devotion to a subversive cult of murder and child-sacrifice. How do we
make sense of this central, integrating feature of evil—and of ritual itself as a representation of evil?

Inevitably, these images of evil ritual have been constructed, in either popular or official lore, according to prevailing notions of proper
liturgy, sacrifice, sacrament, or ceremonial behavior. As much as evil
rites designate the devotees as monstrous, by their sheer adherence to
ceremony itself they become somehow recognizable—evil as a function
of inversion, not incomprehensibility. But through all the cultural constructions of evil ritual—among witches, Jews, Satanists, heretics—and
the popular responses to them, there is a deeper element of speculation
about humanness and savagery, about local maleficence and a greater
evil, and about ritual itself as an ambivalent aspect of society and
tradition. For the many images of evil or savage ritual across cultures

ultimately serve as negative means for imagining ritual and religion as constitutive forces in culture: what they do for people and the efficacy they carry.

Across these scenarios ritual both epitomizes the Other and signifies the Other's most profound danger to us.[5] On the one hand, the elaborate mythic scheme of the witches' Sabbat and Jewish ritual murder derives from the most archaic images of difference. Not only has the Other customs the very inverse of ours, but those customs are integrated with his culture, his gods, and his traditional behavior through ritual expressions. In antiquity, ritual expression meant sacrifice, the central religious act by which a community achieved reciprocity with the supernatural world by transferring some body or substance. But sacrifice often implied—in the imagination of the Other—transgression of humanity, ecstatic states when such barbarians would come together and, through frenzied dance, lose their reason and engage in bestial acts of violence. In this sense, sacrifice—or ritual in general—served as a potential point of danger: what "they" might do to "us." Ritual might then imply the deliberate mockery or inversion of human—"our"—customs, and then (as early modern Europeans imagined) an alternative supernatural world, a dangerous and chaotic one, reciprocity with which might bring real and destructive powers into the arena of the human and domestic.

Ritual as a Point of Otherness

It is not just that the Other, living on the world's periphery, can resemble in many ways an animal in his sexual, culinary, and political proclivities, but even more that he has a body of custom and ceremony that sanctions such behavior. The Irish "are cannibals as well as gluttons," reports Strabo, and they "consider it honorable, when their fathers die, to eat them and to fornicate openly both with other women and with their mothers and sisters." The Jews, Tacitus claims, are "uniquely lustful"; and while their unseemly disgust for outsiders forbids sex with them, "among themselves nothing is prohibited."[6] A covert and innate concupiscence thus describes even a relatively familiar people, whom one might meet in one's city. An enemy's cruelty and even monstrosity would be signified by imputations of cannibalism, for in this act he became like a demon. The warlike nature of the Scythians, the perennial barbarian for Greco-Roman writers, was encapsulated in their disorganized modes of sacrifice and in their customary inclination to sacrifice humans. Rituals of human sacrifice epitomized *xenoktonia*, "killing of the stranger-guest," a crime of mythical proportions in Greek tradition but imputed as religious custom to Scythians and other peoples on the edges of the world. To the extent that a properly ordered culture engages in properly ordered sacrifices, these alien cultures do keep ritual traditions and customs—thus they are above animals—but differently enough from the Greek and Roman models to cast them as entirely Other . . . and to afford literary entertainment.[7]

This last point emerges most vividly in the novels of the Greco-Roman world. One finds in this literature (as well as in other aspects of culture) a particular concern with boundaries, foreignness, and especially foreign religions that seems to have followed the rise and expansion of Roman imperial authority in the first centuries CE. The theme of cannibal cultures on the empire's periphery provides the dramatic foil to an anonymous third- or fourth-century legend of the Apostle Andrew, who is sent to Myrmidonia, a city whose inhabitants "ate no bread and drank no water but ate human flesh and drank their blood. They would seize all who came to their city, dig out their eyes, [and] make them drink a drug prepared by sorcery and magic" that would make them animal-like.[8] Novelists like Achilles Tatius and Lollianos offer lurid scenes of human sacrifice to demonstrate the religious Otherness of the bandit gangs into whose clutches heroines tended to fall.[9] For example, in the second-century CE novel *Leukippe and Clitophon* the bandits

> had an improvised altar made of mud and a coffin near it. Then two of them led up the girl, her hands tied behind her back. . . . First they poured libations over her head and led her round the altar while, to the accompaniment of a pipe, a priest chanted what seemed to be an Egyptian hymn; this at least was indicated by the movements of his lips and the contortions of his features. Then, at a concerted sign, all retired to some distance from the altar; one of the two young attendants laid her down on her back, and

strapped her so by means of pegs fixed in the ground, . . . then he took a sword and plunging it in about the region of the heart, drew it down to the lower part of the belly, opening up her body; the bowels gushed out, and these they drew forth in their hands and placed upon the altar; and when they were roasted, the whole body of them cut them up into small pieces, divided them into shares and ate them. . . . I [the narrator] sat gazing in my consternation, rooted to the spot by the horror of the spectacle.[10]

The perspective in which we are invited to participate here combines curiosity and revulsion: surely, we realize, we are in another realm of human culture—on its very periphery, in fact. Yet our curiosity is drawn to the ritual precision of the atrocity. It is without doubt a sacrifice, but quite the extreme of our own. Another novel heightens that extreme distance by following the ritual disembowelling and consumption of a young man with an orgy, as if to signify that no standards of bodily purity surround the ceremonial offering of the body, and yet this is what bandits do to create social cohesion.[11]

These deliberately fantastic scenarios from Roman antiquity, using bandits as countercultures, paralleled a tendency among historical writers of the same period also to impute sacrifice and ritual cannibalism to cultures deemed disorderly or subhuman—especially nomads. The boundaries of humanity that might be apparent in such cultures' different economic and domestic lifestyle are revealed and epitomized in ritual acts that are fundamentally atrocious.[12] The historian Cassius Dio, for example, imputes to both Jews (who staged a revolt in the early second century CE) and Egyptian "herders" (a kind of nomad) human sacrifice and cannibalism, practiced as central binding rituals.[13] Several centuries later, an anonymous monk living in the Sinai Desert depicted the central religious ceremony of a mysterious, apparently subhuman Bedouin tribe as revolving around the ecstatic slaughter of a camel:

They three times circumambulate [the victim], which is lying down. And a certain person begins both the procession and hymns. . . . On the third circuit, when the multitude has not yet stopped the hymns but the last part of the song is on their tongues, he quickly draws the sword and strikes the tendon, and immediately tastes the first blood. And thus the rest of them, rushing foward with daggers, cut off bits of skin with the hairs, hack off and snatch the first pieces of flesh, move into the organs and entrails, leaving none of the sacrifice behind undigested that could ever be visible to the sun. For they avoid neither bones nor brain matter, overcoming with endurance the hardest stuff and cracking resistant matter with ease. *This, then, is the* nomos ["law" or "custom"] *of life and worship for the Barbarians.*[14]

A descent into bestial disorder, a true blood-orgy, is preceded by a series of deliberate ceremonial acts. The overall scene encapsulates this people's *nomos*. In fact, this camel-sacrifice scene is quite famous in Western intellectual history, for it formed the basis of theories of sacrifice developed by the nineteenth-century Semitic scholar Robertson Smith, followed by Sigmund Freud and René Girard. The blood-orgy around the camel offered the key, these thinkers believed, to all acts of sacrifice and sacred killing. Yet the scene belongs to the same imaginative tradition of depicting alien cultures through their putative central rituals as altogether different and fundamentally savage. Here especially the sacrificial beast is the domestic camel—too close to be proper food—and there is no discrimination as to what parts are eaten. Although the rites begin in ways familiar to a monastic writer and his audience (procession, hymns, circumambulation), they quickly slide into chaos: a scene of utter depravity in food-consumption that can only be compared to Euripides' picture of the ecstatic *sparagmos* ("[flesh-]tearing") of the Bacchae. The *nomos* of the religion is chaos, a ritually sanctioned descent into bestiality that neatly melds the culinary and the devotional.[15]

These classical and late antique materials show an overt cross-fertilization of themes of ritual Otherness across geographical, historical, and fictional writing. On the periphery of Roman culture lay cultures prone to cannibalism and human sacrifice, imagined either as ecstatic or deliberately systematic rites. Monstrous ritual implied an ambiguous humanity, an association with beasts in one sense, yet an all-too-human devotion to sacrificial precision in another sense. Closer to civilization, one found such monstrous rituals especially among nomadic peoples or those peoples imagined as interlopers, like Jews. Roman culture became increasingly fearful of such monstrous rituals and their claims to subversive power encroaching on the center itself: from devotees of Bacchus in 186 BCE Rome to Christians around the Roman

FIGURE 2   Theodor de Bry, scene of Tupinamba cannibals. From *Grands voyages*, Book III: Americae (Frankfurt, 1593), 87. Cambridge, Massachusetts. Courtesy of Tozzer Library of Harvard College Library, Harvard University. While the women casually feed their children with body-parts in expressions of maternal intimacy, their nude poses offer the viewer a combination of horror and erotic freedom similar to depictions of witches in Europe (cf. figure 7).

Empire in the second and third centuries CE, the subject of the infant-cannibalism rumor we saw above (pp. 73–74). But even in these cases of outright panic—orgiastic human sacrifices in our very neighborhoods!—it is important to note a feature of the ancient novels: *voyeurism*. Underlying all these literary representations of monstrous ritual is a horrified fascination with ceremonial abuse and murder, emerging in the alleged witness's position, the lurid details, and the eroticized victims.

Through the early modern period and into modern times peripheral cultures have likewise been composites of bestial traits—nudity,
cannibalism, even beast-like appearances—and fantasies of sexual
freedom and Edenic harmony. Sixteenth-century reports of Brazilian
Indians were absorbed into a geographical tradition fascinated since
antiquity with images of subhuman culture. Consequently, the methods of cannibalism—were victims hunted or bred?—became the focus
of ethnographies of the New World, complemented invariably by
woodcuts that arranged nude Indians in pornographic tableaux of cannibalistic butchery and cooking.[16] (See figure 2.) As in Strabo and
other ancient geographers, cannibalism was paired with sexual excess
or inversion in order to depict a culture completely lacking "our"
mores, yet cohesive in its own ways. "Ignorant of all forms of civil society and religion," the literary historian Frank Lestringant summarizes,
the savages of sixteenth-century travel-literature

> fornicate freely, shamelessly and openly, without respect for the bonds of
> blood: "they have as many women as they wish [he quotes one text]. Son
> couples with mother, and sister with brother, any man with any woman;
> any and every time they wish, they divorce from their marriages, and in no
> thing do they keep order."
>
> These peoples, as well as enjoying freedom of divorce and the absence of
> an incest taboo, are voraciously anthropophagous, and here again they ig-
> nore all frontiers and taboos.[17]

These are cultures that engage in abhorrent acts "by nature" and as
collective expressions. As sixteenth-century illustrations depict it, Indians do not even need to go into ecstatic states or to precede their
culinary or sexual abasements with processions. It is simply custom, as
the Indian king seems to indicate to his European guest as they watch
nude women dance before the sacrifice of one's first-born child. (See
figure 3.) But this geographical fantasy soon gave way to a missionary
effort. And from the missionary perspective, that distanced image of
the cohesive customs of cannibalism and incest proved less comprehensible than the more sinister idea that a series of formal rites, mysterious and bloody, integrated the Indians' perversions. Indians now
were Devil-worshippers, with priesthoods, sacrifices, atrocities, and sexual behavior all brought together in service to Satan. This perspective

FIGURE 3   Theodor de Bry, scene of sacrifice of first-born child while women
dance. From *Grands voyages*, Book II (Frankfurt, 1603), pl. 24.
Cambridge, Massachusetts. Courtesy of Tozzer Library of Harvard
College Library, Harvard University. As the Indian king gestures
to the European soldier and one mother's firstborn is prepared for
slaughter on the altar to the left, the Indian women dance freely
and suggestively in a ring. Highlighting such (alleged) customs in
popular books represented the Indians as both alluringly libertine
and atrociously bestial, while the image of naked women's dances
in anticipation of child-sacrifice corresponds to depictions of the
witches' Sabbat (cf. figures 4c; 5-F, H).

gained most credibility when applied to cultures like those of the
Aztecs and Mayans that indeed had sophisticated, centralized religions. And yet the view of a Devil-worship that organized all the

perversities of heathen culture clearly drew upon fantasies of the perversities of the Other on the edge of the earth so popular in sixteenth-century literature.[18] It also elaborated, we might say, that more basic belief, often recorded in small societies, that the people "over there" are Devil-worshippers or particularly dangerous sorcerers who use children in their potions.[19] In these perspectives, it is ritual that becomes the central point of difference, that brings together a range of bestial, inverse, or perverse customs. Ritual portrays horrific acts as essential to a culture and habitually pursued by those adhering to that culture.

We have seen how this fascination with ritual as the centerpoint of Otherness began in classical literature and flourished in early modern Europe, especially in Europeans' encounters with Central and South American cultures (which did have distinct, and sometimes bloody, ceremonial practices). By the later nineteenth century, description of "primitive rites" had become an opportunity for prurience into worlds of a dangerous yet exciting debauchery. Thus an 1869 Portuguese novella conjures the Afro-Brazilian Umbanda rites:

> The dance, now spreading, comes again to a boil; the obscene Negress and her partner move lewdly. Interrupting their violent dance, they carry to each and all the vase or gourd containing the beverage, telling them to "drink *pemba*" and each one takes a swig of the dangerous and filthy pemba. Those who are sick from sorcery, the candidates to the office of sorcerer, those who use sorcery for good or bad ends subject themselves to the most absurd, repulsive and indecent ordeals, and to the most squalid of practices. . . .
>
> . . . and in the delirium of all, in the infernal flames of depraved imaginations, are evidenced, almost always shamelessly, an unchecked, ferocious, and torpid lewdness.
>
> All this is hideous and horrible, but that is how it is.[20]

As anyone familiar with American movies will recognize, these same themes also took root in modern American culture, where foreignness—its nature and especially its place—preoccupied a nation perpetually encountering "savages" around its borders. Popular cinema and books from the 1920s through the 1980s repeatedly highlight some savage ritual—usually an exotic human sacrifice performed by drum-maddened natives—into which a white woman has fallen. These scenes of orgiastic ritual maintain the simultaneous allure and horror of peripheral lands, as in in the "Kong sacrifice" rites the explorers witness in the beginning of *King Kong* (1933), or even—more horrifying—of a secret savagery that continues beneath the surface of colonized worlds, like the "Thugee" cult, replete with drugged slaves, human sacrifice, and mindless devotion to a terrifying idol, that the hero discovers in *Indiana Jones and the Temple of Doom* (1984).

Haiti in particular was made the subject of such depictions of savagery revolving around ritual. Because of its multiply ambiguous status as a black republic within reach of the United States and as the site of both African and Catholic cultures—both deeply suspect to Protestant American eyes—a series of books and films starting in the early twentieth century revealed a land of cannibalism, sexual depravity, nudity, obscene and wicked rituals that involved human sacrifice, and the ever-present quest for group ecstasy through drums, chanting, and trance—all integrated as elements of "Voodoo." That *voudoun* exists as an historical religious formulation remains a fact separate from *Voodoo's* popularization as an eroticized and dangerous cult of the periphery (in the same way that evidence for actual Brazilian anthropophagy offers little context for the popular sixteenth-century depictions of Brazil as a land of cannibals). Books such as W. Seabrook's *The Magic Island* (1929) and R. Loederer's *Voodoo Fire in Haiti* (1935), and films like *White Zombie* (1932) and *The Serpent and the Rainbow* (1988) confronted American audiences with the stirring notion that the cannibalistic and orgiastic rites of savage lands lay at their doorsteps—and even came inside. In the 1987 films *Angel Heart* and *The Believers*, Voodoo cults were imagined as practicing their nefarious rites right in American cities.[21] Both films, moreover, cast these homicidal cults in plainly erotic undertones.

Through such scenes, which have always carried a pseudoethnographic air, as if they were but distillations of known cultural traits rather than exotic fantasy, an image of savage ritual has been preserved since antiquity. When such rituals are imagined to take place on the periphery of civilization, they are a source of horror and allure (and often an inducement to conquer or missionize). When they creep inside, carried perhaps by immigrants from the edges of the earth, they pose a threat—even a conspiracy, as their savage cravings begin to turn on us, the host culture. Their human sacrifices and cannibalistic urges in our very midst fill us with horror. And yet that horror comes partly from our *fascination*—even, as the next chapter will describe, identification—with these transgressive impulses to invert the moral order. The Other, the Savage, who bears our projections and inversions is now in our neighborhoods; and this new location requires that we repudiate it sharply. Thus, through rumors and literary depictions of horrific ceremonies, we re-evaluate the allure that the savage's rites *might* offer, off on the periphery. Now they pose a grave danger and immediate threat.

Ritual and the Monstrous Realm

The rites of the dangerous Other, whether witch or foreigner, involve first of all inverted feasts and sacrifices and the breaching of sexual and ceremonial boundaries. But beyond these central elements, the bizarre repertoire of ritual acts imputed to the savage Other consists of a bricolage—an experimental assemblage—that combines the inconceivable with the forbidden, the ludicrous, the suspect, and the unattainable. This bricolage of inversions conjures an entire monstrous realm, which is itself organized around certain rites. It is a world intrinsically set apart from ours, where the disgusting is prized and the horrific celebrated. It may be populated by the physically monstrous—one-eyed giants, bird-headed demons, wolf-men—thereby offering culture a way of conceptualizing the inhuman in terms of appearance and basic natural classifications (as we saw in chapter 2). It also conceptualizes an entire culture of monstrous tendencies, from cannibalism, orgy, incest, or predatory sexuality to riches, powers of vengeance, invisibility, and flight.

This monstrous realm serves imaginatively as our opposite, as the antithesis to our orderly culture, and in this way it rather resembles the savage Other—that distant cannibal of ancient and early modern geographical fantasy that we saw in the last section. And yet they differ in their functions. On the one hand, when imagined as threats to explorers who venture off to the periphery, savage and monster both strike people with simultaneous horror and fascination. On the other hand, monsters' essential *dissimilarity* from humans reduces the allure—that is, the fantasy that "they" do things we must not (but could). The monstrous, as many critics have observed, is often imagined as some-how essential to the perpetuation of the cosmos—even sometimes a sympathetic creature, a safe projection of our own impulses. But at other times—as demons, werewolves, vampires, and fairy changelings—monsters are felt to be a tangible presence, a real threat; in such cases they provoke terror and the impulse to avoid or destroy it at all costs.

The classic supernatural night-witch is just such a monster, with an-imal attributes or appearances, predatory sexual urges, and hunger for humans (especially children). Most importantly, where we may be fa-miliar with the rituals of local wise women and cunning men who con-coct healing potions and protective remedies from local materials, the night-witch assembles her ritual preparations from excrement, corpses, and infant-parts. Out of such monstrous ritual acts the witch gains power, riches, and the ability to wreak catastrophe on neighbors. And in this way this monster has a foothold in the social world rather than being entirely a creature of the wild and the periphery. She may even, as some stories tell it, have a tragic past among us that brings her back now to prey, or she may simply depend on us for sustenance, like a par-asite. The night-witch is thus a monster who can dissimulate as a neighbor. And like us in our communities, she and her ilk may com-prise a veritable society of parasitic evil, distinguished not only by their perverse sexual acts but also by ceremonies that systematically invert and parody our social order: dancing naked and feasting on chil-dren or human corpses, for example.[22]

In this way, the monstrous realm, like the realm of the savage Other, is often organized and rendered coherent for audiences through images of ritual. Indeed, it is the elaboration of these rituals as representa-tions of the monstrous—horrific, ridiculous, enviable—that preoccu-pies those experts in evil from chapter 3, who discern in the world an evil more pervasive than a single old witch. In both early modern Europe and contemporary Christian Africa, the linking of witchcraft and Satanism has invited more and more details, perversions, and odd-ities into the fantasy of the monstrous realm's core ceremonies. Ritual itself becomes a way for articulating what, in a world of multiple ambi-guities and fears, is *entirely* Other. By ceremonial affiliation with the Devil, an ambiguous world becomes clearly evil.

THE SABBAT AND ITS RITES

We will spend some pages on the construction of the witches' Sabbat in early fifteenth-through seventeenth-century Europe, because this fantasy of ritual evil—evil conspiracy integrated through ritual, as in Pierre de Lancre's scenario at the beginning of this chapter (p. 74)— is perhaps the most elaborate and systematic the world has seen. It was also the most terrifying and effective in mobilizing responses, and so it is worth dwelling on the implications of *how* the Sabbat myth came to be.

Most European cultures had active notions of a cannibalistic night-witch who preyed on children and the pregnant. Night-witches could fly, look like or use animals, and in some versions meet in some cere-monial capacity.[23] Such notions of predacious, supernatural witchcraft certainly informed local accusations of witchcraft: not so much who was a witch but what kinds of affliction a witch might wreak in the vil-lage, and what places and hours one should avoid for fear of encoun-tering witches. But the project of assembling an image of diabolical witchcraft—generally the work of learned experts—involved weaving these popular notions with other kinds of lore. As Norman Cohn and others have noted, these additions to the picture of Satanic witchcraft came from such literary traditions as heresiography—that is, images of heretics as cannibalistic, orgiastic, and diabolical that were preserved in ecclesiastical texts. To these ideas were added the familiar accou-trements of real, everyday magical practices and all those weird sub-stances that people imagined sorcerers to use: "eye of newt and toe of frog, . . . finger of birth-strangled babe" and the like. All this diverse, unintegrated lore about demons, witchcraft, sorcery, and everyday magic were brought together in a total picture of a realm of evil: every-thing harmful, suspect, or simply ambiguous belonged to the domain of the Devil, its efficacy due to the perpetrator's devotion to the Devil.[24] As the early Swiss witch-finding manual *Errores Gazariorum* (1436) imagines, the realm of the Devil is one of total monstrosity, from the substances prepared to the havoc planned, and everything revolves around a central ceremony:

> After the seduced person pays homage to the presiding devil, he is given a
> jar full of ointment and a staff and certain other things with which the

seduced man must go to the [ceremony (*synagogus*)], and the demon teaches him how and in what ways to anoint the staff. That unguent is made by a mystery of diabolic malignancy out of the fat of small children who have been cooked, and with other things, as will be seen.

Further, when the unguent made of the said fat of children has been combined with the most poisonous of animals such as serpents, toads, lizards, and spiders, which are all mixed mysteriously as said above, and if a person is touched once with this unguent he immediately dies by an evil death, sometimes for a time in a persisting illness, sometimes dying quickly.[25]

All things take place in this witches' Sabbat: inversions of proper behavior, sacrilege of official liturgy, the preparation of horrible crimes, and—at the core—the ritual sequence that integrates those witch-activities familiar to all. Indeed, as Martine Ostorero has noted, there is a structure to this fifteenth-century tableau that balances the authors' concern for inverted liturgy with the more widespread horror of sexual, culinary, and infanticidal monstrosity. The *Errores*' Sabbat, she observes,

> is developed through progressing towards the abominable, the inhuman and the sacrilegious: the murder (of infants) is replaced by diverse crimes perceived as "contrary to nature" (cannibalism of infants, orgy, incest, sodomy, homosexuality); then, after the sacrilege of the profanation of the Eucharist, the ceremony culminates in the supreme crime, that of high treason (apostasy). There is thus constructed an inhuman and unnatural picture of the witch, defined as child-killer, cannibal, beast, and apostate.[26]

Once established in ecclesiastical literature by the early sixteenth century, this bricolage of Sabbat horrors continued to expand in its details of atrocity and inversion. Those under torture might contribute features of local witch-lore, while church demonologists and witch-finding experts might impose details of relevance to current theology. Women's habitual inclination to fornicate with demons, alleged in the late fifteenth-century German *Malleus Maleficarum*, would prove demons' corporeal existence; hence much depended on the extraction of testimony to this effect.[27] Overall, the Sabbat crystallized the monstrous wherever it travelled: scriptorium, torture chamber, or crowd. It offered elite and folk alike opportunities to imagine parody, sexual transgression, and yet also to crystallize real fears of demonic conspiracy. By the seventeenth century the manuals that laid out the now-voluminous testimony of Sabbat details were swollen with popular tales of fairy culture, carnivalesque parodies of ecclesiastical culture, and elaborate fantasies of the disgusting and perverse. The perverse Sabbat rites begin to seem as ludicrous as they are demonic. Francesco Guazzo includes illustrations of such acts in his 1608 manual, the "witches" dressed as an elite countersociety. (See figure 4, a–c, and compare figure 6.) Authors like Nicolas Remy (1595) and Pierre de Lancre (1612) describe in detail the orgies, their discordant musical accompaniment, the foul meals, the strange dances and costumes, and the perverse ritual acts that extend throughout the Sabbat rites: "For they turn their backs towards the Demons when they go to worship them, and approach them sideways like a crab; when they hold out their hands in supplication they turn them downwards; when they converse they bend their eyes toward the ground; and in other such ways they behave in a manner opposite to that of other men."[28] The rites of the monstrous realm are bizarre, resembling nothing in this world. Out of the mutual speculations of fascinated inquisitors and tortured suspects grabbing at any images they can think of, an image is assembled of witches' essential weirdness. And like the weirdness that the anthropologist Bronislaw Malinowski famously defined as essential to the composition of Trobriand magical spells to signify their exotic potency, so the weirdness compiled in depictions of the Sabbat signify the potent Otherness of the Sabbat and its world.[29]

As with stories of the New World savage, the image of the Sabbat led to the development of an iconographic tradition. Artists stressed both the erotic and disgusting aspects of witch-cults, carefully attending to details of female nakedness, unnatural acts, and symbols of inversion.[30] Shortly after its first edition, De Lancre's *Tableau de l'Inconstance des Mauvais Anges et Démons* included an illustrative engraving of the Sabbat by Jean Ziarnko (1613). (See fig. 5, pp. 92–93.) The engraving captured the whole canivalesque aspect of De Lancre's Sabbat tableau. It was now something almost familiar, performed by *grands Seigneurs et Dames*, as if at a splendid party. With its masks, musical

FIGURE 4
Woodcuts from
Francesco Guazzo,
*Compendium
Maleficarum* (1608):
(a) Witches present
child to Devil; (b)
Ritual kiss of Sabbat;
(c) Obscene
demonic dances at
Sabbat. In this early
witch-finding
manual, witches are
depicted as of both
genders and dressed
in elite finery,
counterposed to the
monstrous nudity
of demons (cf. figure
5-D, L). London.
Courtesy of British
Library.

instruments, and a great dinner table, the historian Margaret Mc-Gowan describes, the Sabbat made

> complete contrast to the tedium of everyday life, reminding some of a wedding, and others of a magnificent court with suitable accompanying festivities. . . . There followed a banquet where some say tasteless food was consumed, while others fall into raptures over the limbs of children and toads they had eaten. Then came the lascivious dances, performed naked and back to back, before the ceremonies culminated in a frantic sexual orgy, broken only by the crowing of the cock.[31]

In this way the witches' Sabbat became not only a coordinated concept of danger, of a Satanic conspiracy's very core, but an elaborate

---

On following spread:

FIGURE 5   Jan Ziarnko, engraving of witches' Sabbat, to accompany Pierre de Lancre, *Tableau de l'inconstance des mauvais anges et démons* (Paris: Nicolas Buon, 1613). Ithaca, New York. Courtesy of the Division of Rare Book and Manuscript Collections, Cornell University Library. Details include: (A) Satan enthroned as five-horned goat, along with (B) the Queen of the Sabbat and another mistress, to whom a naked witch and demon present a child for initiation (C). The Sabbat involves (at lower right D) a banquet of human body-parts, hearts of unbaptised babies, and diverse vermin, and is attended by female witches and their demon-lovers; and it is followed by a backward, naked dance of the women and their demons (F): "they dance . . . with the most indecent and dirty movements they can." To the left (H) more women and girls dance, naked and backwards, to the sound of a cacaphonous musical ensemble (G); and below them (L) can be seen an elegant masque for lord- and lady-witches. In the center (K) more children arrive with a naked witch on the back of a goat to be dedicated to Satan, while to the lower left (M) the initiated witch-children tend to the toads they have brought to the Sabbat for senior witches (bottom center, I) to mix in a maleficent brew.

vision of the monstrous, linking the fantastic with the familiar, the sexual with the culinary, the horrific with the hilarious, and the human with the bestial. If the Sabbat's construction was originally motivated by ecclesiastical concerns to show the reality of the Satanic realm, it came to epitomize an alternative, monstrous domain—distilled to a bizarre sequence of rites.

The development of the witches' Sabbat over the fifteenth and sixteenth centuries allowed the conglomeration of multiple sorts of inversion and monstrosity, from the most learned—sacraments, pledges of devotion, Satanic hierarchy—to the most popular: infanticide, weather-sorcery, flight. The rites of the Sabbat brought the terrors of the child-eating night-witch together with the carnivalesque pleasures of an elves' party in the woods at night. By the end of the sixteenth century the Sabbat was the shared myth of friars, priests, and, in many places, laypeople. While it assumed slightly different shapes in different places for different communities, the terrifying image of a central rite of evil had the capacity to bring together multiple concerns about demonic subversion "here" and "in this age."

THE COHERENCE OF DEVIL-WORSHIP AND THE INCOHERENCE OF MODERNITY

Historians of the Sabbat myth in the great European witch-hunts have noted the importance of Satanism to the whole picture of a conspiratorial witchcraft—that diverse and ambiguous folklores about the customs and nocturnal rendezvous of witches, fairies, ghosts, or even sorcerers are radically demonized through association with the Devil.[32] A similar process occurred in areas of Africa in the late twentieth century, in which the combination of traditional witchcraft beliefs with ecclesiastical notions of a Satanic realm led to a frightening picture of Satanic conspiracy operating through real people and real accoutrements of modern life, whose evil was epitomized in perverse rituals. As in early modern Europe, public depictions of this Satanic realm and its rites incorporated familiar notions of the powers witches can gain and the elements of life they can harm. Riches, technology, political authority, and prophetic abilities all serve as rewards for the devoted witch, who now preys not just on fertility and children but also on the civic infrastructure, railroads, and automobile safety. Most importantly, the witch attacks not only because she is a witch, but now out of a sophisticated (and notably anti-Christian) dedication to the Devil.

As in early modern Europe, the propaganda of such modern Satanic fears consists of tracts and official reports, widely read in Nigeria, Ghana, and Kenya. The two most influential texts, a 1987 Nigerian booklet and a 2000 Kenyan Presidential Commission report, both combine traditional African images of witchcraft with a range of modern accoutrements deemed suspect and, permeating the whole tableau, a new and ramified connection of evil to Satan-worship. As in the earliest European depictions of diabolical witchcraft, these texts show Satanic power extending to everyday ritual preparations and the local ritual experts of traditional culture.

The most widely read of these modern "revelations" of Satanic conspiracy is Emmanuel Eni's booklet *Delivered from the Power of Darkness* (1987). Eni claims that before his conversion to Christianity he was initiated into an occult world of Devil-worship, based in India, that met in an anonymous building in Nigeria's capital. This diabolical realm was under the control of a figure named "Queen of the Coast" who dwelled in an undersea city, a distortion of the popular west African water-spirit Mami Wata, who in this case is identified with the seductive powers and accoutrements of modernity: she has laboratories and computers and uses a special television to discern whether victims might be Christian.[33] In the process of his induction to the Devil cult Eni notes details of the cult's activities that clearly bring together older witchcraft beliefs and the ambiguous trappings of modernity. The first cult member he meets, "Alice," is well-stocked with appliances: "She had four refrigerators [sic] and on opening one, I saw human skulls, different parts of the human body both fresh and dry. Inside the ceiling were skeletons. In another corner of one of the rooms I saw . . . a water-pot filled with blood and a small tree in the centre of the pot, a calabash and a red cloth by it (p.11)." The places of Satanic activity are thus marked as ritual spaces, with the familiar equipment of African traditional rituals—or Christian caricatures of that equipment. When Eni accompanies Alice to his first cult meeting,

I was instructed . . . to enter backwards. I obeyed and entered with my back, she also did the same. The hall was so large with about 500 young men and women seated in a circle, and seated above them was a man whose head could only be seen and without a body, as the leader. Some of these young people were students, undergraduates, graduates, teachers, etc. Alice pressed a botton [sic] on the wall and a seat came out from the ground and I sat. (p.11)

These Satanic caricatures of technology work in tandem with more traditional notions of witchcraft substances:

1. A concoction that looked like putty was rubbed on our bodies. This qualifies you as a full MEMBER.
2. A glass shot of oil-like liquid was given to us to drink. This qualifies you to be an AGENT.
3. A gun-powder like substance was rubbed on our heads. This qualifies you to STUDY THEIR MYSTERIES. (p.12)

Even older notions of cannibalistic ceremony and disgusting substances are central parts of this otherwise modern Satanic cult:

Early one morning, [Alice] told me there was an important ceremony to be performed in the house. At 2:00 a.m. she brought a crawling child, a girl, alive. Before my eyes, Alice used her fingers and plucked out the child's eyes. The cry of that child broke my heart. She then slaughtered the child into pieces and poured both the blood and the flesh into a tray and asked me to eat. I refused. She looked straight at me and what came out of her eyes cannot be explained in writing. Before I knew what was happening, I was not only chewing the meat but also licking the blood. While this was happening she said: "this is a covenant between us, you will never say out anything you see me do or anything about me to any human on earth. The day you break this covenant your own is gone (p.13)."

Eni's pamphlet thus proposes an extensive Satanic cult, intrinsically hostile to "Christians" in African society and at the center of which take place monstrous ceremonies such as had traditionally been imputed to witches, but now framed and administered through the accoutrements of modernity. Furthermore, the Satanic cult is supposed to afflict society through the ostensible benefits of modernity—hotels, make-up, lingerie, stores, teachers, automobiles—and familiar African institutions like maternity centers and prophet shrines. Thus affiliated with modernity and recast as Satanic, traditional witchcraft notions became updated and legitimized. Moreover, the Satanic cult Eni reveals is as extensive as it is hidden in the interstices of modern life. Its administrators live off in India; its agents work throughout Africa and especially in cities.

Delivered from the Powers of Darkness has had an observable effect on local concepts of witch-societies and Satanic threat in Ghana and Kenya, for it both articulates Satan's power in familiar terms and expands the danger that malevolent powers pose in permeating the world.[34] The booklet's influence is also reaffirmed through popular African cinema, many of whose films reveal Satan's power as alive in merchandise and riches, single urban women, and undersea goddesses.[35] But the cultural process of Christianizing and modernizing traditional witch-ideas had already taken place in Kenya through different channels. Rumors of a government-sanctioned Satanic conspiracy had permeated the country though the 1980s and 1990s, while church leaders of various denominations were identifying Satanic cults as a principal danger to Kenyan society and youth morality, and witch-cleansing movements themselves continued unabated in some regions of Kenya.[36] Finally, in 1995, the president—himself implicated in some rumors—established a Commission of Inquiry into the Cult of Devil Worship in Kenya, which delivered its report in 2000. Satanic cults, the Commission declared, amounted to a serious problem for Kenya; more than just an alternative religion, they were seducing educated youth and causing train-wrecks and other accidents.[37] The report drew extensively from American and British evangelical literature on putative Satanic cults but wove into the now standard American anticult fears of brainwashing and Satanic conspiracy elements of traditional witch-belief:

The process of initiation into the cult involves the following: members are taken to some secluded place at night for initiation; the initiates start by stripping naked in the presence of other members in preparation for the rituals; prayers are conducted by the "high priest" in an unfamiliar language; incisions are made on the initiate's body to drain blood; the blood is mixed with some substance and then given to both existing members and the initiate to lick. This is an oathing ceremony meant to bind members to the organisation and to keep its secrets; a human being is either killed during the ceremony, or a fresh human body is brought in, then some pieces of flesh are cut from it and served to the members. This seemingly, is intended to instil fear [in]to the initiates to discourage them from withdrawing from the cult or divulging its secrets, and to give them courage to partake of human flesh and blood; human blood is also given to members to drink as part of the ritual.

It was also claimed that the members of the cult usually conduct their prayers at night in dark places while in the nude. They pray with their hands raised and in an unfamiliar language, which is not associated with any known local dialect. For instance, a group of boys in a certain high school who were suspected to be involved in devil worship, were found at night in a corner near a water tank, apparently praying, in some unintelligible language with their hands raised and in a state of trance.[38]

Cult members would thereby gain powers to turn into animals, the report asserts, and could afflict Kenyan society in its very infrastructure:

Some members of the cult were said to have powers to cause fatal road accidents. Some of the accidents which have taken place in the country were said to have been caused by the devil worshippers. Such accidents include the Mtongwe Ferry disaster, the Ngai-Ndeithya train accident and the Kenya Prisons Officers accident at Ruaraka. It was also claimed that those who instigated ethnic violence in some parts of the country, which led to loss of many lives were, in fact, responding to the wishes of their master the devil.[39]

The idea of a Devil-worship conspiracy thus links a series of national catastrophes with a conspiracy of evil. More specifically, this conspiracy consists of ritualized inversions and atrocities. Satanic conspiracy brings together traditional notions of witches' predatory cravings with evangelical Christian notions of Satanism and the realities of modern experience—its allures, dangers, and powers. At the same time, the national character of this Satanic conspiracy reflects concern about organized global institutions and corporations. Rather than the technological accoutrements of modernity, as in Emmanuel Eni's pamphlet, it is the modern institution and its powers to threaten state and infrastructure that make the report's scenario of Devil-worshippers a curiously contemporary threat.

These examples from early modern Europe and contemporary Africa demonstrate the flexibility of the monstrous realm and its central rites. In these assemblages of official demonologies, traditional images of sorcery and witch-powers, and familiar aspects of modern life we find an ongoing bricolage of monstrosity. Bricolages are never simply arrangements of things but attempts to make sense of them through relationship, comparison, and synthesis. Here the bricolage of the monstrous allows cultures, through various media and by many self-proclaimed experts, to turn over elements of cultural experience for examination, parody, or repudiation, to play with notions of inversion and disgust, and to conceptualize the "worst possible things" in terms of an evil underworld and its ceremonies. Ambiguous cultural experiences—like banknotes, television, or the resurgence of traditional ritual practices in Kenya or Ghana; or dancing or the unorthodox use of sacraments in early modern Europe—are thrust into the realm of cannibalism, perversity, and infanticide. The realm of inhuman ceremony explicates the nature of the Devil, while modernity's stresses and Christianity's efficacy both give new significance to notions of a society of witches.[40] One might say that this notion of witch-society represents a point of projection, framing evil as an identifiable world in order to make sense of—even play with—the ambiguities of ritual and social relations in this world.

Ritual, then, represents what "they" do—the Satanists, the conspirators, the denizens of that underworld—as more than personal malevolence or greed but as part of a larger service to some evil god who will reward them with power. Rituals signify their attachment to the conspiracy. Rituals also signify that particular atrocities or misfortunes have a context in the conspiracy's plan: missing or ill children, obsessed spouses—their souls have been robbed to make diabolical concoctions. Recent anthropology, indeed, has noticed how rumors of cannibalism, organ-harvesting, and the disembowelling of innocents for rituals that empower the imagined predators, which are current in Central America as well as Africa, invariably serve as ways of thinking about modernity itself—global capitalism and its exploitative evils. Anxieties about political corruption or new entrepreneur classes, for example, or about commodities and status all become folded into narratives of bloodsucking, child-eating, and the collection of body-parts for sorcery. People who seem to gain power and commodities purely through their capitalist wiles or political corruption must, it seems, be engaging in secret rituals using innocents' organs. Women who abandon traditional gender roles for the sexualized attire and behavior of Western modernity must, it is believed, be witches, in thrall to the Devil, seeking victims among traditional family men. Thus evil ritual offers a recognizable context for the ambiguity of modernity to begin to make sense: evils emerge from witches'—now Satanists'—need to collect ingredients for power or, as the Kenyan report reveals, to destroy culture itself.[41]

Rituals, those hallmarks of tradition and hoary ceremony, serve both as the integrating axis of some realm of evil—what makes "their" acts truly evil—and as a convenient context for framing uncomfortable aspects of modernity as expressions of evil. Out of the central rites of evil spring all manner of misfortunes "distinctive of this age." This feature of Satanic rituals emerged quite vividly in the Satanic cult rumors that spread through the United States and United Kingdom in the late 1980s. Lurid Satanic ceremonies linked the new ambiguities of day care (who are these people taking care of my children?), religious diversity (are all these various religious options safe?), and the family itself (how widespread is the horror of sexual abuse, and how intrinsic to patriarchal family structure?). Of course, the ancient Roman rumors around the Bacchanalia and then Christians likewise wove traditional notions of covert sorcery and its disgusting ingredients with new anxieties about civic boundaries, foreign religions, and moral breakdown. Ritual links the dangers of the new with the ostensible antiquity of the traditional, and all with the image of mindless, even frenzied, devotion to some alien god, the inverse of our own.

But the bricolage of the monstrous, the picture of evil, envisioned through these various ceremonies and sacrifices is not an abstraction or a general theory of maleficence. It serves as an account of real affliction and catastrophe. It is the rituals themselves that afflict us, whether by their parasitic dependence on "our" children or by the oaths to evildoing they involve or simply by their sheer perversity. Ritual is objectified in these fantasies as something uncanny and potent. But then what is "ritual" that it could be imagined as such an ambiguous force—the characteristic of the Other, the Satanist, as well as the cohesive acts among "us" that "they" seem to invert?

Ritual as a Point of Danger

In the first part of this chapter we saw how Otherness itself—the foreigner, the monster—was expressed in horrible sacrifices and other sorts of binding ceremonies. Practices that might be central to "our" concept of moral order "they" turn upside down, celebrating their bestial disorder with atrocities. In the second part of this chapter we saw how a whole realm of evil and monstrous behavior might be drawn out and integrated through the image of a central ritual. Misfortunes like child abuse or government corruption, as well as ambiguous facets of experience, like wealth and technology, might all be linked to conspiracy and abject evil through the idea of rituals that people must perform—to which they live perpetually in thrall. In this section we tackle the larger Western suspicion of ritual, a state of social behavior that can conjure mysteries or lead participants into murderous frenzy. What is meant by speaking of a witches' *Sabbat*, Jewish *ritual* murder, or Satanic *Ritual* abuse? If the central rituals of the monstrous races, combined with their sexual and culinary customs, amounted to a picture of total Otherness in classical and early modern literature, where did we get the idea that ritual itself might be a source of danger?

CEREMONIES TOO CLOSE FOR COMFORT

The process begins when those fantastic inversions we impute to "them" in sexual, culinary, and ritual custom become intrinsically subversive to us, so that their danger lies precisely in those differences: what they eat, how they engage in intercourse, and how or what they sacrifice. And this process develops when the cultures to whom we attribute habits both atrocious and alluring seem now to dwell among us, carrying the same habits and cravings.

Rome, again, serves as the historical genesis of some of these ideas, as well as an example of fears that the Other's—the savage's—proximity will lead to great danger. Roman anxieties about sorcery and ritual subversion are evident from the beginning. Over the first centuries of the Common Era we see popular "magic" deemed illegal, foreign religions imagined as threats to civic order, and divination—various means of gaining divine messages through worldly symbols—feared as the most dangerous of rites.[42] Divination, folk magic, and foreignness were equated with *mageia*, subversive ritual or sorcery—that is, deliberately malign ritual acts. And the figure in popular lore to bring these ideas together was the night-witch, that completely demonic being whom we have already met, universally held to be responsible for child-deaths and infertility. In Roman literature she becomes not simply an amalgam of horrific cravings but, now, the mistress of perverse ritual.[43] One classic depiction of the night-witch rehearses the danger that witches pose specifically through their rites of binding people and darkening heavenly bodies. However, the text continues, the most demonic witch of all, Erictho, scorned

> these criminal rites, these wicked practices of a horrible race, . . . as being *too pious*, and she degraded a science that was already tainted *with rites before unknown*. . . . She is ready to commit a murder whenever she needs the fresh blood that gushes forth when a throat is slit and whenever her ghoulish repasts require flesh that still throbs. She also slits women's wombs and delivers babies by an unnatural method, *in order to offer them on a burning altar*.[44]

The point is clear: witches' atrocities are not simply extensions of their chaotic nature, as if of a different culture or a bestial urge, but revolve around sacrifice—central rituals—whose proper procedure depends on what "they" take from "us." Ritual itself can be predacious. Nor was this way of thinking restricted to stories and protective rites; it extended also to accusations. The second-century CE holy man Apollonius of Tyana was accused of "sacrific[ing] a boy to divine the secrets of futurity which are to be learned from an inspection of youthful entrails"—that is, in the manner that "our" priests might examine the entrails of beasts.[45] As Rome assimilated more of the cultures of its empire, so these cultures' bizarre rituals (or those imputed to them)

seemed alternately to provide mysteriously potent ways of doing things
"we" always wanted to do (such as to find out the fate of the emperor),
and to threaten the very integrity and purity of "our" center. Where
proper civic ritual should have order and custom, should be public or
common, should involve a separation of genders, should be accompanied by melodious music, and in its sacrifices should involve the proper
division of substances for burning, eating, and offering, *alien* ritual was
imagined as disordered and excessive, secretive and foreign, cacaphonous, and inverting of proper sacrificial procedures and substances.

Thus there arose in the Roman imagination a disparate realm of
alien ritual, comprising underclasses and foreigners and the secretly
malevolent. It was the very picture of subversion: cults whose very
presence would lead to the breakdown of civic order, seducing the up-
right into following base passions (sexual, homicidal) and mixing
classes and genders in unseemly ways.[46] Hence the impetus to launch
purges against the alleged practitioners of religions that seemed to be
brought in from outside. The Bacchanalia panic of 186 BCE, for example, was believed to bring cacaphonous ceremonies, ecstatic behavior,
orgy, human sacrifice, and civic corruption right into "our" territory.[47]
In the second century CE, popular fantasies of what a subversive foreign cult might do among us grew even more graphic. Christians, it
was said (at least according to their own apologists), would adore their
high priests' genitalia and feast on infants *en croûte* (as in the passage
at the beginning of this chapter); but even beyond these atrocities,

> they gather at a banquet with all their children, sisters, and mothers, peo-
> ple of either sex and every age. There, after full feasting, when the blood is
> heated and drink has inflamed the passions of incestuous lust, a dog which
> has been tied to a lamp is tempted by a morsel thrown beyond the range of
> his tether to bound forward with a rush. The tale-telling light is upset and
> extinguished, and in the shameless dark lustful embraces are indiscrimi-
> nately exchanged; and all alike are involved in incest.[48]

Moral danger, subversion—evil, in the Roman cultural imagination—
lay in the *ritual* accumulation of inversions, which not only conjured
the kind of bestial subculture as might be safely imagined on the edges
of the earth, but placed it among us, beneath us, a scandal to the gods
who bring civic fortune. The rumors were almost systematic in their

depiction of perverse ceremony: *sacrifice* of *children, ceremonial meal* with *incest*.[49] Indeed, these early scenes of ritual atrocity anticipate central features of witches' ceremonies in early modern thinking, wherein cannibalism, as the art historian Charles Zika has pointed out, "cannot be limited to the consumption of human flesh; it involves a ferocious consumption, a bloodthirsty savagery. . . . [A]llusions to the consumption of human flesh are part of a much broader and more spectactular scenario of ritualistic dismemberment and the exploitation of human body-parts for the evil ends of others."[50]

Admittedly, there has been a tendency among some modern scholars to try to find some grains of historical truth in these rumors and accusations: were the Bacchantes really trying to regain some dangerous primal ecstasy? Were the chaste Christians being confused with pseudo-Christian "libertine" sects? Do all these rumors circulate back "to concrete rites that were [actually] celebrated by ethnic or tribal minorites in the southeastern corner of the Mediterreanean, possibly as late as the second century A.D."?[51] These propositions all rely more on a scholarly prurience—a longing for some verifiable "Others" who really did such things—than reliable sources or critical analysis. Even more, such efforts to historicize perverse rituals always underestimate the power and integrity of *fantasies* of alien ritual, which obviously grew more elaborate and anxious as they sought to depict cults penetrating the very interior of civic society. These scholarly efforts to make infanticidal, orgiastic cults an historical fact resemble those same archaic fantasies of the rituals of the Other but now imputed to the *historical* periphery. The Roman Empire itself has become a time and place of voluptuous pleasures and strange cults before the rise of Christendom.[52] But more recent studies of these fantasies of perverse ritual have seen in them a quite deliberate play on what proper sacrifice involves, how the genders or classes should not mix in ritual situations, and the meaning of secrecy, ritual efficacy, and "Romanness" itself. When one feared subversion and foreignness, these were the shapes of those fears.[53]

RITES AND HORRORS OF THE INTIMATE ENEMY

Situations of proximity, then, lead to the imaginative construction and imputation of rituals that invert everything conceivably proper, civic-minded, and human in order to illustrate how the ambiguous alien in our midst is in fact entirely offensive. Even more than subverting the social order, their rites offended the sacred order and its gods and would bring about general cataclysm: as another second-century Christian complained, "they take the Christians to be the cause of every disaster to the state, of every misfortune to the people."[54] But the evil of such rituals changes subtly as the alien cult evolves from the intimate savage to the perceived *rival*, whose beliefs and rites are close enough to threaten confusion of boundaries. As sociologists Georg Simmel and Lewis Coser both laid out in intricate terms, situations of ostensible similarity, yet (to insiders) irritating difference, breed particular hostility; and among early Christians, such hostility against the intimate enemy was expressed typically in Satanic terms.[55] The ritual of the "heretic"—the one who believes differently while masquerading as "us"—is fundamentally the worship of the Devil.[56] And hence, to the extent that *proper* ritual brings about divine beneficence and the *conquest* of disorderly, Satanic powers, heretic ritual carries equivalent power in the opposite direction. Heretics cause havoc and threaten society through their very rites, as is obvious by the things they do in those rites.

Heresiography, the systematic classifying of ideological rivals, arose in early Christianity as a literary endeavor, with each writer building and elaborating on his predecessors' allegations with little more information than his own imagination and awareness of current institutional squabbles. Yet from the beginning heresiographers drew on older Greco-Roman notions of perverse ceremony. Heretics gave themselves to unrestrained licentiousness; their rites aimed at ecstasy and disorder; they practiced human sacrifice and cannibalism; men and women comported themselves in obscene inversions of gender propriety, and—following the abandonment of public sacrifice when the Roman Empire turned Christian—their rites depended on a panoply of disgusting sacraments, from semen to fetuses to menstrual blood. At the same time, the pretense of order and system in heretic rituals became all the more important, both to frame differences in the guise of liturgical similarity and to convey a sense of evil in the prospect of the holiest things turned upside down. The fourth-century CE writer Epiphanius of Salamis offers such a horrific portrait of Gnostics, whom he claimed to know at firsthand:

Their very liturgy they defile with the shame of promiscuity, consuming and contaminating themselves with human and unclean flesh. . . .

. . . [At their feasts:] They set out an abundance of meat and wine, even if they are poor. Having made their banquet from this and so to speak filled their veins to satiety, they proceed to arouse themselves. The man, moving away from the woman, says to his woman, "Arise, hold the love feast with your brother."

And the pitiful pair, having made love . . . then proceed to hold up their blasphemy to heaven, the woman and the man taking the secretion from the male into their own hands and standing looking up to heaven. They hold in their hands the impurity and pray, . . . And then they consume it, partaking of their shamefulness, and they say, "This is the body of Christ and this is the Pasch for which our bodies suffer and are forced to confess the passion of Christ." They do the same with what is of the woman, when she has the flow of blood: collecting the monthly blood of impurity from her, they take it and consume it together in the same way.

Although they have sex with each other, they forbid the begetting of children. They are eager for the act of corruption not in order to engender children, but for the pleasure. . . . But if . . . the woman becomes pregnant, then listen to something even more dreadful which they dare to do. Extracting the fetus at whatever time they choose to do the operation, they take the aborted infant and pound it up in a mortar with a pestle, and, mixing in honey and pepper and some other spices and sweet oils so as not to become nauseous, all the members of that herd of swine and dogs gather together and each partakes with his finger of the crushed up child. . . .

They dare to do other dreadful things as well. When they fall into a frenzy among themselves, they soil their hands with the shame of their secretion, and rising, with defiled hands pray stark naked.[57]

Epiphanius begins from the established fourth-century position that evil lies intrinsically in the different beliefs that Gnostics hold. But here, he reveals, the evils of Gnostic beliefs are encapsulated in their perverse inversion of "our" liturgy, which ranges from systematic parody to an orgy that denies procreation. If "ritual" suggests both order and attention to space and substance, it inevitably also involves much attention to purity. In Epiphanius's own time Christian liturgy depended heavily on purification. Yet in this image of Gnostic inversion it is the impure and disgusting, both acts and fluids, that take place under the ritual spotlight: public intercourse, semen, menses, aborted fetuses—a veritable concentration of bodily pollutions. Danger and disgust arise not from the pollutions themselves, for they are part of human life, but from the sacred attention that the ritual gives to them.[58]

Other competitors were said to prey upon proper Christians to fulfill their ritual atrocities. In the following case, allegations of secret child-sacrifice are imputed to those who, a century after the declaration of a Christian empire, were still conducting the old religious cults in the vicinity of Christians. In one part of Egypt, it was said,

> the pagans were . . . seizing the children of the Christians and slaying them for their idol, Kothos. For instance, one day they waylaid them and he saw them performing the lawless acts by slaying the little children and pouring (out) their blood upon the altar of their god, Kothos. They seized some of them and handed them over to the tribunal. They interrogated them, and they revealed (the truth) without torture, saying: "We call out to the children of the Christians and deceive them and give them morsels of bread and little things to eat in order to shut them up in hidden places so that no one outside would hear their voices. And in this way, we slay them and pour their blood upon the altar and take out their intestines and stretch them (to make) strings for our harps and we sing to our god on them. We also burn the rest of their bodies and reduce them to ashes. And everywhere we know there is treasure, we take a small quantity of ashes and cast them upon it. And we sing on the harps with the little children's intestines for strings. The treasure comes to light at once, and we take what we want."[59]

The details of harps and treasure-hunting derive from growing fears that the old religion was a kind of sorcery employing equipment both strange and familar, while the cult's luring of Christian children suggests not the savage or barbarian Other, whose horrific customs involve only his own kind, but the predatory rituals of the night-witches, now emerging in the shape of rival religion. Whether the subjects are heathens or heretics, then, the monstrosity, subversion, and evil of rival religions is depicted through the details of their ritual process: their perverse mockery of proper liturgy or their need for "our" innocents for ritual materials. There is a continuum in the image of the foreign religion that abuses and eats its own progeny off at the ends of the earth, and the foreign religion among us, that threatens our ordered society by its enthusiastic, ceremonial savagery while drawing our youth into its foreign allures. And out of this image of the "monstrous cult among us," now perpetuated and expanded in Christians' literature, there developed another, more threatening scene: the intrinsically *parasitical* realm of monstrous ritual, craving our progeny and destroying our livelihood—the cult of witches, maleficent people.

ASSEMBLING THE SABBAT TABLEAU

The connection between, on the one hand, Roman and late antique caricatures of alien cults and rival Christian sects, and on the other, late medieval and early modern images of diabolical witch-cults was established most exhaustively in Norman Cohn's *Europe's Inner Demons* (1975). The transmission of these images of monstrous inversion over time and space, Cohn showed, occurred through the copying and application of old texts like that of Epiphanius (above), which were generally regarded not as fossils of a prurient past but as having perennial value for understanding new forms of religious diversity. By the Middle Ages a monk or bishop who encountered alternative Christian beliefs in his region had a standardized repertoire of ritual atrocities to frame both the beliefs and their sophisticated exponents as only the seductive veneer of a far more insidious, diabolical underworld.[60] The core rites of heretics in 1022 Orléans, France, (whatever their actual beliefs and practices beyond a strict Christian piety) were said to involve secret nocturnal orgies and child-sacrifice:

> They gathered, indeed, on certain nights in a designated house, everyone carrying a light in his hands, and like merry-makers they chanted the names of demons until suddenly they saw descend among them a demon in the likeness of some sort of little beast. As soon as the apparition was visible to everyone, all the lights were forthwith extinguished and each, with the least possible delay, seized the woman who first came to hand, to abuse her, without thought of sin. Whether it were mother, sister, or nun whom they embraced, *they deemed it an act of sanctity and piety* to lie with her.

When a child was born of this most filthy union, on the eighth day thereafter a great fire was lighted and the child was purified by fire in the manner of the old pagans, and so was cremated. Its ashes were collected and *preserved with as great veneration as Christian reverence is wont to guard the body of Christ*, being given to the sick as a viaticum at the moment of their departing this world. Indeed, such power of devilish fraud was in these ashes that whoever had been imbued with the aforesaid heresy and had partaken of no matter how small a portion of them was scarcely ever afterward able to direct the course of this thought from this heresy to the path of truth.[61]

As in earlier rumors, the ritual integrates the culling of substances for gaining powers with perversions of proper liturgy and with celebrations of group commitment. Indeed, it was the secrecy and the magical powers that effectively bound the devotees to heresy when—it seemed to the concerned bishops—an intelligent person would realize the absurdity of the heresy's theology. Perverse ritual substitutes for heresy's incoherent theology.[62]

It was Cohn's further contribution to demonstrate the interweaving of these heresiographical cliches in the Middle Ages with perennial fantasies of predatory night-witches, alive as much in late medieval Europe as in ancient Rome.[63] If earlier writers had occasionally merged these two images of evil ritual, disorderly and predatory, there were some fundamental differences between the evil of heretic ritual (with its inversions of proper Christian liturgy and devotion to the wrong powers) and the evil of witches (with their predatory cravings and inverse habits). But in a series of documents emitting from witchcraft inquisitions in mid-1430s Switzerland, we see the two images forced into synthesis, as inquisitors constructed a fantastic image of a heretical initiation ceremony that integrated the popular image of a witchcraft with parasitic effects on the world. The "new heretic" is admitted into the "synagogue" of the "sect" in a public oath-ceremony before the Devil. He swears fealty to the Devil and the sect, as well as to "kill all of those children he is able to injure or kill . . . under three years" and to "impede sexual intercourse in every marriage that he is able to," using the techniques and potions of sorcery—crimes of infanticide and infertility typically imputed to witches. Then follows a celebration consisting of the now well-known series of perversions, eventually to be termed the "Sabbat":

These things having been promised and sworn to, the poor seduced person adores the presiding devil and pays homage to him; and as a sign of homage kisses the devil, whether the devil appears as a human or some kind of animal, on the anus or the ass, giving the devil as tribute a member from his own body after death. These things having been done, that pestiferous sect rejoices together and dines at the reception of the new heretic who is now one of them, and murdered children are devoured by them. This most evil of banquets having been completed, the presiding devil cries out that the lights be extinguished and yells "Mestlet, mestlet." After they have heard this command they join themselves carnally, a single man with a woman or a single man with another man, and sometimes father with daughter, son with mother, brother with sister, and the natural order is little observed. When the unspeakable abominations are over and the lights are relit they eat and drink for the journey home. . . . When some were asked why they did this, they responded that they did this to vilify and show disrespect to the sacrament of the Eucharist. Then, all these things done, they returned to their homes.[64]

Further sections detail the potions that the initiate receives, made of children's bodies mixed with poisons and used to wreak havoc in everyday life. Thus the 'heretics' ritual encapsulates a number of central themes and fears. First, it points to the religious or institutional nature of the group: they are a counterchurch of Satan, with "statutes," and they require initiation and oath-taking.[65] Ritual, as formal as it appears in the oath-swearing component, establishes the solidarity of the group, the dedication of each individual member to the sect and above all to Satan himself. Second, in conjuring this counterchurch, the inquisitors add—on the basis of both heresiographical assumption and testimony under torture—the pollution of the Eucharist as a key feature of the cannibalistic orgy. Third, ritual inversions, from images of initiation to images of holy substances, govern the sequence of horrors and allow, through this depiction of a completely perverse, antihuman domain, a subtle interweaving of older notions of heretic liturgy and the inverse practices of the witch. Finally, out of the rituals come the substances of sorcery: unguents, powders, liquids, all brimming with malign efficacy. This efficacy comes not from traditional lore (like dried frogs or dirt from a crossroads) or the local charisma of a ritual

suggested centuries of secret predation in the service of

CATHOLIC LITURGY AND NEW MODELS OF RITUAL EVIL

In most cases of evil ritual that we have seen so far, from the sacrifices of the savage Other to the witches' Sabbats, evil has appeared in the image of a frenzied and perverse decline into savagery, unstructure, and chaos, mediated by inhuman sacrifices. In this model of evil ritual, evil emits from utter disorder, a combination of mayhem and madness, as the Greek playwright Euripides captured it in the fifth century BCE:

The maenders [the Bacchae] swooped on Hysiae . . .

. . . .

Everything in sight they pillaged and destroyed.
They snatched the children from their homes.

. . . .

In the culminating scene, when the hero's mother tears him

Pentheus was foaming at the mouth, and her crazed eyes
rolling with frenzy. She was mad, stark mad,
possessed by Bacchus. Ignoring his cries of pity,
she gripped his left arm at the wrist; then, planting
her foot upon his chest, she pulled, wrenching away
the arm at the shoulder—not by her own strength,
for the god had put inhuman power in her hands.
Ino, meanwhile, on the other side, was scratching off
his flesh. Then Autonoë and the whole horde
of Bacchae swarmed upon him. Shouts everywhere,
he screaming with what little breath was left,
they shrieking in triumph. One tore off an arm,
another a foot still warm in its shoe. His ribs
were clawed clean of flesh and every hand
was smeared with blood as they played ball with scraps
of Pentheus' body.[69]

expert (like charms prepared
but from the substances' affilia
vation from the central, infa
touch, nor the waxen image,
thing," the witch-finder Henr
symbol of the pact formed by
brings together the heretical Sat
and sorcery in the village worl
witchcraft.

These earliest fantasies of a Sal
opportunites for imagining a c
brought together various notions
tility and children, that individua
there existed particularly horrible
powers could arise from the inversi
lay at the very center of cosmic dar

It is ritual, then, that by its very
the danger of subversion from some
its ingredients and powers, leads con
on us, and especially to take our chi
This same pattern is also applied to
Ages. Much in the way sorcery, ille
typically imputed to the tribe "over t
in medieval and early modern Europ
abilities with ritual spells and invocati
this capacity they needed the ingredi
popular imagination to blood, eucharis
all highly charged substances in Christ
hosts, it was often asserted, they would
bing repeatedly at the child or wafer (v
Nor were these rites or atrocious ingredi
from the Jewish religion; they lay at the
thought, craved such dramas or ingredie
inevitably, allegiance to the Devil. The
gredients upon which they depended thu
Christians. Moreover, the very antiquity
occurrence of these rites all the more c

scope, for it
the Devil.[68]

bestial sacri
been captur
agery, antis
fantasy of
rage, lust, a
already in

Like inva
. . .
Everythi
They sn
. . .

And i
apart—

... she
rolling
possesse
she sei
her foo
the arr
for the
Ino, m
his fles
of Bac
he scr
they
anoth
were
was s
of Pe

We can now recognize in Euripides' description the construction of ritual typically imputed to the savages, the monstrous demihumans, off on the periphery of culture. Ritual's danger lies precisely in its tendency to drag people down into a bestial blood-lust. This theme has underlain the history of images of savage ritual, night-witch ritual, and many features of the witches' Sabbat.[70]

But ritual became the basis of a different kind of danger in seventeenth-century Europe. In this case, Protestant caricatures of Catholicism cast Catholic ritual as a kind of malign deception, even as sorcery, although the actual efficacy of the rites was denied.[71] Unlike ecclesiastical notions of witches' sacraments, which bore considerable demonic power, Protestants rarely attributed power to the sacraments or gestures or priestly liturgy.[72] Indeed, the very falsehood of Catholic rites conjured an image of ritual itself, with its gestures, chants, and procedures, as dangerous and conspiratorial. In the view of early Protestant historiography, "crafty ancient priests . . . had created and perpetuated a series of fake demigods in order to bewilder the laity into abject spiritual and political subjection to the high priest."[73] The consequent image of ritual as applied to the Catholic Church involved a hierarchy of priests bent not on orgy but on deliberate evil, deceit, and mesmerizing their audiences, using a portentous array of gestures, chants, symbols, and robes—often liberally mixed with scatological symbolism, as some early Reformers make clear.[74] In such caricatures of Catholic rites, the formalized ritual process functions as an instrument of subterfuge—keeping its participants in thrall to the priesthood. Ritual gestures are hypnotic and ludicrous at the same time, with no power whatsoever, yet an undercurrent of bloody sacrifice passed down from pre-Christian rites. Increase Mather describes how, during a medieval siege, "the Popish Priests undertook by Conjuration to obtain Water. The Magical Ceremonies by them observed were most horrid and ridiculous. For they took an Asse, and put the Sacrament of the Eucharist into his Mouth, sang Funeral Verses over him, and then buried him alive before the Church doors." As John Wesley put it, a greedy priesthood's seductive "arts . . . were practised upon the ignorant devotion of the simple."[75]

In these caricatures of Catholic rites we depart completely from the sacrifice-induced descent into savage blood-lust captured in Euripides' lines above and in the ancient novels, and to a large degree in the witches' Sabbat. The early caricatures of Catholic ritual stressed their stilted and mysterious character, where the danger, the evil, is based in artifice, delusion, and malicious exploitation. Here indeed is the origin of our contemporary definitions of "ritual" as repetitive and mindless. While Roman ideas of subversive cults and early modern Christian constructions of the witches' Sabbat depended largely on the archaic model—the savage's disordered sacrifice and blood-orgy—many depictions of evil ritual, or depictions of ritual *as* evil, in early modern Europe begin to feature an insidious formalism. For example, notions of ritual that stress its ambiguous yet efficacious techniques and the peculiarity of its ingredients, as in the panics over Jewish host-desecration or ritual murder of children, suggest this formalist model. At the same time, some depictions of evil ritual still invoke the image of the savage's sacrifice when they portray the perpetrators' rage in sacrifice or some natural urge to perpetrate ritual atrocities: "They scourged him till the blood flowed," reports a thirteenth-century monk about the alleged Jewish ritual murder of little Hugh of Lincoln, well before the spate of ritual-murder prosecutions in early modern Germany and Spain.[76]

Modern views of ritual as a context for evil have veered between these two models of ritual as intrinsically evil: as an opportunity for libertine savagery or as engulfed in formalism, repetition, secrecy, and manipulation. While images of libertine savagery have continued to shape reports and fictional portraits of "primitive" societies (such as Haiti, discussed earlier in this chapter), those formalist notions of a ritual hyper-order have led to fantasies of a Black Mass to Satan, modelled closely upon Catholic liturgy through their details of altars, chalices, robes, chanting, and bloody sacrifices, and popularized throughout Europe since the early eighteenth century as an actual occurrence among the dissolute elite.[77] Originally, such images of a counterliturgy reflected concerns about the efficacy of rituals and sacraments: what if one invoked demons the same way one invoked Christ? But also, through the nineteenth century, the Black Mass captured many intellectuals' resentment toward Catholic shame-culture and sexual repression. In this vein, the very idea of church liturgy provided a context for Catholics to *imagine* transgression within a Catholic discourse. The full accoutrements and staging of Catholic rites could then serve imaginatively as the opportunity for sexual perversions. Ritual in this case would not be a state of—or build-up toward—frenzied and libertine savagery but rather a stilted, portentous theater—priests, nuns, chalices, altars, chapels, and the rest—within which one might, paradoxically, think about sexual transgression.

Here, as Georges Bataille has proposed, is the very essence of eroticism; for this scene of utter transgression—of liturgical space with sexual activity—offers the freedom of sexual indulgence (in fantasy) at the same time as affirming the very taboos that make that indulgence transgressive.[78] And a fantasy of transgression it was. Captured vividly in Martin van Maele's pornographic illustrations for Jules Michelet's classic work on witchcraft in an early English translation, ritual formalism became the theatrical context for erotic tableaux.[79] (See figure 6.) "Official" rites provided the tradition-bound, coldly sensuous, and constricting environment for utter release. Yet, at the culmination of the Black Mass in J.-K. Huysman's 1891 novel *Là-Bas*, the literary foundation of subsequent notions of this rite, all the worshippers collapse in a frenzied version of Bacchantic disorder:

> An air of wild hysteria followed in the wake of this sacrilege and overpowered the women. While the altar boys were paying homage to the nudity of the pontiff, the women threw themselves onto the Holy Eucharist and, face down at the foot of the altar, they clawed at it, tore off wet fragments, and ate and drank this divine filth.
>
> Another, squatting over the crucifix, let out a screeching laugh, then cried out: "My priest, my priest!" An old woman tore at her hair, jumped up, whirled herself around then buckled, no longer sure of her feet, and fell down next to a young girl in tears, who cowered against the wall, racked with convulsions and foaming at the mouth, spitting out fearful blasphemies. And [the protagonist] Durtal, terrified, saw amid the smoke of incense, as if through a fog, [the Satanic priest] Docre's red horns: he was now seated, frothing with rage, chewing up the unleavened hosts, which he was spitting out, wiping himself with and distributing to the women, and they were burying them with lustful groans, writhing over each other, in their attempts to violate them.[80]

Thus the image of the Catholic mass as a stilted and repressive performance linked intrinsically to sexual shame breaks apart like so

FIGURE 6   Martin van der Maele, "Sur ses reins un démon officiait, disait le
Credo,"engraving accompanying Jules Michelet, *La sorcière* (Paris:
J. Chevrel, 1911), 123. Ann Arbor, Michigan. Courtesy of Special
Collections Library, University of Michigan. To illustrate a private
edition of Michelet's romantic history of witchcraft and witch-
hunts, van der Maele uses explicitly pornographic poses within a
"ritual" scenario plainly modelled on Catholic liturgy. Unlike de
Bry's and Baldung Grien's implicitly pornographic uses of female
nudity (cf. figures 2–3, 7), van der Maele plainly intends to titillate under the framework of ritual atrocity.

much shattered china to release, not sexual and expressive freedom, but a cacaphony of the basest impulses. It is the antithesis rather than the simple loosening of liturgical repressiveness: a fantasy of defilement rather than libertinism.

By the twentieth century the idea of the Black Mass also reflected the deep distrust and fear of Catholic liturgy harbored among many Protestants. Indeed, even the notion of a secret Satanic priesthood incorporated suspicions of Catholic hierarchy. Pseudo-Catholic motifs indicated a script that a predetermined elite followed for ulterior reasons, such as blind service to ancient rites or mere exploitation. "Their rituals are very formal and established," concludes the psychiatrist Lawrence Pazder in *Michelle Remembers*, "Nothing really spontaneous is allowed to happen."[81] Their identities would invariably be obscured in robes or masks; their ritual materials, as in earlier images of evil ritual, required both innocent outsiders (children, small animals) and substances of disgust (feces, blood, snakes, corpses).[82] And thus in the professional literature on SRA in the late twentieth century, allegedly first-hand depictions of evil ritual like the following come to characterize the evil cults lurking among us:

> After supposedly being forced by the male group leader to stab the girl herself, [Elaine] distinctly recalled how: "one white-robed woman has come forward with a large butcher knife & is repeatedly stabbing the child's body & cutting into where her heart is. At least two other women assist her & at last they take her heart out and put it on a plate. . . . They have been drawing blood from the body and Death gives me a cup and makes me drink some of it then take a bite out of the heart."
>
> Gail . . . recorded in 1989 that: "They did a thing like communion. I recognize the ceremony as similar to what you do in . . . church for communion. (A woman) came in from the left and she carried this little bag and in it was some sort of faeces. I am not sure what it was. It was gross. It was awful and she stood on my right. I was kneeling and she said, 'this is the body of ' . . . and I just blacked out and take it and eat it. And then he said 'this is the blood of my body, take it and drink it,' and then she pushed my head into the abdomen—the open abdomen of this child."[83]

Ritual here suggests a dispassionate, repetitive theater of evil: human sacrifice and dismemberment according to rote rather than the culmination of rage. (One notices a similar construction of dispassion-ate, exploitative cruelty in stories of UFO abductions, in which the aliens' laboratory takes on many of the features of the formalist rit-ual.)[84] The author of this last passage, a sociologist and therapist, pre-sented this testimony as first-hand evidence that secret cults thrive on the margins of mainstream religion and are concocting such weird rit-ual procedures out of perverse interpretations of scripture.[85] Other writers on SRA tried to relate such stories of Satanic cults to those classic images of savage rites on the geographical periphery, both in modern times (like Haiti) and ancient (all those cannibal barbarians that Greeks, Romans, and other ancient cultures imagined to dwell beyond their borders). By tracing the contemporary Satanic cults to such putative origins, the contemporary cults could be shown to de-scend from much more established cults of evil, still practicing their ritual atrocities according to traditional schemes—a conspiracy with an ancient and savage past.[86] In all these quasi-scholarly endeavors, writers try to understand the diverse, allegedly first-hand claims of Sa-tanic cult abuse through association with other exotic ritual traditions, which themselves tend to be the fantastic constructions of Otherness typical to folkloric and literary thinking.

We thus come full circle to the idea that danger arises from the imagined encroachment of the antihuman—from the ends of the earth to our very neighborhood. A fascination with the monstrous cul-ture and its inverse ceremonies when they are in their place becomes horror and panic when that culture is believed to be among us, prac-ticing their ancient customs in the basement of that house down the street or in those local woods. If the foreign cult of ecstatic, bloody de-votions comes into the city, those devotions become potentially preda-tory, and their essential monstrosity, expressed ritually, is viewed as a source of immediate disorder. A similar process occurs when the myth-ical night-witch, denizen of another sort of cultural periphery in her nocturnal child-stealing and -sacrificing, moves into the center, as it were, through personification in a real person: a jealous neighbor or lo-cal midwife.[87] This shift of the monstrous from periphery to center—a process typically catalyzed by a witch-finder, as we saw in chapter 3—will also bring terror to communities, as monsters "good to think with" become all too real predators in our midst, the faces of real evil. In these cases, too, it is ritual that encapsulates the difference of the Other when performed on the periphery but expresses danger now that it takes place covertly at the center. Those rites of evil integrate real experiences and lurid fears, fantasies of transgression and litanies of the "worst things imaginable," the trappings of modernity and the specter of ancient atrocities repeated perpetually.

The point here is not simply the encroachment of the subhuman or perverse but that their rites and religious habits themselves are predatory or subversive. Out of their religious commitments and ritual substances come our catastrophes. The acts that bind them afflict us. Hence it is worth comparing the two patterns I noted in the history of the representation of evil rites: are their ceremonies dangerous because of libertine savagery and disorderly sacrifices or, on the other hand, a dry, manipulative formalism? The addition of these formalist features to the conception of evil ritual, especially since the Reformation, demonstrates a real shift in notions of proper and improper religiosity. With this formalist model, popular terror arises from perceiving evil in some covert institution and its hierarchy, rather than in ancient or primitive custom or urge. It is thus hardly surprising that this image would predominate in modern fantasies of ritualized evil, which encapsulate conspiracy itself.

The Implications of Evil Rites

The concepts of evil rituals we have seen in this chapter, and those monstrous realms that are integrated through obscene ceremonies, all provide cultures a way to define religion itself—to lay out a proper way of celebrating sacred things. Through these negative fantasies people process their questions about the perpetuation of society and the acquisition of practical powers—even if these powers result in danger to us. Operating at the very center of inversion and monstrosity, evil rituals seem to serve three primary purposes for their performers, those denizens of the monstrous realm, those worshippers of Satan: first, their mutual binding and allegiance to a larger cause; secondly, their acquisition of supernatural power; and thirdly, the coordination of their broader (malign) activities. Of course, these functions might well resemble a general definition of "ritual" or "religion."[88] Thus we might recognize in depictions of evil ritual an objectification—albeit in disgusting, subversive terms—of religion and ritual as various cultures imagine (or approximate) these categories.

THE MUTUAL BINDING OF THE MALEVOLENT

Across our examples we find the core rituals of evil serve to bind the malevolent community. To aid in the human sacrifice, to share in the cannibalistic feast, to declare formal devotion to the Devil—all constitute ways of affirming solidarity with the group (as in African notions of witch-cults and Western depictions of the rites of the savage) or with a higher power (as in constructions of diabolical witchcraft in Africa and early modern Europe). As both the *Malleus Maleficarum* and the Kenyan Presidential Report on Devil-Worship indicate, this dedication links individual acts of destruction with the affirmation of a central, sacred force. (Night-witches, of course, practice evil by nature, but some cultures' depictions of their ceremonies invariably conceptualize their glee in, and dedication to, maleficent acts.)[89]

Furthermore, as European witch-hunting treatises make clear, rituals of evil are imagined as having their own structure, even a rite of passage, that presses the totality of inversion into a series of stages. Solidarity and mutual commitment to evil, that is, come not simply through rendezvous but through a sequence: separation from this world, arrival in the place of that realm, and constitution of that realm through others' presence and through leaders. There follow quasi-liturgical acts like response dialogues, chants, gestures of devotion, and a collective merging (in dance or orgy) that alternates with gestures of individual self-submission, like confessions of harm one has perpetrated, or oaths of dedication to evil. At the end, the evil ones depart, back to "our" world, recommitted to the group or Devil and to the perpetration of evil.[90]

MONSTROUS RITES AND THE ACQUISITION OF POWER

The rituals of evil also frame the acquisition of the supernatural power that the witches, Satanists, or other evil society are supposed to hold. Medieval and early modern European witch-finders and their official schematizers put much store in the reality of the diabolical forces that could be wielded through disgusting unguents and stolen eucharistic hosts. The maleficent efficacy that witches and Jews were thought to extract through abusing hosts and crosses proved logically these objects' positive efficacy in their proper liturgical places. Unguents and powders produced from infants—and even infant cannibalism—likewise reflected concern over the nature of eucharistic communion and the protective efficacy of infant baptism.[91] These correspondences between evil efficacy from abused bodies (or even abused pseudobodies like the Eucharist) and sacred efficacy from cherished bodies in their place—that the former somehow proved the latter—emerged in particularly vivid form in the pilgrimage cults dedicated to eucharistic hosts and to children that local Jews, it was claimed, had stolen, ritually stabbed, and hidden. (See figures 9 and 10.) Discovered and rescued from such abuse, the hitherto ambiguous bodies now "worked" to the benefit of Christians.[92] In the case of witches, of course, the efficacy of infants' body-parts could only be demonstrated through the coerced testimony of the accused. But in both cases the definitive abuse of the holy substance took place in a ceremonial context—as part of the gestures of collective affirmation and devotion.

The efficacy of baby-parts, is, of course, even more basic to the depiction of inverse, monstrous ritual, for it involves the use, *as* magical substance, of that member of society most needful *of* magical substance (i.e., protection). It is a plausible generalization that the richest arsenals of practical magic cross-culturally are devoted to perinatal protection. The inverse of this concern is not just the terrifying image of the infant stolen and abused or eaten, but the exploitation of the infant's corpse for efficacious substances themselves. Carried back into our world, these substances would carry malign powers. Hence the preoccupation in Roman literature with witches' and foreigners' use of ritually slaughtered humans, especially infants, to acquire supernatural power. The witch Erictho "needs the fresh blood that gushes forth when a throat is slit" and unborn fetuses "in order to offer them on a burning altar."[93] For Epiphanius's Gnostics, it is semen and menstrual blood, also loaded with perinatal symbolism, that are ritually "transubstantiated" and then, too, become the magical extension of the perverse ritual. So also in Eni's *Delivered from the Powers of Darkness* and the Kenyan Presidential Report on Devil-Worship, the substances prepared or shared in the central ritual setting—typically blood and human body parts—are supposed to transmit power to the partaker. Even in more secular guise, the imputation of a craving for baby-parts to an amorphous, predatory realm has arisen in national panics (as in Guatemala) about the dangers that aid agencies, corporations, and governments pose to "our children."[94]

Speculation on the power of substances that emerge from evil rites is part of a broader cultural endeavor of objectifying religion, its acts, rites, accoutrements, and propositions. It is an imaginative process, projected onto a mythical, if tangible, realm of inversion and the horrific rites at the center of that realm: the cannibalism, infanticide, blood-lust, and incestuous orgies of the foreigner, witch, or Satanist. How remarkable, then, to find this same assertion of the power in evil or ecstatic ritual at the core of many early anthropologists' and psychohistorians' theories of sacrifice. From Robertson Smith (*Religion of the Semites*, 1889) through Sigmund Freud (*Totem and Taboo*, 1913), René Girard (*Violence and the Sacred*, 1972), and Walter Burkert (*Homo Necans*, 1972), and even underlying works of Émile Durkheim, Mircea Eliade, and Victor Turner, a potent ritual state of collective, dissociative enthusiasm, often (or originally) culminating in violence and cannibalism, lies at the very origin of religion itself. The need to recapture that ritual state becomes a problem that culture must resolve or sublimate (Freud, Girard) or approximate by other ritual means (Durkheim, Eliade, Turner).

Yet these thinkers' documentation for such an original state of violent inversion came from the same classical literary fantasies of savagery and subversion that we saw in the beginning of this chapter: a late antique camel sacrifice, and even a fictional drama from classical times about the cult of Dionysus—Euripides' *Bacchae*. Sacrifice, historians and anthropologists now know, does not revolve around killing, not to speak of ecstatic killing, nor even is it the central feature of religions. It was a case of theory inspired by fiction. Yet blood-sacrifice did make compelling fiction, and presenting these scenarios of inversion in secular, academic terms had the effect of legitimizing these scenarios for contemporary Western writers who were trying to explain the alleged evil cults of their own day. People tantalized by the idea of Satanic cults and secret human sacrifices needed only to delve into the speculative work of these scholars. Hence the picture of rituals in which bloody, orgiastic inversions became a source of power provided modern writers, like ancient ones, with a subject of both alarmed condemnation and voyeuristic fantasy.[95]

Both these sentiments consequently informed late twentieth-century speculation on Satanic cults—their origin, nature, and perpetuation. Such cults, some writers believed, sought "power" in their rituals of evil. For example, writers speculating on the reason for Satanic cults' perpetuation since time immemorial returned to notions of some intrinsic power released in the killing of live beings. If a camel could produce the enthusiasm described by Pseudo-Nilus in the scene canonized in the works of Robertson Smith and Freud, how much more power—the speculation goes—could result from a human or an infant, from whose blood-spilling devotees would be infused with a sense of potency and arousal.[96] In the following imaginative explanation for Satanic atrocities in his own day, the psychohistorian Lloyd DeMause clarifies this power of Satanic cult rites as essentially sexual:

> Cult abuse, like all sadistic acts, individual or group, is a sexual perversion whose purpose is achieving orgasm by means of a defense against severe fears of disintegration and engulfment. . . . Only by reenacting cultic rituals can these deeply regressed individuals avoid castration and engulfment fears and reassure themselves of their potency and separateness.
>
> Groups are particularly effective in achieving this traumatic reenactment. The individual identifies with the aggressor and the group and its leader become the murderous, engulfing mommy torturing the child. Actual castration is often inflicted on victims by cults. It is also sometimes inflicted upon cult members, who cut off their *own* fingers and offer them to Satan to make him more potent. "It was considered on honor among satanists to have one or more fingers missing," says one cult member. Sometimes the phallus or the finger is actually eaten, an act very effective in restoring potency. The same principle lies behind all cannibalistic acts of cults. In fact, all cultic rituals eventually aim at the restoration of lost potency. . . .

This delusional absorption of children's power has been the central group-fantasy behind all child sacrifice since the days when early civilizations sacrificed children to prevent the world from descending into chaos.[97]

In this way a contemporary writer can assemble a theory of ritual power to explain rituals that have no forensic evidence. The conceptualization of a realm of monstrous ritual results in a theory of efficacy, produced and transmitted through violence. And indeed, the depiction of monstrous ritual provides a means of thinking about the nature of ritual itself: does it comprise stilted, repetitive forms and gestures? Or does it provide excitement, even a violent excess of dissociative enthusiasm, in compensation for the impotence of everyday life?

EVIL RITUAL AND THE COORDINATION OF CONSPIRACY

Monstrous rituals, we have seen, demonstrate the essential Otherness, savagery, and often evil of an ambiguous or rumored society. They are different or subhuman, that is, *because of* the way they carry on ceremonies; they are evil *because of* what they do (or kill or eat) in those ceremonies. The core ritual, often revealed by a self-proclaimed eyewitness even despite the cults' essential distance or secrecy, indicates the basic nature of the cult. And when the cult operates in our midst rather than on the exotic periphery, its secrecy and persistence, combined with the horrific nature of its rituals, translate into *conspiracy*. The rituals, as indeed the entire religious character of the subversive society, reveal a motivation for evil, a social body dedicated to evil, a plan or coordinated approach to evil, a history of evil, and a rationale for discerning evidence of that evil: in dead or missing children, or simply in the local wise woman and her spells.[98] Conspiracy lifts misfortune and conflict from the level of the particular, the context-specific, to that of the general, as a tentacle of broad subversion. "Only when malice is seen as internally motivated within the sect" of witches, the historian Richard Kieckhefer has pointed out, "does it become reasonable for anyone to see anyone else as a potential aggressor."[99]

All these features are in many ways characteristic of the conspiracy or subversion myth as sociologists like David Bromley and Serge

Moscovici have described it in comparative terms. For example, to mobilize people against conspiracy the conspiracy must be shown to be transcendent—historically, spatially, institutionally, and in its means of effectiveness—of any particular incident of ambiguity or misfortune. The myth outlines how the conspiracy is organized and perpetuates itself socially, and thus how the putative individual malefactor is merely an arm of the collective body. The myth outlines how long, how widely, and how deeply the conspiracy has operated over time, such that there must be a long-term plan underlying individual catastrophes. The myth locates the center or source of conspiracy spatially: a foreign land, a secret realm, even the basement of a house in our very community. And the myth outlines the ways by which the conspiracy affects our society: incremental moral erosion? Destruction of children and means of reproduction? Initiation or enslavement of ever-greater numbers of our youth? Or train-wrecks, storms, poisoned wells, and infertile fields?[100]

The cumulative effect of such an articulated myth of evil conspiracy is generally not a theory of misfortune but rather a terrifying reality, which mobilizes communities and institutions to acts of purification, often utilizing special tactics (torture, close questioning of children, admission of otherwise questionable evidence) due to the immediacy and extent of the threat.[101] An inquisitorial commissioner wrote of the hysteria that swept a Basque region in 1610, following a preaching crusade that laid out the immanence of diabolical witchcraft: "The moment a person is accused [of witchcraft] on the basis of the statements of two, three, or more children, a large crowd of people rush to his house and in the name of justice they seize him, submitting him to monstrous and cruel tortures because of the hatred and bitterness felt towards anyone accused of this crime."[102]

Attributing religious motivations and a central ritual to the conspiracy myth both simplifies and exoticizes the conspiracy. Real and imagined maleficence in the community now derives not from envy, social tensions, or hereditary malign powers like the evil eye but rather from internal motivation: dedication to Satan. From antiquity through the early modern period an alternate society and its relative humanity might be known by its religious elements. Even in contemporary cases of Satanic subversion it is the religious element of Satan worship that serves to classify a conspiracy of sexual abuse as a recognizable component of horrific ancient cults. Religion and ritual are inevitable cultural components of the Other, however monstrous. Yet religion and ritual are also horrific things to uncover. The very notion that witches, foreigners, or Satanists are in thrall to an ancient cult, in whose ceremonies they forswear humanity for a sequence of perverse and bloody acts, renders the conspiracy more resilient (as religions are purported to be), more dangerous (as religious motivations are thought to be unassailable), and more enthusiastic (as the Other's rites invariably bring him to addictive states of ecstasy) than, say, conspiracies of a more political or racial character. Protestant caricatures of secretive institutions and manipulative priesthoods only ramify the dangers of subversive religion in modern times. Hence we find in one Satanic abuse therapist's manual an elaborate picture of the Satanic organization that stands behind the widespread abuse of children and terrorizing of child advocates::

The power that exists in Satanic (and Luciferian) cults is reportedly reflected in an organized hierarchy with incremental ranks. These positions may vary somewhat from one group to another, but some which appear common include the following: page, knight, priest (or priestess), prince (or princess), high priest (or high priestess), king (or queen), savior, and god (sometimes goddess, . . .). As one increases in rank, one is taught more about the programming cues or "triggers" used in ceremonies with the other followers of the cult. Some of these triggers are relatively generic and thus can be used with a relatively large number of people . . .

Those who increase in rank are not only taught a variety of triggering stimuli that they can use in controlling others (via such programming methods), but they are also deprogrammed so that their responses to these lower-level generic cues are less powerful. Thus, survivors who are higher ranking in the Satanic (and similar) cults are "trained" with more highly specific and idiosyncratic programming cues so that the majority of other members will not readily have control over them. Such control remains with the elite, who are higher in rank and skill.[103]

Is there not something reassuring about the rigid order these authors have projected onto the horrible specter of cult atrocity? We are reminded of the elaborate demonologies ancient institutions used to render supernatural attack more comprehensible, as we saw in chapter 2. But modern attempts to systematize a Satanic conspiracy myth went further. Another writer suggested that Satanic cults "program" victims from early childhood to work as prostitutes, bookkeepers, and legal advisors, amassing enormous financial resources for the cults and aiding them in maintaining secrecy. The conspiracy and its organization permeate society, therefore; but at the core—what actually enslave the army of prostitutes and financial advisors—are the cannibalistic, incestuous rites.[104]

Indeed, the image of the perverse ritual and the devotion that the rites are supposed to inspire among the wide society of cultists give the myth of conspiracy a particular coherence, casting all its members as essentially savage. As one historian of European witchcraft ideas has noted, "The Sabbath is, all at once, the theatrical and ritual synthesis of the antisocial, antireligious, indeed antihuman components of the imaginary structure that is the witches' conspiracy."[105] The image of Jewish ritual murder likewise redefines an amorphous suspicion of an ambiguous Other as the predatory cravings of a subhuman body in the midst of orderly Christian society.[106] And in modern American and English depictions of SRA, the image of Satanic rites rationalizes cultural panics over sexual abuse by casting that abuse as a subsociety's *ritual*. Even more, this potent spectacle of Satanic rites makes the abuse the very binding ritual of a conspiracy, while at the same time presenting that spectacle as somehow revelatory of conspiracy. The remembering, the rehearsal, and indeed the systematic scrutiny of incest, cannibalism, infanticide, liturgical parody, and uses of excrement, blood, and corpses all become important components in realizing the Satanic conspiracy.

Here, in fact, we approach a second level in the construction of evil rites: the effect of gazing on or imagining the perverse. To what extent does the fascination with the perverse cultures "on the edges of the earth" arise from a kind of pornography of inverse customs, both sexual and culinary? When these cultures move into our own spaces, does our voyeurism cease out of the inclination to purify? Or is our inclination to purify motivated by the intimate presence of people who now confront us with their alluringly inverse customs? What is the fascination with the obscene and lurid when it is performed "ritually" and secretly? The next chapter will explore the element of fantasy and repudiated desire that weaves through all the legends and literature of evil rites.

5 Imputations of Perversion

The Imaginative Resources of the Monstrous

DURING THE HEIGHT of the recovered-memory disputes in the early 1990s, in which SRA often figured as an example of the horrors therapists could recover, SRA therapists often posed the question, how could people conceive of such perverse atrocities *without* their being true? How could people make up such horrors? Infanticide, cannibalism, torture, animal and human sacrifice, orgy, incest, bizarre sexual acts, pseudosacramental use of feces, urine, blood, and corpses—it all seemed quite beyond what these middle-class, married, suburban women or their therapists could concoct on their own.[1]

Other rumors of perverse cults in history have likewise inspired scholars well after the fact to try to find some core of truth or historical practices behind the allegations: that some early Christians really *did* have incestuous orgies, that some Jews really *did* sacrifice Christian children for their blood, or that the witch's Sabbats envisioned in late medieval and early modern Europe *were* demonic reconstructions of actual heathen cult rituals.[2] For scholars who have thus argued for some grain of truth behind alleged perversions, the significant feature has often been their so-called ritual context, which appeared to lend the atrocities, and the perpetrators' commitments, a kind of history, a cultural necessity, and even a bizarre theological sense. Ritual would suggest the repetition of some archaic needs for transgression or even the continuation of ancient heathen cults of human sacrifice. My argument in chapter 4, of course, has been quite the opposite: far from giving rumors of monstrous perversity an historical authenticity, images of evil ritual have a structural, imaginative function, integrating the whole scenario of monstrous anticulture, as well as a distancing function, rendering participants and atrocities more alien, more consuming, and—if the ritual were to take place near us—all the more evil. But ritual also provides a point of familiarity. Even if we regard them as inhuman and disgusting, the perversions we impute to savages and witches become, through their ritual structure, somehow comprehensible as something people might, somewhere, do—a kind of parody of our own rites. Thus our own ritual structures—sacrifice, Eucharists, vestments, dance, chanting, meal-sharing—become the very means for us to imagine those disgusting reversals that signify a realm of monsters.[3]

IMAGINING PERVERSION

So then let us return to the overall picture of transgression that weaves through all these rumors, accusations, and learned manuals for discerners. I shall refer to it as the *tableau of perversion*. Endlessly variable, the scenes of atrocity revolve around incestuous orgy and cannibalism, especially infant cannibalism. They extend in historical and culturally specific ways to styles of dance, use or preparation of disgusting materials, obscene parodies of proper religion, and inverse sexual behavior (sodomy, necrophilia). Sometimes, as in the Jewish ritual-murder accusations, the full tableaux are condensed into gory sacrifices with only sublimated eroticism.

We have seen that versions of this tableau imputed to the libertine or savage races envisioned on the world's periphery served to bolster our—insiders'—sense of moral and cultural propriety (as well as our legitimacy in conquering those savages). We are civilized; they are the antithesis—beast-like. For example, in antiquity, what we do as custom—sexual, culinary, or mortuary—becomes, in contrast to the Irish or the Scythians or Egyptian herders, not arbitrary but the very essence of humanity.[4] When ritual comes to figure more centrally in the tableau (most recently in depictions of Africans and Haitians), images of ritual excess and a lack of control serve even more to elide savage and beast. Early modern missionary and literary depictions of savages show normally austere tribal kings and queens reduced in the course of orgiastic rites to quivering, sexually omnivorous animals. Sometimes the bestial Other creeps nearer, to dwell among us, acting as normal citizens do during the day. Then rumors of the Other's secret perversions and ritual atrocities align him clearly with that subhuman savagery and all its dangers that we associate with the periphery of the world while underlining *our* civilization and humanness. The Other's rites are so far beyond the bounds of "religion" and "culture" that they cannot be considered acceptable variants of either.[5] While we celebrate mindfully and peacefully, in purity and daylight, hedging round our children with divine protection, the Other descends into orgiastic depravity under cover of night, to the sounds of drums or some other cacaphony, coating himself with slime and disembowelling children and other innocents. Imputations of perversion set some Other firmly in the realm of savagery, monstrosity—beyond the pale in all fundamental domains of morality. Lest an audience think otherwise—lest they would view the Other as neighbor, citizen, human, familiar in habits but for some acceptable cultural differences—an articulated scenario of cannibalism, sexual perversity, and moral inversion makes clear the degree of difference.[6]

But it would be naive to suggest that tableaux of perversion have merely carried a utilitarian purpose in distinguishing the culture of the insiders as human as opposed to that of outsiders. For the mere act of contemplating such wholesale transgression, then portraying its details in literature, art, or inquisitorial tract, inevitably involves a voyeurism, a fascination with what perversions count as culture for the Other. The Maka people of the Cameroon imagine an antiworld of night-witches whose perverse nocturnal ceremonies, replete with cannibalism and homosexual acts, signify their monstrous anticulture. Yet this ceremony, according to the anthropologist Peter Geschiere, "is an image that obsesses [them]. They speak about it with horror, but also with curiosity and even excitement."[7] In the ancient world, novels like that of Achilles Tatius (quoted in the beginning of chapter 4) that depicted the erotically charged atrocities of alien tribesmen as threats to chaste Roman maidens served obviously to titillate their audiences with spectacles of transgression framed plausibly as customs on the edges of culture.[8]

By late antiquity the topic of cruelty itself, the historian Daniel Baraz has argued, was contemplated only through graphic scenarios— martyrdoms, the torments of hell, the atrocities of barbarians—rather than moral speculation, and any of these images could invite the

identification and sadistic excitement of the viewer.[9] The literature of
New World exploration and the naked, cannibal savages revealed there
also meant to arouse embarrassed enjoyment as well as horror. In text
and illustration both, revolting scenes of culinary preparation of human
bodies were set in a kind of Eden, with nude men and women lying
about, pursuing domestic duties, or dancing. Yet it was a violent para-
dise: cannibalism at the hands of voluptuous or aged naked women
conveyed an eroticized terror. In the sixteenth century, such images of
cannibalism and infanticide among women in the New World (e.g., figures 2 and 3) were also influencing the popular visual depiction of
witches and their ceremonies. Artists like Hans Baldung Grien portrayed ceremonies of nude women in insidious yet erotic poses, cooking and devouring infant parts and penises, and generally condensing
in their revels all that Europeans deemed supernaturally malicious,
from miscarriage to impotence to storms.[10] (See figure 7.)

As we move to documents of a more sinister type of perversion—
like demons and Satanic cults—it is clear that the unpacking of
transgressive detail, from the dismemberment of infants to the forced
rape of passive victims, involves a voyeuristic complicity in creating
the tableau. The tableau of perversion appears to illustrate why its perpetrators are beyond the moral pale—to substantiate pure evil. And
yet it also functions in reverse: the designation of a realm utterly beyond human comprehensibility allows imaginative participation in the
perversions and atrocities to take place safely.[11] In other words, knowing something is evil allows us to contemplate it without the fear that
we may be enjoying it, for we must be condemning it. In the 1990s, so
the psychologist Janice Haaken has suggested, women's erotic fantasies
deemed improper or unimaginable among most feminist and evangelical Christian communities could emerge in an "acceptably demonic"
form as SRA memories. While alleged victims and therapists disavowed
them as fantasies, they rehearsed the scenes and images compulsively—a
veritable folk pornography. And it was a useful pornography, for it
served also to consolidate group boundaries and ground moral claims:
"*We* are the ones who know these perversions take place," feminist
SRA believers seemed to declare, "*we* call upon society to acknowledge and purge itself of these perversions."[12] At other times, the obsession with details of monstrous perversion has been justified as

FIGURE 7 Hans Baldung Grien, *The Witches' Sabbat* (1510), chiaroscuro woodcut, 37.8 × 26.0 cm. Boston, Museum of Fine Arts, W. G. Russell Allen Bequest 69.1064. Photograph © 2006 Museum of Fine Arts, Boston, Massachusetts. Baldung Grien's images of witches consistently emphasized the dangers and allures of female nudity, combining various ages, contorted poses, and sexual insinuations.

edifying, beneficial even beyond the sensation of vicarious transgression. Through the ritual atrocities imputed to Jews, for example, the Eucharist could be imagined as the living—crying, bleeding, healing—body of Christ.[13] Through dwelling on the ravenous sexuality of female witches, one could comprehend the corporeality of the demons with whom they fornicated.[14] Thus people at multiple levels of culture could experience, enjoy, even profit intellectually, from the tableaux of perversion while framing their voyeurism not as fantasy but as an exploration of evil conspiracy.[15]

SAVAGE AND/AS MONSTER

As we begin to acknowledge some element of voyeurism and transgressive enjoyment in contemplating the tableaux of perversion that are affixed to the savage, the foreigner, or the subversive cult, we come to an essential point in the cultural imagination of evil. Here are monstrous *people*—Jews, Satan worshippers, denizens of the periphery like Scythians or, in American imagination, Appalachian mountain men—and the perversions and atrocities we impute to them indicate their subhumanity. Yet those perversions and atrocities, those indicators of monstrosity, draw on the same reservoir of images and symbols as the *supernaturally demonic*—vampires, werewolves, demons, and night-witches. Whereas monstrous people are dangerous by virtue of their bestial acts, the supernaturally monstrous preys on us by its very nature. Monstrous people are physically human, their monstrous tendencies usually hidden. But demons and monsters are at most (and at worst!) only *apparently* human, their physical natures being grotesque combinations of human and bestial features, whether fangs, claws, hair, or scales. Demonic sexuality, whether female or male, is rapacious, devouring, and grotesque, and demons' predatory appetites, especially for children and fetuses, are voracious.

If Western culture tends now to encounter these supernatural monsters only in movies and literature, and only occasionally now with true horror, they have been all too real in village life through history, and even now cross-culturally they can be the very image of predation and maleficence.[16] They often lurk quite near, embracing in their blood-thirst all the predatory terror of modernity itself, as recent vampire panics in Malawi demonstrate: the vampires used syringes.[17] Often, when villagers discuss these demonic figures they speculate with both horror and fascination about the demons' innate malice: for example, the celebrations they hold to eat infant flesh, their perverse sexual antics at these celebrations, the cravings they bear for human blood, or the disgusting ingredients they use for their sorcery. Or villages might discuss these demons' origins as pathetic humans, before being overtaken with evil cravings.[18]

Clearly the traditional conceptions and fears of such out-and-out monstrous beings have historically overlapped with, and influenced notions of, the savage, sorcery, and everyday witchcraft, such that a person imagined as dangerous in tendency and commitment comes to be "demonized"—assimilated to the category of the supernaturally monstrous. Such demonization of real people lies at the root of witch-panics in late medieval Europe and contemporary Africa.[19] But more importantly, the very construction of monstrosity in each type of evil—monstrous people and demons/monsters—depends on the same themes: sexuality (incest, rape); monstrous orality (cannibalism, cooking infants); impurities (blood, corpses, excreta); and inversion (nocturnal activity, parodies of proper behavior). Furthermore, in each case, the depiction of some monstrous threat out of these deeper components is both an intellectual exercise and an exciting, cathartic one, for it involves, first, the distortion of sentiments deemed ambivalent or socially unacceptable (envy, lust, even infanticidal aggression), second, their projection as monsters of some kind, and third, their reification as predators in our very midst, forcing our concern and hence our gaze.

In the rest of this chapter, then, we will explore how the imagination and imputation of monstrous perversions function in society. We normally think of monstrosity as a category of size or appearance— gigantic or half-beast or misshapen. However, these physical attributes only symbolize the monster's predilections: to incest, cannibalism, cruelty to children, destructiveness—acts utterly beyond the pale of comprehensible motive. The mother who kills her children in contemporary America is labelled "monster" as easily as the grotesque Lamia, the child-killing demon of Mediterranean cultures; the mass murderer-rapist-cannibal is assimilated to the same monstrous zone as the Cyclops. Sexual perversity, cannibalism and oral voraciousness, and broader schemes of inversion all stem from the deepest levels of human fantasy, while at the same time they come to hold particular meanings for audiences in imperial Rome, early modern Basque country, and contemporary America and Africa. My point is not the universality of meaning nor the complete discreteness of each historical symbol of Otherness, but rather the utility and allure of deep psychological images of threat and transgression in articulating Otherness, modernity, and even holy things.

Constructing the Monstrous

In his 1975 "Psycho-Historical Postscript" to *Europe's Inner Demons*, Norman Cohn pointed out the clear links between the chief perversions of heretics' rites and witches' Sabbats in ecclesiastical literature and motifs of atrocity and perversion used in Grimms' Tales and Greek mythology. All these narratives returned to motifs of child cannibalism and sexual boundary-crossing in ways that invite the psychoanalytic proposition that any depiction of perversion and horror allows the expression of repressed desires and impulses. That is, desires and impulses that we might deem immoral preemptively, even before we are entirely aware of them, these depictions of gross transgression and atrocity bring to awareness and explore in narrative form— sometimes at a safe distance, sometimes too close for comfort.[20] The repression of those desires and impulses, it must be added, is itself maintained through their distortion. Cannibalism and incest are the acts of demons and monsters and witches, not us, and they are relegated to a realm entirely Other: mythology's origin times, the romantic "once upon a time" of Tales, the peripheral lands of Africa or Haiti, or the utterly evil realms of Satan-worship or Jewish ritual murder. Studies of the monstrous must respect the different spatial, temporal, and even ritual ways that these basic fantasies of transgression can be safely worked through. Yet a comparative approach to demonic tableaux of perversion will inevitably confront some element of desire mixed into the horror of these Other realms.

Along with cannibalism and sexual perversity, ethnographers have noted especially in modern ideas of witch-cults a fascination with inversion itself: not only what is eaten and who copulates with whom, but every aspect of what witches (or demons, or Satanists) *do*: their dances, their music, their singing, their transportation. Everything is turned upside down: they eat what we find disgusting, they mock what we find sacred, they expose what we do in private, they abuse what we protect, they congregate when we stay at home. It is as if the wholesale inversion of cultural norms carries an intrinsic excitement, which compounds both the overall picture of the monstrous and the prurience of contemplating it.

SEXUAL INVERSION

Sexual monstrosity has been a key motif among the various tableaux of evil we have encountered. Epiphanius's fourth-century CE depiction of Gnostic liturgy (quoted in chapter 4) has nude priests and priestesses copulating, masturbating, and using their fluids as sacraments.[21] This tableau was only a more stylized version of the mindless orgies that Romans imputed to Christians in the second century, following the ritual toppling of a candle, but Epiphanius's (and subsequent heresiographers') pornographic scenario is picked up and nuanced by sixteenth- and seventeenth-century witch-finders in their depictions of Sabbat perversions.[22] The late fifteenth-century *Malleus Maleficarum* imputes sexual monstrosity to women in general, their orgies with demons merely an extension of their natural lust. Out of this demonic lewdness come not only sick babies and impotent men but also storms and droughts, yet it is monstrous female lust that provides the entry-point, as it were, for demonic power.[23] If lust and perversion were missing in the Jewish ritual-murder stories of the early modern period, both the trials and the printed images that circulated to illustrate the crimes often depicted the genital mutilation of the child. Later versions of the story—such as the 1969 rumors that Jews were enslaving young women behind their stores in Orléans, France—allowed greater presence to the latent eroticism of the Jewish ritual-murder rumors. These versions suggest that predatory lust may always have been implicit in the stories of Jewish ritual atrocity.[24]

Of course, the widely published stories of SRA placed sexual monstrosity at the center of the tableau of evil:

> I was carried to the toolbench where gibberish was spoken by the four robed adults around me. Rather than water sprinkled, a small, black, wriggling cocker spaniel was held over me and disemboweled with a dagger-like instrument. . . . The long white taper was lit and ceremoniously held over me, wax dripping carefully onto each of my nipples. It was then inserted, still lit, into my vagina. In this way I was welcomed into the faith.[25]

The detailed depictions of sadistic perversion that run through SRA testimonies actually recall the 'savage abductions' that made such popular reading as far back as Greco-Roman antiquity (as we saw in chapter 4) but most evocatively, and with most inflammatory effect, in the narratives of white women "taken" by Native American or African tribes. The reader or audience participates in the abduction, rape or marriage, and sights of tribal customs and rites through the eyes or body of the alleged eyewitness. In the most popular abduction narrative from early New England, Peter Williamson's *French and Indian Cruelty* (1757, with multiple reprintings through the end of the eighteenth century), the author describes in titillating detail coming upon a young woman ravished by savages:

> [N]o heart among us but was ready to burst at the sight of the unhappy young lady. . . . For, oh! What breast, tho' of the brutal savage race we had just destroyed, could, without feeling the most exquisite grief and pain, behold in such infernal power, a lady in the bloom of youth, blest with every female accomplishment that could set off the most exquisite beauty! Beauty, which rendered her the envy of her own sex, and the delight of ours, enduring the severity of a windy, rainy night! Behold one nurtured in the most tender manner, and by the most indulgent parents, quite naked, and in the open woods, encircling with her alabaster arms and hands a cold rough tree, whereto she was bound, with cords so straitly pulled, that the blood trickled from her finger's ends! Her lovely tender body and delicate limbs, cut, bruised, and torn with stones, and boughs of trees as she had been dragged along, and all besmeared with blood! What heart can even now, unmoved, think of her destress, in such a deplorable condition; having no creature, with the least sensations of humanity, near to succour

or relieve her, or even pity or regard her flowing tears and lamentable wailings.[26]

In such stories of abducted maidens, the eroticized savagery that is inflicted upon her in her story condenses a larger savagery—the bestial (or monstrously cruel) anticulture of the abductors' world. In combining victim, reader, savage, and often eroticized ritual treatment (native weddings or concubinage, for example), the savage-abduction narratives epitomize the notion of a monstrous and predatory anticulture. In sixteenth-century descriptions of the New World, for example, Indians would be depicted alternately hunting and cooking humans, dancing, and copulating—always nude—before the shackled and appalled European alleged to have witnessed the scene.[27] (See figure 2.)

Yet at the basis of these tableaux of savagery lay the Edenic fantasy of a world with *no* taboos, where the mores that make us human simply never developed, and latent urges to libertinism and cannibalism became normalized. The Satanists revealed in SRA testimonies like the one above apparently resemble us and live among us, yet they throw off our shared taboos for ulterior reasons: the higher, if insidious, purpose of ritual, its cultural necessity and magical rewards. In both cases—savage and Satanist/witch—our contemplation of their transgression takes place in tandem with an insistence on the taboos broken. That is, in order to depict the horror in inverting sexual taboos, the sexual taboos themselves must be implicit—suspended for the duration of the rite but not collapsed entirely. It is the secret place or time of the rite, in fact, that is supposed both to invite transgression and to intensify it.[28] These human monsters, we imagine, must eventually return to life among us. In the case of the savage, we contemplate his unfamiliarity with taboos in connection with our own urge to conquer and civilize—that is, punish—him. Either way, taboos against sexual libertinism and perversion are upheld as the rationale for imagining sexual perversion.

The temporary, stylized suspension of taboo in these fantasies, these tableaux of perversions, is thus conceptually safe, for sexual mores remain theoretically fixed for all people regardless of lapses. But even more, as Georges Bataille observed, such transgression gains an erotic allure directly proportional to the anxiety one experiences in maintaining the taboo. Indeed, he argues, real erotic freedom for some people in some cultural contexts can only be imagined or performed as transgression.[29] Here we may count, among many examples, the nuns of Loudun, whose possession states consistently bent toward performances of erotic transgression, and the equally sexually cloistered women claiming SRA, for whom gothic scenarios of rape and torture attributed to Satanic cults provided the sole medium for sexual fantasy.[30] When people thus engage imaginatively and erotically in tableaux of sexual transgression and inversion—even sexual monstrosity in the case of SRA—tableaux that are relegated totally to a world of darkness and evil, their excitement arises specifically from the anxiety surrounding that transgression. At the same time, that transgressive engagement with tableaux of perversion *affirms* the very taboos that set those tableaux apart from us as evil or savage.

The sexual perversions in so many tableaux of monstrosity—ancient Bacchae and Christians, witches, Jews, Satanists, savages—are thus not simply projections of latent impulses and desires, but, even more, erotic fantasies of transgression. The rigidity of human mores becomes the basis for temporary—demonic, ritual, ecstatic—freedom. In medieval and early modern clerical culture, for example, the sexualized female body could be contemplated freely in distorted, demonized form, such that the repressed desires stimulated in such contemplation are disowned. Medieval clerical demonology is awash in Incubi and Succubi, voluptuous and repugnant witches, demonic fornication of every conceivable sort. But these images, the historian Dyan Elliott points out,

> are no longer recognizable as objects of desire. Therefore, in a certain sense, the images that return [from the level of unconscious impulses] have been so successfully fused with the demonic that they are no longer perceived as mere women and thus, in their repugnant guise, are no longer subject to the censorship that would accompany objects of libidinous desire.[31]

This same effort to construct a space for sexual voyeurism within the imaginative realm of the demonic took place during witch-finding procedures, which often revolved around the naked female body. Stripping the accused provided inquisitors a way to confront the full, demonized femininity of the witch directly—her demonic sexuality, rage, voracious hunger, maternity and antimaternity, all the inversions of her malicious being displayed in real flesh for the inquisitor's response. His own excitement before the spectacle of the naked woman would actually be repudiated through this demonization, his self-disgust transformed into disgust for her. Embodying his desire, she becomes something to be repelled or punished. Indeed, the inquisitor's response involved not only a hateful gaze but also a physical response to the naked female body—torture—that was itself sexualized.[32] "In this sadistic game of showing and concealing," the historian Lyndal Roper observes, "the witch forced her persecutors to apply and reapply pain, prising her body apart to find her secret."[33]

Excitement in the spectacle of inverse, predatory female sexuality has not been simply the provenance of male ecclesiastical culture. For women too, the wanton demoness or witch affirms the boundaries of sexual decorum in society while evoking fantasies of sexual and spatial freedom.[34] Women's discussions of the sexually transgressive night-witch in all her horrifying guises—aged, ugly, misshapen, or part-beast—play with notions of female sexual aggression, enjoying its spectacle while repudiating it, situating sexuality apart from beauty or nubility, allying it with images of the revolting. Many of the cultures that harbor such ideas also regularly impute sexual voraciousness to women, especially older women. For women, the exaggerated cravings of the night-witch thus serve to critique or lampoon male stereotypes of older women, or even male lust itself, here inverted as a demoness who molests unsuspecting husbands. Women's own imaginative play with notions of female demons and witches can thus combine ambivalent images of male lust with moral judgments about the relationship of sexuality to child-bearing (and its cessation), to widowhood, and women's decorum.[35]

These larger patterns of imagining sexual inversion are invoked at particular historical moments to think about sexual transgression as fantasy, threat, and metaphor. The *Malleus Maleficarum*'s oft-noted attention to women's lust not only stoked male clerical anxieties about sexuality and impotence, to be projected and reeenacted in each witch-investigation, but it also provided a way of thinking about *demons*' bodies. The clearest evidence of such bodies, Walter Stephens has argued, came from the very act of copulation with women, whose naturally lewd ways were supposed to invite the demons' presence. In the *Malleus Maleficarum*, "the witch's reaction of 'carnal delectation' demonstrates that she is being acted on, and, the more intensely she enjoys, the more intensely real is the agent who is acting on her."[36] Here, then, is the transgressive image extended, although in no way diminished, for the purpose of higher demonological speculation.

These late medieval and early modern tableaux of perversion cast desire itself as only a disorderly element in the realm of evil, projected far from the domain of the one who contemplates perversity. So also in the consistently pornographic imagery of SRA, the drawn-out scenarios of sexual violence and perversity are done *to* a passive, often drugged and bound, victim within a framework of complete Otherness, the Satanic cult ritual in its secret or liminal arena.[37] The element of fantasy in these scenes is far more complex than the simple projection of wishes into another world. For example, the construction and validation of the scenes involves the rapt audience of therapist or support group, and the scenes themselves may articulate deep psychological matters (identity, family status, even genuine abuse) beyond erotic transgression. But that central theme of SRA narratives, the victim's utter passivity at hands of evildoers—her invasion by impersonal, often masked forces—opens the imagination to several kinds of transgressive stimulation: the experience and repudiation of desire, infantile experiences of anxiety and pleasure, and even an identification with the monstrous Other against the suffering victim.[38] Here we might note a far less violent form of such fantasies of passivity and sexual invasion that has arisen in contemporary times among those people claiming extraterrestrial abduction. In the typical UFO-abduction narrative, the victim is taken, immobilized (although often allowed partial awareness), laid on a table, and then subjected to probings to remove or insert reproductive material, all under the impassive "eyes" of unearthly beings. It would seem that the image of one's passive sexual invasion and transgression—an entirely different subject, it should be noted, from real rape experiences—has become a fantasy in search of an appropriate "reality" in a culture anxious about erotic imagination.[39]

These themes of sexual invasion and passive transgression that permeate SRA claims also translate essential experiences in modern

Western female sexual development. As Janice Haaken has noted, the body comes to be imagined at a distance, "as an alienated realm of disturbing sensations and as a site of invasive encounters." Fantasies, anxieties, and sexuality itself, she explains, all become projected onto a distanced—sometimes alluring, sometimes grotesque, sometimes despised—female body through the course of adolescent development. Thus the various images of bodily fragmentation, female vulnerability, and masculine monstrosity that fill SRA testimonies offer refractions of female sexual identity, projected into lurid tableaux of Satanic ritual and human sacrifice.[40] SRA tableaux become ways of thinking about one's sexuality emerging from close familial confines much in the way the sadistic stories of the Grimms' Tales articulated the anxieties and aggressive fantasies of a younger stage of development.

But SRA stories also involve deeper, more infantile levels of sexual preoccupation: what psychoanalysts call "primary-process" thought. Images of feces and anal invasion, of forced oral ingestion, and of poked and prodded orifices permeating such testimonies convey the angry and desperate fantasy world of the infant described by Melanie Klein. A patient describes her attire for Satanic initation as "an obscene mixture of feces, urine, and blood, packed and smeared from my head to my toes"; another gives her psychiatrist a drawing of a nude child—herself—lying quietly on a table surrounded by candles while disembodied hands insert sharp objects into her; while numerous patients envision themselves forced to eat feces, blood, corpses, animals, and fetuses at the behest of terrifying authority figures.[41] It is in this very realm of primary-process fantasy that the sexually perverse and the cannibalistic (to which I will turn shortly) become combined. That is, while the adult mind tends to separate sexual from oral monstrosity, the infantile mind experiences them in collapsed and dialectical forms. Of course, this collapse is often maintained in adult culture: early modern images of nude witches, for example, who collect and roast both baby-parts and castrated penises, or legends of monsters who eat nubile women, or night-witches that both eat babies and castrate men.[42] Such primary-process fantasies of oral-anal-sexual transgression have a universality and a horror that psychoanalytic theory has proved singularly capable of interpreting. Kleinian themes of infantile experience and emotional response arise repeatedly through the life cycle of imagination in both individual terrors and those shared among societies, like monsters and witches.[43]

Indeed, as highly repetitive with images of sexual monstrosity, oral and anal invasion, and sadomasochistic arrangements as SRA testimonies could be, they also provided considerable space for pornographic creativity and idiosyncrasy. The sociologist Stephen Kent collects from his informant "Gail" this detail from her alleged Satanic wedding ceremony: "What they were trying to do in this particular ritual, this wedding ritual, was to simultaneously blow air up each other's buttocks."[44] The Satanic frame—the myth of evil conspiracy—allows a particular inventiveness in imagining erotic transgression, especially since it claimed to represent decades of intrafamilial cult activity, not just brief abductions. While therapists (and some scholars like Kent) managed to integrate some of these bizarre visions into larger theories of conspiracy, other details were simply cited—and visualized and rehearsed—as further evidence of Satanic monstrosity.

In its openness to individual fantasy, the culture of SRA experts and media recalled the ways that European witch-finders would augment their published depictions of the witches' Sabbat with new discoveries taken in trials. From witch-trials in late-sixteenth-century Burgundy, Henri Boguet gleans that

> there are also demons which join in these dances in the shape of goats or rams, as we learn from many witches besides those we have just mentioned; and particularly Antoine Tornier observed that, when she danced, a black ram held her up by the hands with his feet, which were, as she said, very hairy, that is to say, rough and rude. . . .
>
> I may safely leave to the imagination the question whether or not every other kind of lechery known to the world is practised at the Sabbat; what is even more remarkable is that Satan becomes an Incubus for the women and a Succubus for the men. This is a fact to which George and Antoine Gandillon have testified and, before them, Antoine Tornier, Jacquema Paget and several others.[45]

Clearly the accused, whether coerced or desperate for local respect, were contributing their own fantastic details to the official theories of Sabbat rites and demonic intercourse. How the Devil was dressed, the delights of the dance, the seductions that drew them in, kisses and carresses, as well as inventive carnal acts—the invitation to participate imaginatively in that Sabbat realm led the accused to draw from their own reservoirs of fantasy.[46] Nor should we assume that they spouted private fantasies purely to relieve the pain of torture, for some suspects seem to have come to believe in their claims to Sabbat participation. In fact, a closely studied incident of Satanic Abuse prosecution has some bearing on these extraneous Sabbat details. In this case, which took place in Washington State in the late 1980s, a devoutly charismatic Christian police officer accused by his daughters first of sexual abuse, then of Satanic cult abuse, began to "remember" graphic pornographic scenes to substantiate the daughters' accusations, even—one psychologist discovered—when these accusations were deliberately concocted by investigators. Thus, from the suggestion—under highly coercive circumstances and to a man committed to a fundamentalist worldview and to his own essential sinfulness—that he had orchestrated sex *among* his children before an audience, or that he had committed homosexual acts, or that Satanic cult rituals took place, the accused would enter an observable trance state and consequently produce graphic "memories" based entirely on his own sexual imagination, an eroticism utterly proscribed in his charismatic subculture yet legitimate in the projected form of cult atrocities.[47]

The stimulation that Sabbat tableaux and these modern analogues offer individual pornographic creativity emerges differently where children are the ones encouraged or coerced. In the late 1980s social workers earnestly sought links between the perverse Satanic cults that adults were reporting and the massive day care "fronts" for Satanic cults they believed that they were uncovering. Under coercive, prolonged, and suggestive questioning, children of quite young ages were invited to "recall"—in essence, to imagine—perversion and molestation. Yet the imagery of sexual transgression that children provided revolved around simple anal and genital themes—hardly the gothic horrors of SRA—and a certain exhibitionism, mixed liberally with such typical children's anxieties and pleasures as masks, costumes, clowns, animals, and airplanes. Lacking the dark frame of Satanic ceremony, the meticulous sadism, and the wholesale repudiation of eroticism, the children's imagery of sexual inversion amounted to a quite different tableau from that projected by adults.[48] Adult interviewers, of course, did not recognize either elements of fantasy or, in fact, any possibility of children's sexuality, attributing the sexual details they extracted instead to the adult perversions of Satanic cults. Indeed, they viewed the children's "reports" of day care center perversions as both more innocent (because of the frivolous nature of the children's "screen memories" of airplanes and zoo animals) and more terrifying, as the interviewers endeavored to discern through the children's inconsistent "memories" the horrors they had allegedly undergone.

But at other times when children's distinctive eroticism has emerged publicly, communites have not displaced their anxiety onto Satanists and witches but labelled the children themselves as demonic. A case in early eighteenth-century Germany began when some parents in the town of Augsburg became aware of their children's sexual interests and, perhaps, play. The details of witchcraft that subsequently emerged in trial, the historian Lyndal Roper has observed, revolved around the most infantile of sexual themes: anal and oral preoccupations, exhibitionism, masturbation, and subversion of their parents' sexuality. But instead of constructing a Satanic conspiracy *behind* the children's sexual behavior, as in the SRA panic, the adults of Augsburg regarded the children themselves as in league with the Devil—the fantasy world they revealed as indicating their complicity in diabolical witchcraft. The trials thus consisted in getting the children to frame their sexual interests in terms of Satanic devotion. While their testimonies reveal the typical preoccupations of children's sexuality, the adults were confused and threatened by the revelation of this fantasy world and responded brutally.[49]

These last cases of children's perverse images show once again that the idiosyncrasies of social position, gender, age, and indeed individual psyche sustain—like an endless reservoir of fantasy—those tableaux of sexual perversity so essential to depictions of an evil realm. And these realms of evil themselves serve not only as horrors in their own right but also as a safe—extramoral—framework for imagining transgression without admitting the human possibility of such acts. Imputed to the realm of evil, transgression can be embraced as one's own recalled experience, or as a subject for learned contemplation. Or (perhaps most often), one can repudiate those horrible transgressions, burning them away in the body of the one who could have willfully committed such sins.

CANNIBALISM

Cannibalism, especially infant-cannibalism, lies equally at the heart of tableaux of perversion. Heretics eat babies, witches eat babies and penises, Jews drink children's blood, Satanists abort and eat fetuses. Infant-cannibalism might represent the very crux of the tableau of evil. We might be tempted to see the witch's desire for infant flesh as simply a creative rationale for the catastrophic (if common) loss of pregnancies and children to capricious misfortune.[50] However, it is worth noticing the attention to the cuisine of infant-cannibalism, which can be as elaborate as in "Hansel and Gretel." Second-century Christians are believed to encase an infant in dough and invite a novice member to pound the mixture until the blood flows out, at which point they collapse in a blood-orgy and tear the body apart.[51] Gnostics, to the fourth-century Epiphanius's lurid mind, engage in even more disgusting cookery:

> [E]xtracting the fetus at whatever time they choose to do the operation, they take the aborted infant and pound it up in a mortar with a pestle, and, mixing it with honey and pepper and some other spices and sweet oils so as not to become nauseous, all the members of that herd of swine and dogs gather together and each partakes with his finger of the crushed up child.[52]

So at essence it is not that "they" eat any particular children (ours, hers, mine) but rather that they *eat children*.

This image of infant-cannibalism was developed in particular detail in late medieval witch-finding manuals. As in depictions of South American savages, attention was often directed to the grill or the spit (as in figure 8), familiar cultural accoutrements and symbols of good feasting, on which the replacement of a pig with a child focused attention and horror on the inversion. In other cases the actual cuisine receded from status as central horror, as in the late Roman examples above, to a stock component of the Sabbat meal, while real attention might be directed instead to the witches' use of baby-parts—fat, limbs,

FIGURE 8   Witches cooking children. Woodcut from Francesco Guazzo,
Compendium Maleficarum (1608). From reprint by Dover Publications, New York, 1988. The horror of infant-cannibalism is juxta-
posed to the fine clothes of the witches, their serene attention to
cooking, and instruments (spit, cauldron) associated with more
prosaic cuisine.

ears—as a source of supernatural power. Indeed, baby-parts became a
kind of Satanic sacrament, a symbolic combination of the horrors of
monstrous cannibalism and the horrors of an alternative, diabolical
realm of practical power.[53] In these particular tableaux, malign sorcery
and parody of Catholic sacraments became the real context for
witches' preying on infants, not hunger for children's flesh. But infant-
cannibalism seems always to have remained the latent element in
these elaborations, as we see in the famous 1613 engraving of the Sabbat accompanying De Lancre's *Tableau de l'inconstance*: there on the
table, among the finely dressed guests, sits a platter of baby-parts (see
figure 5, locus D, p. 193).[54]

The craving for children's blood imputed to Jews in medieval and early modern times also clearly had much to do with beliefs in the physical power of Catholic sacraments, the reality of their transubstantiation to blood and flesh, and the magic of blood.[55] All three ideas were continually worked out in medieval legends of Eucharist abuse, in which Jews would steal or buy illegally a sacramental wafer, ritually stab it, then discover that it would bleed, cry out, or even transform into a small child.[56] But cannibalism—in this case, the sublimated cannibal impulses surrounding the Eucharist—again did not lie far behind this distorted projection of liturgical magic. The blood of the abducted child, like the blood of the Eucharist that the child represented, had to be incorporated orally. As the child's murder took on the appearance of mock crucifixion in early modern times, meant to take place around Easter, so the blood had to connect to Jews' ambiguous meal-rites at the same time of year, such that it was supposed to be drunk or spread on matzah or baked with it.[57] (See figure 9.) The fact that these cannibalistic elements continue to emerge in ritual-murder rumors from the fourteenth through twentieth centuries suggests that these elements were always latent, even when learned experts turned the rumors into opportunities to press the power of the sacraments. Indeed, one can find ritual cannibalism imputed to Jews already in pre-Christian antiquity, as an indication of their cultural Otherness.[58]

Yet cannibalism as something imputed to the Other—we make a clear distinction from the unusual and highly circumscribed traditions of ritual anthropophagy documented in a few cultures—is never simply a means of articulating moral and natural difference. There is the form of the Other's predatory hunger: Jews, witches, demons, monsters, and savages will eat *our* children if given the opportunity, but not their own. Early Christians, heretics, and contemporary Satanists eat their own children. Cannibalism can thus signify a form of Otherness—they eat *their* own—or a predatory impulse *from* a state of Otherness: they eat *our* own. It would seem that the specter of cannibalism per se stands prior to the fear of cannibalism as something the Other brings against us.[59] A realm in which such impulses are tolerated, normative, and natural is at the same time so utterly inverse and, historically, so universally fascinating that it must reflect some element of ourselves that

vier adder funff tag nach Oftern im Zehende iar/ein erſten kynnd/van vier oder funf iarenn alt gekaufft/vnnd zu Ofterburg in Meyer indens hauß in der Sinagog im die adern gelaſſen/mit nadeln geſtochen vnd aber damit gehandelt wie oben.ſein halß abgeſtochen vnd alſo iemerlich vom leben zum tode gebracht.

⁊ wie ſye das kynd mit nadeln ſtechen vnd darnach im den halß abſtechen

Zum letzten So haben die vntrewen iudē als Mofch von Pritzwalck/ Sloman/Jacob vnnd Gos von Brandem burg vnd ſmol von Plawenn eis criſtē kyndt vonn funf oder ſechs iaren.vff reminiſcere der mindern zal im Newnden iar zu ſichgbracht vnd daſſelb zu Brandemburg die adern vnnd furder den halß abgeſtochen.

FIGURE 9   Image of Jewish ritual murder in Brandenburg, Germany. Page from printed tract *Sumarius* (1511), 14. 18×10 cm. Berlin, courtesy of Verein für die Geschichte Berlins. Photograph: Jens Ziehe, Berlin.

we project into these tableaux of perversion—a transgressive fantasy of uncontrolled voraciousness.

The profusion of cannibal witches and monsters in children's tales would suggest an association between the cannibal fantasy and the primary-process world of sensations introduced above: infantile rage and rapture expressed in terms of oral incorporation and self-consummation. It evokes a stage of raw, overwhelming sensation, undirected and ambivalent, terrifying in its intensity, as one imagines eating and being eaten almost simultaneously, preserving individuality yet seeking annihilation in some greater force.[60] If such fantasies are generated in infancy, however, they never lose their resonance in life. As children's literature and modern horror movies demonstrate, this kind of fantasy tends to be revisited imaginatively throughout childhood and adolescence: Max, the hero of Maurice Sendak's widely published children's book *Where the Wild Things Are* (1963), who first threatens to eat his mother and subsequently joins a society of friendly monsters, who in turn threaten to devour him out of love; and Dracula movies, where monstrous feasting on victims provides a point of adolescent identification because of its now erotic overtones.[61] The universality of cannibal monsters in folk demonologies and geographies ("cannibals live *there*"), art, initiation and festival rites suggests that the image never loses its presence for individuals and societies alike, as both an object of fear—its chaotic rage and predation—and of identification: devouring those who are loved or who transgress. (In psychoanalytic terms, the cannibal monster is both *id*, sexualized power and rage, and *superego*, the terrifying force of discipline.) So also the corresponding image of infants dismembered and devoured by such a monstrous force maintains its allure, not only as the epitome of horror but also through people's latent identification with the rageful monster. Depictions of Jewish ritual murder and of the gory infant-dismemberments of Satanic cults are preoccupied with the defenselessness and, often, eroticized innocence of the child-victim. Antiabortion literature and posters in late-twentieth-century America likewise showed an obsession with the dismemberment of fetuses. Such preoccupation points certainly to audiences' sympathetic identification with defenselessness; but it also—perhaps more—reflects their *transgressive* identification with the people or force that would kill, dismember, and eat the totally defenseless—a "worst possible thing imaginable," here contemplated in detail. Such demolishing rage against infants signifies at the same time a taboo of mythic proportions and something familiar. To transgress that taboo imaginatively assumes a disturbing eroticism.[62]

Approached from this psychoanalytic direction, cannibal monstrosity becomes not some archetype of the unconscious but a particularly potent way of articulating Otherness. Rather than simply one term in the total vocabulary of the monstrous, cannibalism intrinsically calls forth the projection of latent impulses and fantasies—among both societies and individuals—about devouring, dismemberment, and rage. And if ancient and early modern European cultures would disavow cannibalism as a disorderly impulse projected onto the Other, among some native North American peoples this projective aspect is quite explicit: cannibal monsters are said to reflect real fears of human-on-human predation (Algonkian) or familar aspects of the mythic cosmos that, however disorderly, must be integrated with society by ritual means.[63] The monstrous cannibalism occasionally imputed to a particular Other is thus acknowledged as familiar. More recently, in some parts of contemporary Africa, imputations of ritual cannibalism to prominent politicians, successful persons, and shadowy cults also carry an intimate resonance. Here the specter of monstrous cannibalism invokes perennial anxieties about the body as itself a commodity to be bought, sold, and consumed.[64]

Cross-culturally the treatment of cannibals—those people believed to embody cannibal monstrosity—often takes the form of annihilation and erasure, purifying land and society from these dark fantasies and the bodies that represent them. Depictions of New World cannibal savages motivated conquest and missionary crusades. Indeed, conquest and mission depended on tableaux of cannibalism, perversion, and Satanism to comprehend indigenous peoples as enemy subjects.[65] The host-stabbing, child-crucifying, blood-drinking Jew, it has often been observed, stands for Christendom's own need to render sacraments from an abused body—Christ's—and consume that body and its blood. Jews would be tried and executed or simply massacred for committing the very atrocities that, by rumor, brought salvation and holiness to German towns.[66] Overall, societies mobilize against the very imagined

subcultures—witches, Jews, Satanists, savages—that allow them a legitimate public context for contemplating cannibalism, dismemberment,
and infanticide in primary-process fantasy. The imputation of such
acts serves ostensibly to reveal impurity and predatory threat, but
there is also a transgressive thrill in envisioning those acts. The thrill
is protected by the claim, "this is what *they* do," and by the certainty,
"this is certainly not what *we* do." And in the end, the horror, as
thrilling as it is, must translate into action against the cannibal monsters, to save the babies and eliminate perversion from God's midst.

SPECTACLES OF INVERSION

Sexual perversity and cannibal monstrosity serve both as
symbols of a broader inversion and as deeply resonant worlds of fantasy
and terror in their own right. Because of their centrality in tableaux of
evil and their more explicit roots in fantasy, I have chosen to explore
these images of inverse behavior separately before considering inversion more broadly as a means for constructing monstrosity and for
transgressive fantasy. For many African peoples, for example, incest,
homosexuality, improper coital positions, cannibalism, and corpse-
eating make up key horrors in an overall tableau of night-witches and
their inversions, which includes things they drink, how they sleep,
what they wear or do not wear, their bestial shape-shifting, their nocturnal habits, and the places they gather. By assimilating misfortune,
and occasionally local malcontents, to this realm, communities designate this range of acts as intrinsically monstrous—beyond the moral
framework of the village or even that imputed to outsiders. (Outsiders
might be criminal and disloyal, but they are still comprehensibly human.) In contrast to our conniving neighbors and criminal outsiders,
beings of this sort prey and afflict out of their monstrous nature, by
which they even enjoy and celebrate the harm they do. In this way
they are not "bad" in a relative, comprehensibly human way, but
"evil," beyond understanding and undeserving of judicial mercy.[67]
Yet this imaginative assemblage of a realm of total inversion serves
more than simply to set off the horrific from the comprehensible. The
capacity to imagine inversions lies at the very roots of social thought,
marking off cultural territory on every plane, from "neighbor versus

foreigner" and "human versus animal" to "now (a time of morality, perhaps) versus then (a time of giants, incest, and cannibalism), and ultimately a realm of pure evil versus the realm of civilization and morality.[68] The universality of tableaux of inversion, often focused on the witch or demon, does not make it banal. They are powerful, exciting assemblages that invite our consuming attention as well as our embarrassment and disgust. To invoke Bataille again, imaginative inversion offers the experience of transgression from the vantage of taboo, the projection of desires within a frame of censure.

How, then, do spectacles of inversion provide a medium for transgressive enjoyment? Images of the witch's Sabbat in seventeenth-century illustrations—themselves based ultimately on coerced local testimony of Sabbat frolics—would certainly demonstrate that, as much as the Sabbat was an inverse world of cannibalism and infant-limbs, it was also a splendid affair. Rich lords and ladies in fine dress and masks, finely laid tables, clusters of musicians, even debauchery—there at the palace of Satan was a party such as none could imagine in proper Christendom, or perhaps more accurately, such as church officers were busy proscribing in village festival and urban revelry. (See figures 4 and 5.) Its imagined "place" of desirability had then to become the place of evil, the witches' Sabbat.[69]

A Satanic realm likewise provides a distancing context for imagining sensuous delights in modern African charismatic Christianity. Both movies and popular pamphlets like Eni's *Delivered from the Powers of Darkness* depict a world of traditional sorcerers, spirits, and witches who actively seduce men with riches, sex, appliances, cars, cash, and business success. Here Eni describes the appealing, if ultimately insidious, accoutrements of the Satanic world:

> I saw psychiatrists and scientists all working very seriously. The work of these scientists is to design beautiful things like flashy cars etc., latest weapons and to know the mystery of this world. If it were possible to know the pillar of the world they could have, but thank God, ONLY GOD KNOWS. I moved into the designing room and there I saw many samples of cloth, perfumes and assorted types of cosmetics. All these things according to Lucifer are to distract men's attention from Almighty God. I also saw different designs of electronics, computers and alarms. THERE WAS

ALSO A T.V. FROM WHERE THEY KNEW THOSE WHO ARE BORN AGAIN CHRISTIANS IN THE WORLD. THERE YOU WILL SEE AND DIFFERENTIATE THOSE WHO ARE CHURCH GOERS AND THOSE WHO ARE REAL CHRISTIANS.

I then moved from the laboratories to the "dark room" and "drying room." The dark room is where they kill any disobedient member. They kill by first draining the person's blood and then send the person to the machine room, where he/she will grind to powder and then send the dust to the "sack room" where they will be bagged and kept for native doctors to collect for their charms.[70]

As the last paragraph makes clear, the Satanic world demands malfeasance and participation in disgusting rituals involving body-parts, while the heroes of such stories are always rescued into Christian salvation. Their joy and awe in contemplating Satanic riches are transient. Yet, as the anthropologist Birgit Meyer has observed, these lengthy depictions of transgressive enrichment and pleasure offer a safe arena for fantasy, for it takes place in a proscribed, "evil" world. The projection of Satanic delights

> offers a free space in which to explore new possibilities, to . . . play out (openly or in disguise) hidden fears and desires, and to play with contradictions without the necessity of turning them into a coherent, ordered system. Collective fantasies usually expose ideas in the framework of an "imaginary world" and often employ the "realm of darkness" in order to express and clarify existential questions.[71]

This whole complex of fantasy and proscription moved from media to direct performance in the late 1990s, as young women began to stand up in some Nigerian Pentecostal churches to "confess" their participation in Satan's gloriously modern realm before being "born again." These women gave presence to that new feature in Satan's realm, the sexually voracious Jezebel who could seduce men from family and Christ with promises of both riches and sex. For the Pentecostal congregations the transgressive fantasy of the alleged witches' allure—in their nubility, tight clothing, and make-up—took on a vivid reality through these confession performances. Satanic riches were voiced and embodied by young church-members, yet distanced and denied through the girls' culminating testimony to Christ. In addition, the women's highly eroticized depiction of their witch-powers—"My private part usually disturbs me whenever I see a man because of the power I have in there," one self-defined ex-witch announces before an enormous congregation—allows the women themselves to identify with the fantasy and its images of a dark, powerful, and modern female sexuality.[72]

These women's embodiment of transgressive behavior recalls another prominent way in which the contemplation of inversion has allowed the direct experience of transgression: the tendency of the demon-possessed to express themselves with often highly sexualized or impudent behavior. Demonic possession has a public, demonstrative function, as I will explore further in chapter 6, for it makes evil forces take on a real, embodied form in a social setting. Demonic possession performances also reflect the details of local cosmology—that is, the nature imputed to demons, the meaning of their invasion, and the ritual process involved in cleansing them. Anthropologists have also addressed the tendency of possession cults—wherein demons are either mastered or expelled—to thrive among women and the disenfranchised, a social fact that partly explains the "rebellious" aspects of possession performance.[73] But my concern here, in the context of tableaux of evil, lies with the possessed person's own engagement in the performance of inversion. Are the insults, blasphemies, and lascivious expressions merely a socially inscribed ecstatic "discourse," or is there an actual erotic involvement in this mode of complete and public transgression?

Whether in contemporary Western "deliverance" ceremonies or in the innovative Christian exorcistic cults that have arisen in places like Sri Lanka, a central component of "being" the demon is committing verbal and gestural sacrilege with some gusto: lewdly insulting priests and images of the Virgin Mary or imitating sexual acts like masturbation.[74] Given that these acts are often those explicitly proscribed within the institution sponsoring demonic deliverance, their performance as demonic transgressions both conveys the demon's particular perversity and releases carnal impulses from especially tight constraints. The context of demon-possession (and of a church that defines multiple taboos on sexual impulses) provides an outlet for utter inversion, for performing the most proscribed activity—and for doing publicly, in a sanctuary, acts associated with the private realm. Indeed, we might consider more generally how the process of experiencing demonic possession and then gaining deliverance is inevitably preceded by the subject's acceptance of the multiple taboos that the leadership defines upon its members, from gendered etiquette to the scope of blasphemy and the rules of sexuality. Young women participants in a Catholic or Protestant exorcistic cult are expected to be virginal, demure, and submissive, whatever their individual social worlds or personalities. Thus the very potential for transgression, and all the erotic feelings incumbent in inverting new taboos, appears at the very entrance stage to the exorcistic process.

But in one of the most studied incidents of eroticized demonic possession, that of the nuns of Loudun (1634), it was not entrance to a new system with new taboos that triggered transgressive behavior but rather the presence of a sexually charismatic priest—the accused sorcerer, Urbain Grandier—working among cloistered Ursuline nuns. Grandier's charged presence among the nuns was followed by a team of demonological experts, who added to the nuns' studied awareness of demonic impulses an extravagant system of demonic identities and proclivities.[75] The nuns came to believe that an evil realm had insinuated itself into the convent and into their bodies, and this tangible evil realm became a context for engaging in perverse behavior. "The devil would often beguile me," confessed Jeanne des Anges, the Superior,

> by an enjoyable little feeling I had from the agitations and other extraordinary things he brought about in my body. I took an extreme pleasure in hearing it spoken of, and was pleased to appear more wrought up than the others, which gave great strength to these accursed spirits, for they take great pleasure in being able to amuse us with the sight of their operations, and in this way they gradually creep into souls and gain great advantage over them.[76]

This same nun was acutely aware of the gossamer boundary between experiencing her own annoyances and fantasizing their expression as demonic blasphemy. Feeling irritated, for example, that the new convent priest was offering communion through the grille rather than directly, *it entered my mind* that, to humilate that father, the demon *would have* committed some irreverence toward the Very Holy Sacrament. I was so miserable that I did not resist that thought strongly enough. When I went to take communion, the devil seized my head, and after I had received the holy host and had half moistened it, the devil threw it into the priest's face. I know perfectly well that I did not perform that act freely, but I am very sure, to my great embarrassment, that I gave the devil occasion to do it, and that he would not have had this power had I not allied myself with him.[77]

The tangible presence of the demonic becomes not just terrifying but inspiring: a context for imagining, then embodying, a rush of feelings that would otherwise be simply suppressed. Even latent impulses to transgress or rebel emerge through the adoption of demonic identities: insulting priests and bishops, cursing sacraments and God—all the "worst things imaginable" become imagined, performed, and, at some level, enjoyed.[78]

Thus representations of inversion, from the speculative—like everyday discussions of night-witches and demons—to the iconographic, the judiciary, and these last, performative versions, provide opportunities to fantasize transgressive delights (or "worst possible behavior") in a form that is safely relegated to a realm of evil: "It is not me who has these thoughts; it is the demons who put in my mind what they do habitually" or "it is the witches or Satanists who I saw really *doing* such things." There is a thrill in contemplating these bricolages of inversion, whether in the physical nature of monsters or the exhaustive tableaux of witches' Sabbats and Satanic ceremonies. The features of perversity point at the same time to evil and to us—our own culture—whose deepest mores provide the material of inversion.

Conclusions

The various tableaux of monstrosity, inversion, and perversion that are typically imputed to the Other, the realm of evil, function then as projected fantasies of transgression, involving the most basic, primary-process images. These tableaux allow identification both with victims—especially children—and with the monsters and their deliberate acts of cruelty, cannibalism, and perversion. Although we may be most familiar with monsters from literature and cinema, incidents like the SRA panic of the 1980s and 1990s remind us that the fears that inspire tableaux of perversion and allow us this process of identification can reappear in quite real form. Indeed, from ancient notions of Christians to modern notions of savages, few of our examples have been merely stories. In their tangibility to audiences, inspiring panicked hunts for the perverse monsters among us, these tableaux demand some response, especially given our transgressive identification with victim and monster. The demon must be expelled in violent contortions; the witch or Jew must be carefully tortured and burned; the savage cannibal must be punished. We are driven to attack those we impute with monstrosity, and sometimes do so by means of the very atrocities we imagine them doing.

In a striking account of mutual savagery between colonists and Indians in the Putumayo region of Peru in the early 1900s, the anthropologist Michael Taussig describes the capacity that thinking about cannibalism has to provoke anxious revenge and even a measure of identification. In Peru, as in Africa, the image of cannibalism had taken on multiple terrors both for indigenous people and colonists. The Other's cannibalism, Taussig explains, encapsulated all the ways that colonial enterprises "devoured" Indian people and their souls, on the one hand, and all the ways that Indian culture and the jungle itself devoured colonial people, on the other.[79] But it was the colonists themselves who, from their own combination of power, terror, and voracious rage, struck against the cannibal Indian with—Taussig suggests—an almost "erotic passion":

> The interest the whites display is obsessive; again and again [the early-twentieth-century Columbian traveler Joaquin] Rocha scents cannibalism in the murk around him. He is frightened in the forest, not of animals but of Indians, and it is always with what becomes in effect the insufferably comic image of the person-eating Indian that he chooses to represent that fear of being consumed by a wild, unknown, half-sensed uncertainty. Among the whites, to stamp out cannibalism is an article of faith like a crusade, he says. Cannibalism is an addictive drug; whenever the Huitotos think they can

deceive the whites, "they succumb to their beastly appetites." The whites have therefore to be more like beasts, as in the story retold by Rocha concerning Crisóstomo Hernández killing all the Indians of a communal house down to the children at the breast for succumbing to that addiction.[80]

Such colonial savagery, Taussig continues, occurred repeatedly in the Putumayo. The whites' atrocities reveal not only an anxious tendency to strike the savage preemptively but also a kind of imitation of his savagery. Colonists' own impulses and the impulses they projected onto the Indians fed on each other, exploding in massacres like the following, conducted by a Peruvian rubber plantation's private militia:

> At the next house they reached they caught four Indians, one woman and three men. Vasquez, who was in charge, ordered one of the *muchachos* to cut this woman's head off. He ordered this for no apparent reason that [the consul's informant] James Chase knows of, simply because "he was in command, and could do what he liked." The *muchacho* cut the woman's head off; he held her by the hair of her head, and flinging her down, hacked her head off with a machete. It took more than one blow to sever the head—three or four blows. Her remains were left on the path, as were the severed heads and truncated bodies of other people caught in this raid; [the chief] Katenere's child, decapitated for crying, and a woman, an adolescent boy, and three adult men—all for walking too slowly. The company men were walking very fast because they were a bit frightened thinking of the Indians pursuing them.[81]

Thus, Taussig concludes, "The terror and the tortures [the colonists] devised mirrored the horror of the savagery they both feared and fictionalized."[82]

In this world of legend, panic, and military response, the threatening monstrosity of the cannibal savage serves as a rationale for engaging in savage massacres, but also as a projection of colonists' own impulses to devour and control. We have seen more widely, too, that depictions of child-eating monsters, perverse ceremonies, and the inversion of all things amount to an Other constructed from inside us. Rage, erotic conquest and self-loss, urges to annihilate and be annihilated, and the fearsome delights of transgression itself—all these conflicting sentiments, impulses, and fantasies are worked out in disavowed, monstrous form. Our mores are preserved while gazing at the spectacle of their suspension in a tableau of evil.

My shift to psychological considerations in this chapter is justified on three grounds: the consistency of the images that appear through history under the category "evil" or "monstrous" or "savage," the voyeuristic obsession with details through which people sharpen their terror of monstrous things, and the sheer pornographic inventiveness that arises when people are given free imaginative (or performative) rein to contemplate tableaux of perversion. To be sure, recognizing the psychological basis of the fantasy and its projective dynamics in no way mitigates the plain terror with which people respond to witches and demons, the Satanic, the conspiratorial, or the savage. If anything, psychoanalysts would point out that these psychological elements reinforce the terror, for it is a recognizable terror, of primal threats to self and self-control.

But there is another dimension to these psychological dynamics of transgression, projection, and voyeurism. To paraphrase Lévi-Strauss again, these monstrous constructions of the Other are "good to think with." As cannibalism, perverse sexuality, and wholesale inversion are assembled into monstrous tableaux, depicting another's thorough evil while projecting fantasies of transgression, cultures (and their leaders) are able to work out ideas and concepts important for social cohesion—especially during times of contested morality. For example, what makes a savage a savage? Projecting bestial sexuality and cannibalism onto the Scythian, the Amazonian, the African, or the Haitian combines the process of constructing Otherness with the thrill of contemplating transgression. What is the sexual nature of the family—father, mother, siblings, neighbors? The dark scenarios of SRA articulate—for patients, victims' groups, and therapists—the deepest anxieties and transgressive fantasies of paternal and maternal sexual aggression, mixed "ritualistically" with siblings (posed as victims, child-witnesses, and even perpetrators) and neighbors.[83] What is "my" sexuality—a separate and shameful part of myself or fully incorporated? Is it aggressive or passive? SRA fantasies, like those elicited from accused witches in early modern Europe, likewise express individual eroticism in terms of masked aggressor, frightened witness, devoured victims.[84]

Many such tableaux, we have seen, also work out the nature of sacred things—and purity itself—within a realm of perversion. The Gnostics' use of semen and menstrual blood, witches' use of infant parts, the Jews' disorderly stabbing of Eucharists and children—all these refer, in their repellent, violent imagery, back to a pure ritual system. That ritual system provides the conceptual basis for the transgressive parodies. Moreover, the very efficacy of that ritual system (e.g., the power of the Eucharist) is *verified* by the inverse potency of its opposite. At the same time, that pure ritual system guarded by the church carries with it the inevitable potential for transgression and inversion (as real-life carnivals were prone to show, as well). Indeed, the legendary atrocities of Jews against wafers and children became essential elements in the popular construction of sacraments' efficacy, especially in Germany: the atrocities produced pilgrimage shrines, commemorative celebrations, and new local martyrs. Tableaux of perversity and monstrosity provide an essential component in the narrative of triumphal holiness.

Finally, these tableaux, so full of gruesome displays of abuse, dismemberment, "infant cuisine," and bestial devouring, provide ways of thinking about *children*—and not simply as the real-life victims of miscarriages, diseases, and accidents. In folklore the child is ever the counterpoint to the witch and that figure through whom we experience the witch's (or Jew's, or savage's) monstrosity and terror. The child's purity and innocence provide the first point of audience identification in the construction of all these tableaux of perversity.[85]

> . . . twice a day [the hymn to Mary] filled his little throat,
> Going to school and coming back again,
> Praising Christ's mother with all his might and main.
> As I have said, this child would go along
> The Jewish street and, of his own accord,
> Daily and merrily he sang his song
> O *Alma Redemptoris*; as it soared,
> The sweetness of the mother of our Lord
> Would pierce his heart, he could not choose but pray
> And sing as, to and fro, he went his way.[86]

Thus Chaucer leads into the gory slaughter of the little boy at the hands of Jews, followed by the mother's anguish. We are always invited to contemplate the almost paradoxical innocence and purity of the child in advance of some graphic depiction of his murder. Indeed, it is this same engagement with the child's innocence, then slaughter—as counterpart scenes—that inspired a twentieth-century anti-Semitic author to fasten onto the story of the fifteenth-century Simon of Trent and his alleged ritual murder and consequently reinvest it with historical credibility: "The brutal child murder of little Simon kept coming back to mind," confesses Philip de Vier.

> Then a stark reality dawned. . . . Most of these were children, entirely helpless to defend themselves against a gang of savage child-abusing killers. The realities of the blood, guts and gore, not to mention the appalling fear and terror felt by the victims, began to hit home. Little Simon became a focal point for this as we wrote the book. . . . These are not just ancient tales. They are real stories of real victims, their families and communities touched suddenly and violently by the dark talons of terror and evil.[87]

De Vier means, of course, Jews. Children's innocence becomes the context for merging an atrocity tale, one's prurient engagement with it, and a passion to unveil conspiracy, even (at other times) to persecute and obliterate the alleged defilers of that innocence.

Even when they do not suffer, children function as essential witnesses to such tableaux, their youth and purity giving them a kind of unassailable translucence into scenarios so graphic that an audience fears contemplating them directly.[88] "Numberless witches," the early seventeenth-century witch-finder Henri Boguet declared, "have been discovered and brought to their just punishment by means of a child," the eight-year-old Loyse Maillat.[89] In some medieval tales of Jewish Eucharist abuse, it is a Jewish boy who observes the crime and then converts, a symbolic doublet, the historian Miri Rubin has noted, of the Christ-child appearing and bleeding in the stabbed Eucharist:

> People were moved by the vision of the child in the host and by the complementary image of a child observing it, both chastising presences which evoked suppressed questions and doubt. Around these children—the Jewish boy, the child on the altar—strong fears of abuse and loss could be crystallised. . . . Christ and child, Christ as child, introduced victimhood and with it, of necessity, crime and danger.[90]

Such symbolic complementarity between child-observer and child-victim recurred in SRA narratives in the 1980s and 1990s, with the innocent child-observer often reenacted for therapist or audience by an adult with her ostensibly retrieved memories. Like the host-abuse narratives, the SRA narratives would align the traumatized innocence of the one child with the slaughtered innocence of another, as the adult-as-child described watching her infant siblings be sacrificed and eaten. In the panics over day care center abuse in the late 1980s, however, an actual child had to play both parts. Maverick child-advocates interviewed young children so coercively for details of perverse ritual scenarios that many children ultimately provided what was demanded, mixed liberally with elements of primary-process and wishful fantasy. For the child-advocates, the perversions they believed to exist only took on reality through these children's testimony. At the same time, the advocates' prurient obsession with extracting more and more perverse material suggested to many observers a personal investment in witnessing, experiencing—through the innocence of the children—a world of utter transgression, and many such advocates became utterly engulfed in these stories.[91] Through these children and the stories they had imposed on them, the advocates felt themselves right on the other side of evil.

But if in the initial phase of contemplating these tableaux of evil the child-victims provide a point of identification, of sympathy and vicarious participation, at a later stage (as we saw with cannibalism) the audience comes also to identify with the monster, the perpetrator, the devourer of the child. Chaucer's little boy is not only carefree and innocent; he is also the paragon of a popular orthodoxy, devoting his free time to memorizing a hymn to Mary. He signifies an exaggerated morality whose transgression lies just at the point of imaginability. The child-victims of Jewish ritual-murder legends *must* be stabbed, bled, implicitly crucified in order to become efficacious martyrs; and the audience must do it in narrative, even if the dark subject, the perpetrator, is split off as a cabal of bloodthirsty Jews. In folklore there is a continual alternation between the child-victim and the monster—predator, cannibal, rapist, witch—that can only indicate (as psychoanalytic critics have observed) a process of working out destructive impulses and identity through the narrative. That same process of simultaneous identification continues through what we might call the performative extensions of that narrative: for example, a martyr-cult or a witch-trial, in which audiences continue to identify with both perpetrator and victim.[92] Indeed, it is only *because of* such transgressive identification with the monster (and our denial of that identification) that the monster actually takes on such terrifying proportions.

Obviously the psychoanalytic interpretation would not imply that SRA advocates and witch-finders had any awareness of this latent human process. It is not rage toward children but contemplation of the perverse and evil that brings such ambivalent sentiments of horror and voyeuristic excitement. The experts in evil show they have the capacity to *imagine* infanticide and other atrocities, but they deny their own imaginative complicity, attributing the atrocities only to *real* cults *really* doing such things. Yet there have been many times in history when children's status as innocents has reversed, revealing instead cultural suspicions of the child as himself capable of witchcraft and Satanic pacts (which may have been latent all along). Nicholas Rémy's highly reasoned 1595 witch-finding manual discusses at length the reasons why seven-year-olds should be executed for associating with the Devil.[93] In the example described earlier, the German city of Augsburg saw mass incarcerations of children as witches, accused by the parents themselves, who focused on their apparent sexual games and talk as evidence of diabolical witchcraft. Here children's sexuality and aggression were not polarized to childhood but rather sensed anxiously as a component of childhood. If in earlier scenarios of children's victimization at the hands of witches, Jews, and monsters, the community's identification with the child reinforced its rage against the split-off, monstrous aggressor, here in Augsburg the citizens recognized the children's ambiguity. As Lyndal Roper concludes,

> The children's world of fantasy with its unmediated aggression was disturbing to parents because it forced them to encounter childish emotions—hatred of a new partner, fascination with sexuality—in situations where parents were implicated. . . . [The parents] seem to have become sucked into their children's imaginative worlds, responding by becoming ill from

the dirty objects in their beds, beating their children to excess, viewing the children's activities as diabolic and in one case starving them to death to drive out the Devil. . . . [R]ecognition of the separate nature of childhood, we might say, opened up a space for *negative* projective self-recognition.[94]

No doubt there were elements of such negative projection in earlier times and other places, where it was the children who were victims and yet their imagined abuse served as fodder for graphic fantasies. But here, too, in Augsburg, a tableau of evil and perversity allowed the articulation, albeit in a disowned, negative, and distorted form, of real ambiguity and conflict over the nature of children. Children do not simply represent a cultural boundary—the vulnerable purity of the innocent next generation—but, even more, they provide opportunities for adults to experience feelings that transgress those boundaries.

In the largest sense, this chapter has argued for the appropriateness of acknowledging that fantasy and imaginative transgression play a role in the construction and reception of images of organized evil. This argument has been paved, of course, by those historians of European witch-finding movements who have opened themselves to psychoanalytic theory as a way into the perverse sexual and cannibalistic imagery of the Sabbat; by those modern psychologists who recognized the role of fantasy—for both therapists and patients—in recovering "memories" of Satanic cult perversions; and also by those interpreters of the universal figure of the night-witch, a monstrous version of sexual horror and allure, voracity and disgust.[95] Figures of the night-witch, the monster, the savage, and the Satanist fundamentally represent projections of wishes and fears shared widely among members of society and articulated in distorted form as monsters "out there," preying on us. This imaginative reservoir of devoured babies, incestuous orgies, gruesome hags, and disgusting meals wells up from primary-process imagery of eating and being eaten, passive desire, rage and terror of rage, which psychoanalysts associate with the earliest childhood emotional experiences. We draw on this imaginative reservoir to interpret foreigners and the savage, to flesh out demonic beings responsible for misfortune, and to reify the numerous cultural anxieties about children, subversive cults, and conspiracy that collide at certain historical moments (like late 1980s America). At each such historical moment, these fantasies of an evil realm will be defined and rationalized according to some immediate cultural idiom: the salvific power of sacraments and blood, the language of conspiracy and an anti-Church, the accoutrements of modernity and political power, the memories of the sexual-abuse victim. It is thus to be expected that primal human fantasies, rendered in collective terms or even as the systematic revelations of experts in evil, would assume specific forms. Still, our attention to historical innovations and contexts should not blind us to the underlying power and transgressive fascination that these tableaux have exerted on their inventors and audiences over time. In rising up to purge obscene Satanic rites and their devotees from society, people have inevitably caught sight of some element of themselves: the very vision of obscenity and inversion from which cultures want somehow to be rid. Our purification from such fantasies, as it were, comes about more easily through the medium of others' bodies. At the same time, spectacles of perversion in a realm of evil, among monsters and savages, offer cultures a safe context for contemplating transgression, because the moral rightness of the *uninverted* world is preserved as the center of all things.

6 *The Performance of Evil*

THE IMAGES and myths of evil on which I have been dwelling are not the types people keep at a distance. Like the demons that permeate the landscape in chapter 2, evil forces and conspiracies emerge in the world of real men and women. Demonic forces become visible in the people who writhe and bellow in possession, as well as in the exorcist who seems to perceive exactly which creature he is commanding. Witches emerge in the individuals who finally come to confess, describing lurid Sabbats and horrifying conspiracies that they had (it seems) personally witnessed, and it is the witch-conspiracy incarnate that we see dressed in heretic garb and clustered in the ox-cart en route to the pyre. Jews' insidious plans to retorture the Lord on a regular basis, to deprive us of the eucharistic remains of his physical body, even to duplicate these atrocities with a little child, might come to certainty every time we see a group of them together, near a church, or if a child goes missing. Satanists and their atrocities become all too real as we watch the (self-proclaimed) victim remembering the secret rites in which she had been forced to participate—and now shaking, weeping, shouting at unseen leaders as her memories come alive. Or, after absorbing experts' advice like the following, we ourselves begin to see Satanic confederates all around us, gesturing, signalling, even pretending to help us:

It is helpful to know the accessing methods of secretive organizations and/or cults. Following are some known methods. Look for odd hand gestures, such as opening a book, making the shape of a gun with the pointer finger and thumb and "shooting" it, using the cut sign (hand drawn horizontally across the throat), tapping something (a book, the wrist [as in asking for the time], . . . drawing something in the air [like a letter of the alphabet or an unknown sign]). Winks or facial expressions: . . . Though some of these may or may not always signify triggers, it is important to be aware of them.

Authority figures are often perpetrators. . . . Doctors are sometimes associated with cults, to give medication, to keep someone alive while bringing her to the brink of death, to perform "magick" (e.g., fake) surgery. People who work for the FBI, lawyers, police, people high up in government, have been said to be satanic cult members.[1]

Evil becomes something tangible in the faces one sees and the crowds one walks through. Each suspicious person brings to mind the whole panoply of atrocities and dark rites one knows to exist. How can evil conspiracies and Satanic cults become so real? This chapter examines the multiple ways that evil, in this lurid, ritualized, quasi-religious form, gains a kind of reality through social acts and social experience: through *performance*, in fact. People present the reality of evil to each other as something they have witnessed, something that has taken them over, something they see before them, or something the pursuit of which binds them together, mobilizes them to action. If in chapter 3 we saw the development of a myth of evil conspiracy through some expert's dramatic discernment of evil—and his invitation, as it were, to audiences to embrace that myth—and in chapters 4 and 5 we saw the elaboration and internal coherence of that myth, in this chapter we look at the *realization* of that myth by and among people.

Performance and Demonic Realms

In perhaps his most famous essay, the French anthropologist Claude Lévi-Strauss tells three stories of Native American men who appealed to supernatural beliefs in order to extricate themselves from awkward social situations. An Amazonian shaman, a foreigner in his community, who had secretly visited his original band, tells his new community in scintillating detail about his abduction by an eagle spirit. A Kwakiutl man, skeptical of shamanism, apprentices himself to a local shamanic guild in order to learn and expose its illusory arts, and yet there he picks up one technique that makes him famous throughout the region as a preeminent ritual healer. Struck by his own success in healing despite his assumption that he was merely doing tricks, he embraces the role of shaman and its powers. And a Zuni boy accused

of witchcraft and finding no way of convincing people of his innocence, embraces the role of "witch" with such elaborate intensity that
his rapt audience of accusers lets him free. As his audience became
"progressively aware of the vitality offered by his corroboration of their
system (especially since the choice is not between this system and another, but between the magical system and no system at all—that is,
chaos), the youth, who at first was a threat to the physical security of
his group, became the guardian of its spiritual coherence."[2] In each
case, Lévi-Strauss observed, the acknowledgment of a social role and
the affirmation of some group's worldview served both to alleviate anxiety and to put the actor in an indispensable social position: embodying the system of spiritual coherence. Performance—of a traditional
role and, through it, the supernatural worldview—was critical to social
well-being, especially in crisis situations.

Traditional healing rites involve these same dynamics, revitalizing
and articulating communities' spiritual coherence. A shaman, for example, uses a variety of techniques (trance, song, ventriloquism), instruments (drums, rattles), and language styles to bring into patients'
and audiences' immediate experience a world of spirits—a world in
whose active involvement with community affairs the audience is
deeply invested. Through the shaman's dramatic techniques the spirits
rustle, chirp, speak, sing, and fight. He performs the spirits *mimetically*,
and reframes patients' and audiences' relationships with those spirits.
In this way, such ritual experts relieve ailments, heal social ruptures,
and allay anxiety. They provide a means for the supernatural world to
present itself to those who need it.[3]

Anthropologists who study these kinds of roles have developed the
term "performance" to describe the reciprocal impact of ritual expert,
audience, and patient on one another. As the expert fulfills and nuances the role of "man of spirits," the audience begins to participate,
engaging in dialogue, response, and coordinated gestures with the ritual expert and, through him, the spirits. Thus the spirits become a tangible reality for all. "Performance," as I will reiterate in this chapter
several times, is always a reciprocal expression of a culturally recognizable role before some audience; it involves that audience's participation; and through that role a mythical (in the sense of paradigmatic)
realm of spirits is made real. It should not be taken to imply a

self-conscious pretense or deceit or isolation from immediate social influences, even if (as in the cases Lévi-Strauss discussed) some performers may begin with some skepticism toward their roles.

My route into the performance of evil in the form of an organized, Satanic conspiracy will pass first through two different types of performed evil: demonic possession and the confessions of apostate cult members—that is, returnees from realms of the religiously bizarre. These cases give us a sense for how myths of evil realms can truly come alive through people's proper enactment of roles—and more specifically how Lévi-Strauss's observation about the power in demonstrating a worldview's validity in insecure times can apply to the way evil has been socially exhibited.

EXORCISM AND THE PERFORMANCE OF EVIL

No more vivid theater for the manifestation of evil exists than exorcism, a ritual process found cross-culturally (India, Central Asia, North Africa), but most emphatically in modern charismatic Christianity. Participants—the possessed—*enact* the demons that others have discerned in them with such vivid acts as spitting, growling, shouting obscenities, and insulting authorities. The supernatural world that is enacted is not one that participants want to consult or cooperate with (like the spirits channelled by shamans), but rather something to keep at a distance. Yet for all who are involved, the enactment of demons with names, characters, horrible features, and rebellious utterances affirms the *reality* of a realm of afflicting spirits and the *power* of the exorcist and his sacred words to combat them. The participants are encouraged in their beliefs in demons and exorcistic power. Indeed, a basic belief in demons turns into direct witnessing of their activity. "Demons may cry out with loud voices," one popular contemporary deliverance manual asserts, describing how the authors

> were engaged in a deliverance when a seventeen-year-old girl came forward. She remarked that she had been involved in witchcraft. I had her take a seat directly in front of me. I opened my Bible and began to read from Deut. 18:9–15, which declares that witchcraft and similar practices are an abomination to the Lord. As I was reading verse 15 which says that

God will raise up a Prophet (Jesus) and "unto him ye shall hearken," a piercing demonic scream came forth from the girl. I looked up quickly to see her hands like claws coming at my Bible. Before I could react, her long fingernails tore throgh the page of my Bible on the very verse I was reading! We began to command the *demons of witchcraft* and related spirits to go in the name of Jesus, and she was soon set free from their oppression. . . .

On other occasions we have seen *rhythmic* and *dancing spirits* manifest themselves through motions of the body, especially in the swaying of the hips. One young woman whose body vibrated from the manifestation of the rhythmic spirit, disclosed afterward that she had been a professional dancer. . . . This spirit proved to be the ruling spirit within her. The devil has his counterfeit and perversion for all that is good and right.[4]

The demonic world comes alive through these behaviors, such that observers do not see (or are instructed not to see) the person but the demon in the person. At the same time, the person—the actor—is thrust into the role of performer of spirits, a role developed over the course of the ceremony according to the demands of the exorcist. In larger, group-exorcisms (such as those that take place at Kudagama in Sri Lanka, discussed in chapter 3), the exorcist gives free rein to individuals to enact and define demons on their own—to call upon their own internal sense of transgressive behavior, dissociated and personified as demonic beings. The following was observed, for example, at a deliverance ceremony at a major evangelical college for those afflicted by demons of sexual perversity: while the exorcist

continued praying, the sound of wretched sobbing filled the air. Then several people began howling and screaming, and within minutes the crowd was utterly transformed. The auditorium was filled with howling and thrashing, incessant braying, ejaculations of profanity, and primal shouts. . . . A primly dressed brown-haired woman who looked to be in her mid-thirties threw herself to the ground and began pummeling her genital area. A slim, tanned guy in his forties . . . sank to his knees and went into a prolonged fit of screaming and thrashing. . . . Three or four people within my view were simulating masturbation.[5]

Through such a concentration of individual demonic performances, of demons emerging in so many bodies, the presence of the demonic world comes alive, and a visitor open to such a spirit-world may well come to sense some alternative being within her, too, simply by the power of the situation. Demonic deliverance is always a process of acting spontaneously and in response, shaping a demonic personality out of one's own impulses, an exorcist's demands, the responses of others, and some larger sense of what demons do. And by thus affirming—even extending—a supernatural world that may be familiar but not always tangible to a group, the possessed person reinforces that group's overall worldview and confidence: demons are real and we know it.[6]

CULT APOSTATES AND THE REIFICATION

OF CULTURAL ANXIETIES

Lévi-Strauss's examples also suggest that more abstract or unformed beliefs might also be reinforced through a similar kind of role-enactment. The Amazonian shaman affirmed through his story that shamans could be prey to spiritual attack, and the Zuni boy that witches worked in such-and-such a way with such-and-such materials— convictions each vital to the worldviews of their respective cultures. In more complex, secularized, or culturally transitional societies, traditional moral beliefs that are under threat may, for many people, require affirmation and redefinition rather than denial: gender roles and stereotypes, perhaps, or the danger of foreigners. People crave stories of the promiscuous woman punished, the ambiguous stranger shown to be a corrupting menace, and the new secretive community shown to harbor child abuse and debauchery. More than that, people crave individuals to embody those stories publicly. This need for affirmation of inchoate beliefs, especially in such narrative forms, thus opens up roles for performance.

For example, during the 1970s a number of Americans who had left "cults"—the prevailing pejorative classification for deviant religious groups attractive to young adults—described quite publicly their experiences with brainwashing, psychological control, abuse and starvation, and other atrocities, all of which had been stereotypically attributed to such groups during this era of religious experimentation. A study of these "cult apostates" and their harrowing reports found that they had left the religious movements under highly fraught, even violent circumstances (like forced "deprogramming") and that they were, in effect, repaying society for these extreme efforts by affirming society's assumptions about cults' evil ways.[7] In their roles as survivors and witnesses to cult atrocities—as veritable personifications of common social fears about deviance and of myths of rescue—these individuals gained importance, even a kind of public charisma. They had been on both sides, as it were, of a line between religion and cult, truth and falsehood, that many in the culture wanted anxiously to exist.

A person who embraces the role of ex-member, even ex-leader, of a deviant cult provides essential proof that such cults exist as the culture imagines them and that they do the things that culture imputes to them. And this brings us to a series of cases directly pertinent to the subject of the enactment of evil: that is, the various people who, in the late twentieth century, claimed prior office in *Satanic* cults. They, too, demonstrated the atrocities that audiences believed to exist out there, although in this case *without* there being organized religious groups in these apostates' backgrounds. The Satanist cults with which they claimed past affiliation bore little sociological resemblance to the various groups embracing Satanic identities during the 1970s and 1980s.[8] Indeed, in many cases ex-Satanists' claims to have presided over human sacrifices or to have undergone sacrificial abortions have been specifically disproven. And yet what might be unsupported in critical investigation is fully believable as a dramatic background to the ex-Satanist's account of her Christian salvation. She offers her story of horrendous cult atrocities—child sacrifices, orgies, corruption—that she has repudiated, of her involvement in absolute evil, to (Christian) society as admission to full membership and salvation.[9]

At the time when these ex-Satanists began to emerge in the media in the 1980s, the notion that Satanic cults pervaded culture was most at home among evangelical Christian groups, which celebrated conversions that involved particularly dramatic transitions from sin. Indeed, it is likely that the whole role of "ex-Satanist" took shape within this environment. For American culture at large, the idea that Satanic cults lurked on the extremes of deviant religion only exemplified the range of deviant cults that a diverse society had to suffer. But the evangelical Christian model of the Satanic cult served both as imaginative distillation of broad cultural threats and as a foil to evangelical Christian ideals, offering a lurid tableau of drugs, animal sacrifices, nudity, orgies, and occasionally murder, from which only Christ could deliver the participant.[10]

By the late 1980s, as this evangelical model began to dominate American culture, the specter of Satanic cults came to crystallize new anxieties of the broader culture, such as child-safety, incest recollections, female sexuality, and conspiracy. At this point the individuals who assumed the role of ex-Satanist served to enact much more general and pressing uncertainties within the myth of the Satanic cult. In print and on widely viewed television specials ex-Satanists now described everything from childhood rape and abortion to brainwashing and infant-cannibalism, and in this way they gave gripping "presence" to the culture's inchoate fears and to one theory, Satanic conspiracy, capable of organizing those fears. That most ex-Satanists inevitably promoted evangelical rebirth at the end of their public testimonies did little to marginalize their depiction of the Satanic cults living and working among us.[11]

CLASSIFYING PERFORMANCES OF EVIL

From hostile spirits and exorcisms to ex-cult-members and Satanic high priests, evil has been the subject of performance much like other religious and ritual roles—healing, salvation, and prophecy. In performances of evil the horrible realm that is enacted may be supernatural or, with cults, conspiratorial, and in both cases dangerous, predatory. Whether of demons, Satanists, or witches, the realm involves characters—chiefs and underlings, victims and opponents; there are narratives that explain predation, conspiracy, and motivation. And through the performance of some aspect of that realm, it emerges as a tangible presence for some audience. As they emerge in performance, these myths of evil realms (as we may productively label them, for their paradigmatic value rather than falsity) have a reassuring, even energizing and healing effect on a group, much as Lévi-Strauss observed in the case studies described in the beginning of this chapter. As ritual performances, these enactments of evil offer dramas in which crises are articulated and then resolved in some kind of social setting—an exorcism or witchcraft prosecution as much as a healing ceremony. Indeed, we must recognize the healing or integrative possibilities in frightening and controversial performances just as we do with the ancestral and familiar. Myths of danger and evil conspiracy have the capacity to capture and articulate a host of popular anxieties about children or disasters or cultural tensions. They then set these anxieties within a total picture of the "altogether monstrous": sexually voracious and perverse demons, child-eating witches, utterly depraved Satanists.

There are, of course, different kinds of audiences for such performances. Whole villages or cultures in times of crisis might respond to a performance of evil, or only those select communities, like deliverance ministries, who may strive to live in a state of perpetual spiritual warfare. At the same time, the one who performs a myth of evil before any such audience must inevitably nuance and extend the myth for the sake of relevance. She might, for example, combine Satanism and child abuse, or demons and feminism, or, in earlier times, witchcraft and the Eucharist. But representing evil so directly also involves a powerful ambiguity, for audiences meet the role not only with gratitude and a desire to rescue, as in cases of the demon-possessed, but also historically with horror and a desire to annihilate.

The performance of evil, whether coerced or voluntary, can thus amount to a tense dance with a society's most vivid hostilities and fears, in which the performer tries to give the audience what it desires while preserving his or her own safety, or even gaining charisma in the process.[12] Part of the variability in audience responses comes down to the very range of ways one can enact evil: from the vividly direct manifestation of a demon or ex-Satanist, already discussed, to various *allusions to* the demonic. For example, one might speak referentially of the acts of a demon or witch, or tell a story or legend about demons or witches, or imitate one for fun or deceit, or depict such beings or their victims in art. Some folklorists have classified these expressive allusions to myths of the demonic or Satanic according to the directness and sincerity with which that myth is embodied: for example, acting in such a way as to demonstrate a myth's actuality, like "being" a Satanist or even mobilizing a crowd to hunt witches; or acting in such a way as to pretend the actuality of a myth, as in hoaxes or pseudo-Satanic forms of vandalism; or acting as interpreter of some random occurrence (a cache of bones in the woods, or even a corpse) as evidence of the myth's actuality; or simply transmitting stories that testify to the myth's relevance ("There really are Satanists out there. A friend of a friend of mine swears that . . ."). In such diverse ways a myth of evil can maintain its relevance as mere story, or it can gain immediacy and presence through performances.[13]

Classifications like the one above help us to make sense of the great range of behaviors that draw on or address a myth of evil conspiracy, such as modern Satanic cults. Today, for example, one can see distinctions between youth who embrace a "Satanic style" with jewelry, tattoos, and clothing in order to express feelings of deviance, youth who adopt Satanism as a legitimation for violence (often ex post facto and encouraged by parents or advisors in order to gain popular forgiveness), and the often deranged adults who conceal their crimes under the anonymity of "Satanic cult atrocity." All three of these modes of performance have the capacity to prove the reality of a Satanic cult conspiracy for those who believe it, but in fact they reflect important differences in the actors' motivation.[14]

But to examine the performance of demonic and Satanic mythology in a historically longer and culturally wider context I want to propose a slightly different classification. The enactment of a demonic or Satanic realm—as for any mythic or supernatural world—constitutes a form of *mimetic performance*. This term, "mimesis," has been employed in recent anthropology to describe the acts, dress, and iconography through which Western colonialists and their subject peoples represent each other as powerful or dangerous.[15] I use the category in this chapter in a different sense: to denote the total performance—voice, gesture, staging—through which an individual imitates, or declares to be real through imitation, a myth and its dominant characters. In cases covered in this chapter, that myth concerns a conspiracy of evil, its malevolent devotees, and the rites and atrocities that motivate the conspiracy. But mimetic performance itself can be productively divided into subcategories. *Direct* mimetic performance, in which a person *embodies* some evil spirit or Satanic devotee, differs from *indirect* mimetic performance, in which an individual's actions *address or in some way presume* the existence of mythic evil powers (much in the way an effective pantomime artist can presume and thus suggest the existence of a chair, a rope, or a wall). Furthermore, in modern Western society, an important version of direct mimetic performance is youthful Satanism and its adult corollary, the churches of Satan. But the motivations here differ significantly from other direct enactments of evil. Such contemporary Satanists react to, exploit, even caricature Catholic and evangelical constructions of the Satanic. Hence we can refer to their *direct mimetic parody* of Satanic evil.

Here it is worth another clarification of the term "performance." In common parlance the word suggests deliberate pretense to a role, a self-consciousness about acting one way while normally being another way. The individuals Lévi-Strauss introduces, for example, begin their roles in deliberate conflict with what they know to be genuine, although the conflict diminishes as they embrace their roles. Most of the mimetic roles discussed in this chapter, however, are assumed with the utmost sincerity. They are embraced as greater versions of the self. The possessing demon and the eyewitness "victim" of SRA can represent starker, more charismatic, and sometimes more resolvable expressions of real experiences (for example, real sexual abuse).[16] The confessing witch in early modern Europe or America often assumes in herself the deepest and most perverse collective fantasies of evil, identifying herself fully with images others would repress.[17] In some cases, whether coerced or not, public confessions to ritual atrocities and religious conspiracy constitute complete shifts—"conversions"—from insisting on innocence to confirming audiences' worst fears, with all the charisma incumbent in that role of convert or apostate from evil. Hardly duplicitous, such conversions to the role of witch often exceed mere acquiescence to audiences' and inquisitors' demands.[18] Performance, as I use the term, refers to the manifestation of a myth of evil through public embodiment of a role linked to that myth. The role both affirms the larger reality of evil and endows it with a physical form that can be purified or healed . . . or eradicated. Some indirect mimetic roles I will discuss, like exorcists, demonstrate myths of evil through gesture, movement, and command; and we must likewise presume their sincerity as performers. Recognizing the performative function of these roles in society should never be taken to deny the seriousness of the convictions in an evil realm.

Direct Mimetic Performance

AFRICA: THE NECESSITY OF WITCHES

If the examples with which I began this survey of mimetic performance involved the voluntary enactment of a culture's myths and mythic beings, in history the position of "performing" an evil being—witch, ritual murderer, Satanic devotee—has often been involuntary, involving a process of coercion as the subject is forced into the role. Yet the end-result, I would argue, is the same for audiences: a myth of perverse, demonic conspiracy currently prevailing in the region becomes present through the confession, and then through the series of acts, clothing, and processional devices that publicly transform a person, even a neighbor, into the embodiment of diabolical witchcraft. Public confessions of witchcraft in Africa are recorded at least as far back as the 1890s, when women so accused would sometimes embrace the witch-role (much like Lévi-Strauss's Zuni boy) and then rearticulate witchcraft in such a way as to gain authority before an awed public. Rather than as the horrific night-witch, one Igbo woman who claimed the witch-role used it to declare herself free of colonial authority and commodities (while nevertheless choosing quintessentially modern paraphernalia, like a glass bottle).[19]

Less dramatic freedom was demanded of witchcraft suspects in some African witch-cleansing movements of the 1950s. These suspects were expected to confess acts of infanticide, extractions of victims' organs, and poisonings, altogether fulfilling common regional assumptions about witches. In so doing they affirmed common witch-beliefs and lent credibility to the witch-cleansing movement itself, which might then proceed to purify the suspects and the community with minimal brutality. In this way, the larger process of community reintegration, which in this case drew upon traditional witch-beliefs, required that some individuals "be" witches in order for the community to experience purification and victory. The process surpassed the guilt or innocence of the individual accused.[20]

Of course, as we saw in chapter 3, witch-cleansing movements in the twentieth century have often worked in quite modern idioms, both drawing on Western technology (writing, mirrors, syringes) to find witches and demanding that suspects confess distinctly modern sorts of crimes and powers, like the enslavement of victims, secret access to riches, and even the subversion of government projects. Those forced into the role of witch, moreover, have in many areas come from the ranks of the elderly, those cleaving to ritual traditions and senior status, and the often youthful witch-cleansing acolytes regard them with great contempt.[21]

Indeed, by the 1980s such movements had become both more brutal and, in some places, more reliant on mimetic performances coerced from the accused. A Zambian witch-finder forced those he had accused "to perform a dance said to be done by witches at graveyards, while holding aloft an incriminating power-object" that the witch-finder had "found" in the suspects' houses. The suspects were subsequently cleansed of witchcraft through numerous incisions and other treatments to their bodies. Anxiety about the witchcraft that this witch-finder was claiming to discern was so widespread that dissenters, refusing their roles as witches, were forced into compliance. Through embracing the witch-role and then being cured, individual villagers made it possible for the wider community to experience purification—and for witches, once reified in neighbors' performances, to be replaced into the realm of legend.[22]

A more recent, urban example shows the capacity of public witchcraft confessions to validate public—or at least particular churches'—convictions about evil. As we saw in chapter 5, young Nigerian women testifying to their Pentecostal Christian conversions began voluntarily to depict themselves as ex-witches. And while witches, they affirmed, they used their enormous powers to destroy men sexually and financially. The young women's testimonies wove together common notions of feminine spirits (like the popular West African river goddess Mami Wata) that church members regarded as demonic, with new attitudes about young urban women's sexually immoral tendencies. The testimonies of witchcraft gave dramatic actuality to these popular fears and beliefs, while their consequent conversion to the churches' charismatic Christianity resolved those fears and demonstrated the great protective and cleansing power that Christianity could offer society.[23]

In these African examples, the confession and the public realization of subversive evil form parts of a ritual process, moving from a state of community anxiety toward social reintegration, purification, and stability. Certain individuals must accept and perform evil—fleshing it out with narrative, geography, characters, and motivations—in order for communities to give focus to their inchoate fears. Only through such focus can they then effect some kind of cleansing.

EARLY MODERN EUROPE: THE NECESSITY
OF WITCHES' BODIES

It was perhaps to facilitate a similar ritual process of community purification that several Basque villlagers in the early seventeenth century volunteered their membership in a diabolical witch-cult with great detail.[24] The first voluntary witch, newly arrived from France, may have sought a role for herself as witch-finder, for she used her own alleged participation in Satanic witch-ceremonies to name others in the village, expecting that the route to her and others' purification from witchcraft would occur simply by public confession in church. With apparently little coercion or complaint, at least ten individuals whom she had named likewise gave extravagant details of Sabbat initiation, participation, and acts of magical aggression like infanticide. After these witches' public acts of contrition in the local church, the village apparently reintegrated them with confidence and a restored feeling of safety, much as Lévi-Strauss's case of the Zuni boy. Direct mimetic performance of the witch-role assured villagers of the truth of their growing awareness of diabolical witch-cults, while villagers' commitments to family and neighborly ties allowed harmless procedures for purification and reintegration at the end of these performances. Unfortunately, investigators from outside who got wind of these events saw confessed witches differently, and when some of these villagers continued to volunteer elaborate stories of diabolical witch-craft before these officials—doubtless still in hope of some moderate, purifying sanctions—they were condemned to public burning.[25]

This disjunction between village and official inquisitorial "theaters" and their varying interpretations of the witch highlights one of the central observations of recent witchcraft scholarship. On the one hand, as we saw in chapter 2, small-scale local cultures often do hold elaborate beliefs in malevolent (as well as simply ambiguous) beings that can afflict pregnancies, infants, livestock, and fields, and certainly village tensions might translate historically into the identification of a neighbor or acquaintance or newcomer as the embodiment of such a being. On the other hand, as we have seen also, ecclesiastical and sec-ular witch-finders, working from an ancient and ever-expanding body of literature about the nature of heresy, the powers and manifestations of Satan, and the layout of the demonic world, had begun by the mid-fifteenth century to conceptualize a witchcraft based in Satanic devo-tion and organized like the most pernicious of heresies. As official witch-finding inquisitions moved through areas of Switzerland, Ger-many, and the Basque country, they influenced popular notions of witchcraft through popular preaching and, even more effectively, the production of witches who actively confessed to the things the inquisi-tors asserted they had done. Thus, as local concepts of the witch be-came ever more elaborate, conspiratorial, and evil, the dangers that witches were thought to bear on village and urban life became ever more pressing. In the Basque village just discussed, this elaboration of witch-beliefs gave rise to a sort of local creativity in witch-cleansing—involving local church penance, for example. But in many other places outright panics followed the spread of the official theories of di-abolical conspiracy.

Central to this process was the production of a confessing witch—a figure who, if once known personally to audience or crowd members, now embodied the very tentacles of Satanic conspiracy and predatory evil, and who, for the official theorists of witchcraft, might testify "from the other side" about essential demonic realities. The involun-tary mimetic performance of the Satanic witch thus involved a series of quite deliberate stages, from arrest to execution, as well as different implications for public and official audiences. The removal of the accused from her village environment would already estrange her from a social context in which her behavior and alleged atrocities were embedded in a web of social relations—where, for example, her primary evil might lie in causing a particular neighbor's miscarriage.[26] She would then be relocated in a context of isolated individuals whose evil lay, rather, in Devil-worship—whose function was no longer to produce a plausible, community-embedded defense or show her conformity to a local system of purification (like public contrition or an act of healing), but rather to substantiate inquisitors' theories about diabolical witch-cults.[27] Much like the modern Zambian witch-finder mentioned above, the secular witch-inquisitor in the seventeenth-century Basque region Pierre de Lancre claims even to have "forced children and girls to dance the same way they danced at the Sabbat, . . . forcing them to recognize how the most modest movement was obscene, criminal, and improper to an honest girl."[28] The subsequent stages would render her more and more the Satanic witch, the monster: by carrying her into the room above the ground, as some manuals advise; by stripping her naked; by imposing on her scenarios and terminology predicated on official witchcraft models; and by proceeding to torture her under the assumption that the witch's body is not human but a veritable battlefield for the Devil. "Unless the witch's aura of menace could be maintained," one historian has noted, "the theological superstructure [of diabolical witchcraft] with its delicate balance of supernatural forces would collapse."[29]

Here, then, was forced theater. But it was propelled by an anxiety among the official investigators that a worldview be articulated and clarified, just as in the village environments, where witch-finding inevitably began, audiences likewise needed witchcraft to be affirmed and nuanced as an idea, not to be contested. In her eyewitness testimony to the workings of Satanic cults before the official investigators, the accused witch was not to report how a cow or child died through her curses so much as to clarify the range of antisacraments produced, the sexuality of demons and witches, the precise stages of the Sabbat rites, and the rationale for infanticide. These were the topics that piqued the inquisitors' pornographic fantasies, of course, but more importantly, they also bore directly on the efficacy and the authority of the church's own rites and on the physical nature of the supernatural world—symbolized in the sexual corporeality of demons. By her very presence before the inquisitors and by her testimony to the reality of demonic intercourse, for example, the witch served "to *make credible* the notion that devils have regular bodily interaction with human beings."[30] And when she emerged at the end, having satisfied this learned audience by her enactment of the Satanic witch, her final procession to the pyre—indeed, her very incineration—maintained the role in the more public stage. She was the confirmed Satanic conspirator, the one that must be burned for her own and society's sake, and her corporeal submission in this role to the cleansing technology of church and state gave the public a sense that its institutions had the upper hand in the war against disorder, illness, calamity, perversion, and all things Satanic.[31]

In the spate of witchcraft panics that inquisitors fomented during the early modern period—often with the aid of self-defined witch-discerners—true witches had to be produced, whether voluntarily in local milieux or involuntarily through systematic and brutal transformation. Their presence lent credibility not just to popular anxieties about a witch-conspiracy but also to more abstract ecclesiastical theories of sacramental efficacy and the supernatural world, which the individual witch-performer might verify through her testimony and her very body, medium of the Devil.

JEWISH RITUAL MURDERERS: MIMESIS AND CHARISMA

Students of the Jewish ritual-murder panics that swept parts of England, Germany, and Spain from the medieval through the early modern periods have noted the same combination of ecclesiastical theories and popular rumors about Jews, motivating the production of a role of Jewish ritual murderer, one who has participated in the international conspiracy to abduct and bleed Christian children for religious purposes. For ecclesiastical figures interested in the potentiality of new martyr-shrines or of new incidents of crucifixion by Jews that revive the value of the original one, the rumor of Jewish ritual murder could turn a single child's corpse into a major cult-site and

Easter itself into a period of heightened awe and fear. For layfolk, the rumor placed anonymously disposed child-corpses and popular anxieties for children's safety in the context of a vast historical conspiracy woven intrinsically with Jewish religion, magic, and Otherness. The direct mimetic performance of the Jewish ritual murderer had therefore to tie ritual murder coherently to Jewish tradition and illustrate the conspiracy's workings in regional terms. Much like Lévi-Strauss's Zuni boy accused of witchcraft, for example, one of the Jews accused of murdering eight-year-old Hugh for ritual purposes in thirteenth-century England was offered freedom if he would describe the widespread Jewish conspiracy to steal and crucify little Christian boys—a conspiracy that officials assumed existed. The man proceeded to weave just such an image of cult-subversion, to the great satisfaction of officials and populace. Unfortunately for him, the King intervened, and the man was hanged anyway.[32] Another such performance, in the mid-twelfth century by Theobald, a Jewish convert to Christianity, gave the monk Thomas of Monmouth his most important evidence for establishing a cult to little William of Norwich, alleged child-victim of Jewish ritual murder. As the historian Gavin Langmuir reconstructs the confession,

> Theobald told Thomas that the Jews of Spain assembled every year in Narbonne, where their royal seed and renown flourished, in order to arrange the annual sacrifice prescribed in the ancient writings of their fathers. To show contempt for Christ, to revenge themselves before Christ's death had made them slaves in exile, and to obtain their freedom and the return to their own land, they had to shed blood annually by sacrificing a Christian. Every year, the Jews of Narbonne cast lots to determine the country in which the sacrifice would take place that year, and the Jews of the metropolis of that country then similarly determined in which town of their country the sacrifice would be performed. The lot fell on Norwich in 1144, and all the synagogues in England knew and consented to the act, which was why Theobald had known about it in Cambridge.[33]

Theobald's elaborate testimony, offered apparently without torture or coercion, can only be explained by his liminal status as convert.[34] Like the cult-apostates' depictions of brainwashing and conspiracy in the modern United States, such an elaborate report of transnational conspiracy, religious custom, and cold-blooded planning as Theobald offered both affirmed and developed popular notions of Jews as dangerous foreigners. The report served as an entrance fee, as it were, to full—even privileged—status among Christians, and confirmation that Theobald harbored no lingering alliances with Jewish culture. To reify a myth of evil thus voluntarily can serve as a token of social exchange and a guarantee of charismatic status.[35]

Some three centuries later, however, anxiety about conspiracies and a more passionate pursuit of holy bodies led in Germany to a greater need for Jews to confirm this rumor of ritual murder. The discovery of dead children, or simply long-buried bones, led quickly to investigations of Jewish conspiracy and, through the selection and torture of certain Jews in the city, the forced confirmation of what all had feared to be true: that all the scattered rumors and legends about Jews, blood, magic, and children could be connected through Jews' religious need to procure Christian children's blood. As in witchcraft inquisitions, the judicial goals lay not in getting simple confessions from recalcitrant criminals but in extracting coherent narratives of Jewish conspiracy, the planning involved in selecting particular victims, and the details of the sacrificial or pseudo-crucifixion rites, all of which epitomized Jewish danger, predation, and religious subhumanity.[36] But having confirmed these realities under torture and in such fraught cultural circumstances, the Jewish ritual murderers were met not with gratitude and reintegration but obliteration. "The public execution itself," observes one of the principal historians of these ritual murder panics, "served as a dramatic representation of the evil of Jews and the triumph of Christianity: the convicted were burnt as minions of the Devil, as black sorcerers, and, only incidentally, as murderers."[37]

DIRECT MIMETIC PERFORMANCE: AN OVERVIEW

People who, through mimetic performance, embody the rumors and myths of subversive evil not only reaffirm the public's convictions in the myths but also provide the public (through its institutions) with a concrete medium by which it can purify itself of evil: bodies. Suspects are coerced into the dramatic embodiment of a diabolical witches' or Jews' conspiracy while undergoing metamorphosis—through procession, mode of execution, even published broadsides (like that in figure 9) and songs—into the absolutely antihuman: "that which must be destroyed." Indeed, perhaps the most revealing difference across the various examples of direct mimetic performance of evil lies in the various community responses to the performer: on the one hand, reintegration for his or the community's purification (as in local witch-finding) or for the affirmation of boundaries (as in the apostates' and converts' testimonies); on the other hand, a society's urge to purify itself *of* the performer. Such responses must be due to several factors: the degree of anxiety prevailing in a region at the time; the degree of Otherness projected onto and embodied in the performer—inescapable and monstrous in the case of the Jewish ritual murder, while balanced with familiarity in the case of some local sorceress. Finally, the differing responses to the performers must be related to the procedures available for purification: states and large institutions often carry the means for the brutal extirmination of evil bodies, while witch-finders operating on smaller, more regional scales may offer more socially agreeable procedures for evil to be cleansed from communities, performers and audience alike.[38]

What is perhaps less important as a difference is the degree of volition or coercion in direct mimetic performance: what it takes for the performance to be successful in realizing and situating evil. Apart from the social circumstances in which people might volunteer themselves as witches, for example, which invariably verge on the coercive even if lacking torture, the involuntary performances of witch or Jewish ritual murderer involved a great degree of creativity. Under torture, ritual murderers drew on their understandings of eucharistic power, popular fears of Jews, and rumors of Jewish conspiracy to weave together their narratives. Studies of coerced narratives of witchcraft in the fifteenth and sixteenth centuries, as we saw in chapter 5, likewise show the creativity of the accused in pulling together local beliefs about fairy people and their dances, local ritual experts' claims about spirit-journeys, the maleficent powers of night-witches and local miscreants, and popular versions of diabolical witchcraft.[39] Whether or not subjected to torture, the performer of the myth of evil serves as an *interpreter* of prevailing rumors and beliefs, even lacing this testimony with images of perversion drawn straight from her imagination for the benefit of pornographic inquisitors or audiences hungry for salacious reports of the other realm.

Indirect Mimetic Performance

WITNESSES TO THE DEMONIC

The *indirect mimetic performance* of evil involves acting in such a way as to indicate or presuppose the active reality of demonic forces or some evil realm, but without actually enacting the forces, the evil beings, themselves. The most talented of such performers are the experts in discerning evil discussed in chapter 3, for through their gestures, commands, and assertions of the immanence of evil, audiences begin also to sense its presence. Contemporary Christian exorcists feel and smell the presence of demons and react publicly—their noses wrinkling, their breaths rapid, their expressions alert, their speech controlled and commanding—as if actually stimulated from the outside. Exorcisms themselves involve dramatic exchanges, exorcists against some awesome force channelled through an ostensibly passive subject.[40] In another form of such indirect mimesis, witch-finders in Malawi would find or plant objects in a person's house, which they would then use as centerpoints of a dramatic demonstration of the suspect's active witchcraft.[41] In chapter 3 we looked at the public roles of such discerners in verbally defining and locating evil. In the present section we examine the ways in which performances themselves—acting and responding "as if" the demonic were present—give evil a presence and make local rumors come alive before public eyes.

Of course, the degree to which evil can achieve such presence through indirect mimesis depends on multiple factors: the predisposition of the audience; the availability of myths and rumors of evil; and the effectiveness of the performer, who might appear as a victim of evil rather than its heroic opponent. Through the ministrations of the seventeenth-century Massachussetts church leader Cotton Mather, for example, the children of one John Goodwin maintained their demonic fits for months, even after one old woman they had accused had gone to her death. As Mather describes it, the children would act as if they were being buffetted around the room. The children would scream out that "they"—some shadowy presence—were afflicting them. They would claim to be ordered to act strangely or perversely, even to be forced into self-mutilation. And in one particularly striking performance, one of the girls pretended to ride a horse at the bidding of "her company."[42] At Salem, we saw in chapter 3, girls and women expressed pain and fear when the accused witches merely looked at them, giving shape to audiences' fears and notions of witches' immediate powers. Performing a state of affliction by demonic forces bears many of the same traits as demonic possession, a *direct* mimetic performance, as we saw earlier in this chapter. Either of these roles gained the actor license for rebellion, sexual expression, and even charismatic power through the embodiment of evil spirits.[43] But affliction performances in seventeenth-century New England were nuanced to indicate evil without incarnating it directly. To Mather and others, it was devils and witches that made the afflicted act in such distress, but they did not communicate through these victims.[44] The senior Ann Putnam of Salem even conversed publicly with a witch (in her invisible, spectral form). The terrified observers beheld only Mrs. Putnam talking in an anguished voice, yet they were convinced of the witch's presence.[45]

WITNESSES TO A SATANIC UNDERWORLD

It is through this category of indirect mimetic performance that we can constructively compare the dramatic claims of recovered memories of SRA. For in their extensive range of victimized *personae*—from regressed alternate personalities, to hysterical reenactments of alleged trauma, to deadpan reports of retrieved memories of atrocities—these self-defined SRA survivors always maintain a distance from the actions of the Satanic cult, even if it is meant to reflect a child's eyewitness response to a human sacrifice.

Not only the shape but also the significance of the SRA survivor's performance depends much on her audience. To the general audiences of television talk shows like those hosted by Geraldo Rivera and Sally Jesse Raphael, the victim of Satanic cult abuse had to disclose and prove a realm of pronounced evil beyond anything the audience had

ever imagined. She might make Satanic cults present by enacting alternate child-personalities who would take over her mouth, face, and
emotional states and give her the appearance of witnessing Satanic
atrocities directly, at that very moment. Often she would express terror, as if undergoing the traumatic sights directly before the audience,
or she might use protective disguises, implying that the Satanic cults
lurked close enough still to harm her.[46] In a 1989 episode of the Sally
Jesse Raphael show, however, the alleged victim conjured the atrocities as present events even without an alternate personality. Italicized
phrases in the following transcript reflect her situating of the events in
the present, with gestures visible to the audience. The guest describes
first how she was

> impregnated by a man that worked for them, and what they did was, they
> would always shoot me up with drugs, but when they wanted me pregnant,
> they would quit giving me their drugs and they started giving me fertility
> pills. And what the outcome of that was, I gave birth to two twins—to
> twins. . . . And they prescribed the fertility drugs to me, and they would set
> me up in a room with this man, and—well, actually, he was about 19. He
> was young, too, but I hold him responsible also. I gave birth to—I called
> them, I gave them names myself, because I don't know what they named
> them—Kevin and Wendy. And Kevin was let to live, he was in a bassinet,
> and Wendy they put on a chair—on a table—*and I am very nervous and
> very hurt right now.* And they drove a cross in her chest upside down,
> wooden cross.

The television host repeats, to stress the monstrosity of the act, "In
the newborn baby's chest," and then presses her guest to continue:

> She—they held my head and made me watch. And I was on a delivery
> table, and *they held my head like this, to hold it down,* and made me watch
> them do that. And afterwards, they put me on a stretcher and took the
> baby, Wendy, and buried her out in the yard—after consuming some of her
> flesh for their communion. . . . My son Kevin was let to live for two years,
> and I knew to stay away from him when—when they were around, but
> when they weren't around, I would play with him. And he was sacrificed
> at—on a Halloween when he was a little over two. And what they did was,
> they had—and this sounds really bizarre—they had a spa, and they would

use piranhas in a lot of their rituals, and they took and . . . put his father in a trance and put drugs on him, and they can do that with people. And his father went with him to sacrifice him—my father and the doctor and his father—took and sacrificed my son over the spa with the piranhas. They cut his arm off first and then started dismembering him.[47]

What might strike us today as unstable, even exhibitionist fantasy functioned at the time, on this widely broadcast television show, as a plausible revelation of secret Satanic atrocities. The guest's "memories" were presented and popularly understood in this way, and for that reason we take these transcripts seriously as cultural artifacts. The guest presents the atrocities as living events, happening before her eyes, rather than things of the past. The television audience shares this experience, encouraging one another's shock, horror, and anger in response. Satanic atrocities are thus brought to life in her performance, not consigned to theory or simple belief. With a general audience, enactments of SRA victim-trauma could even challenge people's sense of reality while also confirming an inchoate sense that horrific evils indeed dwell beyond popular awareness. And as we might surmise from the discussion in chapter 5 of the innocent child as symbol, these victims' focus on child-experiences in particular, often via child-personalities, always had the capacity to grip audiences by their identification with a suffering child and their more general anxieties about child-safety.

In contrast to a general audience, a group consisting only of those defining themselves as incest or sexual-abuse survivors would receive such a performance of memories and post-traumatic breakdowns with the earnest credulity it extended as a group principle. But survivor groups also lent credibility to SRA victims out of a conviction that realms of sexual horror existed that they had not *yet* imagined—a group resistance to limiting the reality or degree of evil. In this context, the one who presented Satanic cults—not simply intrafamilial child sexual abuse—as an eyewitness survivor could reflect feelings of sexual ambivalence, self-loathing, and evil held to various degrees among all her audience, but now fully integrated and distanced as the systematic atrocities of a Satanic cult. The well-documented ambiguity of sexual abuse experiences becomes clarified—coherent, *evil*—through the overlay of Satanic conspiracy.[48] At the same time, many feminist critics have noted, the alleged victim's gothic scenarios of torture and passive young girls had the effect of rendering the more typical, unrepressed experiences of sexual abuse almost insignificant—"normal"—by their intrafamilial, un-Satanic details.[49]

SRA survivors also embodied a myth of evil conspiracy for charismatic Christian groups, for whom revelations of Satanic victimhood affirmed—in contemporary, woman- and child-centered themes—the unique threat of covert Devil-worship and the rising power of Satan in a secularized nation. SRA survivors, often replete with demonic personalities, revealed not a demonic hierarchy, as did those delivered in exorcisms, but rather an obscene underworld in which all things perverse and horrific would take place in the name of Satan, but whose effects might still be resolved dramatically through exorcistic deliverance.[50]

The SRA survivor would also affirm and clarify notions of evil for a fourth type of audience anxious for their demonstration: the psychotherapists who encountered such patients in private sessions. If the actual performance was restricted to only two individuals in the therapy session, the results for each were important for the cultural and professional legitimation of SRA as a social problem. The therapist would discover pure evil through the eyes of her patient, while the alleged survivor would find encouragement and shaping of her role as performer of evil through the therapist's credulous interventions.

Indeed, here especially we must be alert to the interactive nature of the mimetic performance of evil realms. Particularly in the case of psychotherapy, few patients maintain the role of SRA survivor without the context of a sympathetic, even forceful "SRA therapist," whose assumptions, techniques, and professional indiscretions give shape to the performance of SRA victimhood.[51] In chapter 3 I examined the SRA therapist in her own role as expert in evil, but here I consider her as an audience transformed through the SRA performance, as she beholds evil through her patients' eyes and affective states in a process that clinical psychologists call "countertransference"—that is, the often intense personal reactions that therapists experience toward their patients and their stories. So if the notion of "audience" is here quite delimited, the performer's effect—on the therapist and indeed on an entire

professional world of evil-discernment—could be considerable, as un-
prepared therapists came to "realize" Satanic evil and then adjust their
practices to heal its victims.

Therapists who have written about their experiences with patients
who break down, dissociate, and tell horrific stories of Satanic cults describe their own feelings of terror, anxiety for their own safety, even a
heightened fear of threats.[52] Following three sessions with "Helen," in
which she revealed what she claimed were SRA memories, the English
psychologist Phil Mollon describes his response as "a mixture of shock,
disbelief, horror, dread and terror—including fear for my own safety. I
experience it as an assault on my sense of reality; and I suggest that this
is what satanic abuse is—an assault on reality and on the child's sense of
reality, an attempt to destroy and possess the child's mind."[53] Other
therapists describe having to choose between total disbelief and total
acquiescence to their patients' stories—an unusual clinical dilemma in
psychotherapy, which has traditionally emphasized nuanced conceptions of reality, memory, and behavior—and indeed, some therapists describe a process of wholesale identification with the reality that the
SRA victims propose.[54] For the Christian psychologist Louis Cozolino,
"to identify with a frightened child, even when that child is hidden
within an apparently well-functioning adult" is the key to finding indi-
cations of ritual abuse. For Mollon, this overwhelming identification
with the patient carries overtones of a leap of faith: "I would rather risk
being deluded by my patients—rather risk appearing a fool—than risk
abandoning the terrified traumatized child within the patient who is at-
tempting to tell their story."[55] These therapists present themselves as
mavericks, out on the edge of clinical psychotherapy. They often spe-
cialize in controversial diagnoses like Multiple Personality Disorder and
advocate treatments that overturn most accepted ethics in psychotherapeutic boundaries. It is often no coincidence that they ally themselves
entirely with patients claiming the most lurid abuse scenarios.[56]

An English psychoanalyst describes his acceptance of SRA stories as
a shift to a greater awareness:

> For those who hear such accounts, the wish not to believe them is often
> very acute. To believe what one is being told by a victim of "satanic" abuse
> would mean facing something for which one has no adequate means to

deal with or to explain. It means accepting that there could be human beings capable of behaving in ways so evil that we cannot bear to conceive of such a possibility. It means facing an outrage to all that we have come to regard as human. It means facing such degrees of deception and corruption of young children that one would no longer know what to believe. It is much less disorienting to think that these accounts could not be true.[57]

The SRA embodied by his patients reveals a larger evil, a realm of atrocity beyond those abuses he had grown accustomed to seeing. His engagement with a Satanic conspiracy even involves a kind of conversion or existential transformation, as he progressively absorbs his SRA patients' lurid experiences.[58] Psychologists have called this process of existential identification with the atrocities a patient claims to have experienced "vicarious traumatization." It is a result of tensions that inevitably build in psychotherapists' countertransference with trauma patients: reactions of protective rage, grief, parental concern, shame, feelings of impotence, even erotic voyeurism. Consequently, the therapist begins to assimilate images of the clients' experiences into her own psyche and becomes overwhelmed with the brutality and exploitation she is striving to heal. "Our world view," describes one manual for trauma therapists, "is altered as we witness so closely the reality of the intentional, cruel, sadistic behaviors of one human being toward another."[59]

Clinical ethics demand that psychotherapists be aware of and own such countertransference responses, lest the therapy come to be driven by the therapist's own fears, fantasies, or overidentification with the patient. Yet many therapists with this altered worldview—the product of sometimes years of harrowing clinical experiences with child abuse—experience the SRA survivor as lending it all a kind of narrative clarity through her revelations. SRA offers the clarifying dualism of a discourse of evil. The patient brings to focus and presence what, at some level, many therapists imagine to exist at the boundaries of the world they treat: absolute evil for its own sake, celebrated in and among families as if normal.[60] "If ever the face of power shows an almost pure evil," one credulous researcher reports, "it is in Satanic cults and their practices. The survivor through recollection embodies or represents what the cult is as a practice of evil. And those recollections are filled with horror."[61] Consequently, the reality of Satanic cults, their abusive rituals, and "brainwashing" displays come to overshadow and even subsume all the therapist's cases of severe child abuse. Professional boundaries collapse; patient becomes therapist; the therapeutic discourse shifts from emotional experience to morality and protection—indeed, to the elaboration of evil itself. Therapists become increasingly beholden to their patients as revealers and witnesses, suspending professional standards regarding the length of sessions, availability after hours, and even physical intimacy in order to protect the patient from Satanic threats. In a typical reversal of usual therapist-patient dynamics, Mollon claims

> that Helen could not have told me about these things until she felt that I could be receptive to them. Moreover, until she told me she could not tell herself. Her perception of the look of horror on my face when she told me of the murder has greatly troubled her. She has felt that she must protect me from further trauma, fearing that I would not tolerate more revelations, whilst at the same time needing to know that I can be emotionally affected by her experiences.[62]

The SRA survivor represents the eyewitness to evil—its victim. She enacts her sufferings before therapist or recovery-deliverance group as a child undergoing ritual atrocities. While reliving the alleged memories she breaks down (or "abreacts") into such hysterical weeping or such deathly passivity that the therapist is incapable of distancing herself from the reality enacted. The patient brings "messages"—letters, hang-up phone calls, strange looks in the street—that "prove" the Satanic cults' continuing efforts to inflict trauma or shut her up or recapture her.

Such audiences, whether sexual abuse survivors' groups or charismatic deliverance groups or simply individual therapists, are transfixed as evil gains a face and a narrative—in the form of rituals and cult-groups—through the enactment of SRA victimhood. And imagining no other alternative means of understanding the victim's performance, they credit it with revelatory powers.

HUNTING ON THE TRACKS OF EVIL

But let us pull back to the actions of the audience: can they, too, serve as indirect mimetic performers, acting as though the demonic or Satanic world were real? Are there ways people can act—often by direction of leaders—that imply the presence of coordinated evil, and by so behaving in implication, create its actuality? Obviously the great range of ritual acts that fall under the category *apotropaia*, "protective magic," serve essentially as indirect mimetic performances of demonic powers. Through the performance of such ritual acts demons are located, named, illustrated, adjured—effectively conjured as real through the use of amulets, avoidance customs, blessings, and gestures. But actual hunts for evil perpetrators, like witches and Satanists, offer a collective experience of evil's tangibility, since these types of action involve unusual and desperate group departures from ordinary life, focused on the finding of evidence imagined to be there.

In Owerri, Nigeria, in 1996, rumors of a conspiracy of cannibal witches among the emergent entrepreneur class exploded in a full-scale panic, with young men roving the streets in search of evidence of ritual murder.[63] In the local Satanism panics of the 1980s and 1990s in the United States and United Kingdom it was customary to deploy extra police and volunteers to avert expected Satanist attacks, or for local police cult experts investigating Satanist rumors to conjure elaborate scenarios of sacrifice, murder, and conspiracy on the basis of scattered bones or graffiti. The scenarios themselves dominated the interpretation of materials deemed "evidence." Then, a formal mobilization of community members served to make the rumors real.[64]

Medieval Germany provides a particularly vivid example of this phenomenon, the reification of an evil conspiracy myth by acting collectively in response to it. As in the Nigerian and modern American cases, collective mobilization—a mob-hunt—served to define the enemy hunted before the imagined evil conspiracy was extirminated in violent lynchings. The evil in this case was Jews' alleged ritual use of eucharistic hosts, and the goals lay both in the discovery and rescue of these Eucharists and the punishment of the conspiring Jews. In one mass-hunt in 1298, a mob of soldiers and volunteers under the leadership of a charismatic butcher rampaged through the countryside in search of the infinitely fragmented host. According to an early-fourteenth-century chronicler, the historian Miri Rubin summarizes,

> the army which moved from town to town, village to village, burning Jewish houses and Jewish bodies, was on a trail of vindication and recovery, in search of *all* the hosts, *all* those parts of Christ's body which had been allegedly disseminated by and among Jews. Thus, as the crowds moved they stumbled upon evidence, in nooks and crannies in smoking houses. The crowd worked as an instinctive avenger, divinely guided but always vindicated by unambiguous eucharistic proof.[65]

Thus the horror and cosmic threat of Jewish ritual abuse of the Eucharist impelled popular action, and that action simultaneously enacted a mythic narrative of evil, directed participants' sentiments of anger and revenge, and drew both the myth and the brutal gestures of resolution out across the landscape. Such mobilizations involved the demonstration of the myth of evil conspiracy, the rescue of its victims (in this case, Eucharists), and the eradication of its maleficent perpetrators, following which came a sense of order and security—even the reward of a miraculous shrine to the rescued victim-Eucharist.[66] Thus all who participated in the hunt and massacre performed—physically if indirectly—a popular rumor of evil predators, a conspiracy of monsters. The myth of evil took shape in the process of mobilizing against it.

INDIRECT MIMETIC PERFORMANCE: OVERVIEW

The indirect mimetic performance of evil offers a compelling glimpse into the mythical realm of evil conspiracy because it so often involves victimhood. The exorcist who shouts at and adjures the demonic is relieving the visible human host of her otherworldly captors. The children dramatizing their afflictions at the invisible hands of neighborhood witches are pathetic victims who cry out for rescue. The SRA survivor emphasizes, sometimes through alternate personalities, her witness to Satanic cult atrocities as a child. Or else, through emotional breakdowns that strike her audiences as obviously posttraumatic, the survivor appears as *continuing* victim and, again, in need of rescue. Our hearts go out to the children and to the adults whose personalities are still explicitly bound in horrific childhoods. Evil and its most predatory impulses emerge dramatically before us.

The hunt for evil, as demonstrated in medieval Jewish ritual-murder crusades perhaps more than the modern Satanist-hunts, also involves victimhood: in this case, the Eucharist, which indeed was often pictured as a child or which, in legends of ritual murder, screamed like a child with each stab of the Jews' knives.[67] Thus to mobilize against the Jews' evil was also to rescue the Eucharist and restore it to a comfortable shrine for pilgrims' adoration.

By including the victim, or simply by discerning the witch and her accoutrements where others cannot, mimetic performance has inevitably called for some ritual process: purification, healing, prosecution. Evil lies before us, not in the person of the performer but *through* her, to the demons or Devil-worshippers wreaking havoc just on the other side. The SRA survivor, the exorcist, the colonial New England witch-victim, the mob in search of Satanists or ritually mutilated hosts all act mimetically—*as if*. Their gestures reflect the presence of a fully formed and active realm of evil. And acknowledging this realm involves some kind of resolution: either its complete separation (as in Satanic abuse therapy or exorcism) or even its annihilation (as in Jewish ritual murder).

Direct Mimetic Parody

Late-twentieth-century Western culture saw a new way of enacting evil: the self-proclaimed Satanist and similar styles and self-presentations like Vampires and Goths. With roots in early-nineteenth-century Decadent styles, this is a phenomenon distinctive of contemporary Euro-American cultures—American, British, Scandinavian, et cetera—where religious morality (and its demonology) is often cast as an oppressive force in everyday life as well as a rejectable option.[68] There is a freedom to develop publicly deviant subcultures, and yet, in contrast to times and places where literature or new music alone might signal deviance, the boundaries of obvious deviance have loosened considerably: it takes more to shock. Hence the symbols of rebellion, difference, group-power, and deviant identity must sometimes be plucked from a more grotesque cultural reservoir: the obviously monstrous and morbid (vampires, corpses, suicides), the mindlessly violent (serial killers, Nazis), and, inevitably, the Satanic. My interest in youth who construct deviant identities in this "Satanic mode"—through dress and accoutrements, public gestures, and pretenses to religious or ritual seriousness—lies principally in their cultural roles as interpreters and performers of society's beliefs about Satan and occult conspiracies, rather than their synthesis of an authentic "Satanic religion." For this reason it is useful to consider the performance of Satanism on a continuum with other monstrous and morbid identities (like Goth, Vampire, and even Punk and Heavy Metal groups), while excluding the more self-consciously religious Neo-Pagans.[69]

Those who enact society's images of the Satanic and monstrous in such florid, often aggressive ways are usually youth (about 15 to 25 years old) who crave feelings of power to compensate for their social position, and inevitably those youth conscious of their own deviance in the local community. Their experiences of deviance and impotence range from family and sexuality to school culture, and these experiences are often compounded by feelings of oppression from, for example, strict and uniform Christian influence in their immediate communities. At the same time, these youth are fully aware of a discourse of evil and the Satanic that has prevailed in many communities in the United States since the 1970s.[70] Social scientists' past attempts to link youth Satanism with drug use and minor criminality have only shown the larger context of powerlessness, deviance, and social frustration in which Satanic styles gain meaning for youths.[71]

Indeed, one of the most common observations of youth Satanists and their Heavy Metal, Punk, or Goth counterparts is the importance of group-identity and group-interaction to the individuals who choose to join them in maintaining the appearance of flagrant deviance. Here are their friends, those whom they trust, those with whom they share experiences of being outside and rejected. Youth Satanism represents a desperate bonding and redefinition among those who feel powerless and separate. Their attempts at creating ceremonies—to gain love, to gain confidence, to curse from afar their persecutors—involve the sharing of private frustrations, mutual encouragement, and the symbolic displacement of rage. Above all, these ceremonies allow a bonding from which the individuals feel otherwise excluded in their lives.[72] Their public performances of Satanism in high school hallways, malls, and main streets are meant to provoke responses of disgust and rejection, overt forms of what the group-members experience individually and regularly, but now enjoyed by the group as a source of power: that is, they can provoke such responses at will.

The accoutrements of modern Satanic identity are not hard to come by, yet in some areas they can spark extreme reactions with minimal effort. Anton LaVey's mass-market *Satanic Bible* (1969) and *Satanic Rituals* (1972) have long been designed as provocative accoutrements rather than thoughtful theology.[73] Jewelry, make-up, and haircuts suggest death, vampires, or a monstrous androgyny; musical styles, posters, plastic skulls, candles, and preserved specimens make strong declarations that deviance is more than idiosyncrasy—that it should be regarded as a culture of sorts. The Satanic group's choices of meeting-places inevitably draw from those that local society fears or rejects: abandoned houses, graveyards, parking lots. Satanic groups thus reach deeply into the reservoir of cultural notions of the demonic, monstrous, and Satanic, and they do so with much help from commercial and popular culture.

But in embracing symbols of the Satanic and morbid, these youth construct their deviance in an essentially *reactive* form: inverse symbols provided by the larger Christian culture, whose aggressive enactment is intended to trigger repulsion and fear. Satanic groups are thus a kind of "reflective subculture," playing with and on the moral boundaries society provides.[74] Imagery of Satan, the Black Mass, death, and even perversity (which tends to remain more a claim than an act) all derive specifically from symbols that society preserves as fearful, and a youth Satanic group's assertiveness with and elaboration of symbols of evil will always depend on how much local society can tolerate before responding with fear and repulsion.[75]

Yet youth Satanism does not simply appropriate and reflect cultural images of the monstrous and morbid. The subculture's deployment of symbols through dress, music, and gesture is shot through with *parody*. By "parody" I mean a type of deliberate mimicry and caricature not only of roles but also of the cultural ideas and assumptions that surround those roles—and as often with a bitter edge as with humor.[76] In this case, youth who appropriate social images of Satanism for their own group-identity, who claim deviance and fearsomeness as a source of power, also *mock* cultural fantasies of monstrosity quite explicitly. Those symbols and images of the Satanic that disgust and shock adult culture are manipulated in such a way as to lampoon their effects: "How ridiculous," their message suggests, "that a goat's head or pentagram or book can send them into conniptions. Their obsession with Satan is so contradictory, given what they do in the name of Christ. Let us show how ridiculous that obsession is by playing with it, teasing them with their own fears." Hence during some real Satanism panics, youth Satanists have occasionally made a point of exploiting fears and Satanism-hunters' self-professed expertise. They plant "evidence," spread rumors of impending atrocity, and appear amid fraught community gatherings in full regalia, altogether exacerbating the signs and rumors on which the Satanism panics are based.[77]

Part of parody in this sense involves experimentation with the internal meaning of symbols of evil: what *is* a vampire, a Satanist, a morbid deviant, a violent outcast, such that society deems them monstrous and uncontainable? If I become this monster, how should I act? If we are all vampires, how do we make a group? Most forms of self-defined Satanism, from youth subcultures to the small "churches" of Satan dominated by young adults, to the public personae of prominent rock musicians like Ozzy Osbourne and Marilyn Manson, involve a self-conscious (if usually quite inarticulate) critique of social fears and their mythical representation in Satanic terms. This social criticism, of course, is no more subtle than appropriating and parodying symbols. Modern Satanic identities are thus fundamentally reflective of and reactive to dominant social myths. They derive both power and group fulfillment from enacting the starkest cultural notions of evil.

Those in society who view Satanism as a distinct threat, like self-defined police Satanism experts, often recognize the parodic aspects of youth Satanism and its social roots in powerlessness and deviance. However, if they acknowledge that youth Satanism is not the very manifestation of evil, they still regard such Satanic "play" as a mind-altering ideology that encourages everything from nihilism to gruesome violence, and such experts have no dearth of examples of youth Satanists who came actually to commit violent crimes.[78] In fact, these cases usually have involved either youth with deeper sociopathic tendencies who had embraced Satanic identities to express their own feelings of deviance, or youth who adopted Satanism during the trial process as a socially meaningful context for unexpected violent crime—as the ex post facto rationale that society craves.[79] That is, their acknowledgment and elaboration of Satanism as a violent scourge reaffirms society's fears about the dangers of Satanic play and offers these criminal youth a potential ticket back to social acceptance—much like the cult-apostates discussed at the beginning of this chapter. But for the Satanism experts these cases demonstrate that Satanism involves a dangerous continuum between youthful experiments and intergenerational child-sacrifice cults. And as youth Satanic styles, in dress and music, cross to other cultures with stricter senses of youth rebellion, this distinctively Euro-American pretense to monstrosity and evil can appear much more threatening. In Morocco, for example, fourteen Heavy Metal musicians and fans were convicted in 2003 of undermining Islam, having been denounced in the popular press as missionaries for an international Satanist conspiracy.[80]

Self-proclaimed, usually youthful Satanists and their counterparts among Goth, Vampire, and Heavy Metal groups thus represent a distinctly modern form of the mimetic performance of evil. They self-consciously don the appearance and accoutrements of the Satanic, the monstrous, and the demonic, and they assert these roles publicly in society as the very manifestations of evil. They seek to "be" visually what society fears the most. Their private activities are far tamer than popular fantasies of Satanic rites, however, revolving instead around ritual experiments in which erotic and aggressive impulses are displaced through symbol, gesture, and feelings of group-commitment. Yet the Satanist performance is not utter pretense, for youth Satanists do articulate their own feelings of deviance, impotence, and rebellion by publicly embracing, as the symbol of group-identity, that perfect symbol of extreme deviance in a Christian society, the Devil.

At the same time such mimetic performance parodies cultural images of the Satanic, showing their absurdity through the ease and ludicrousness of appearing evil. And as parody, youth Satanists perform in continual interaction with local communities. Local communities are often concerned to preserve public spaces and events from the kind of assertive deviance that youth Satanists embrace. The same communities are also prone to panics about predacious Satanists and can be acutely sensitive to Satanism experts' warnings about levels of Satanic involvement. Where the adult Satanic "church"-members are few, lie low, and emphasize self-education, youth Satanists exploit such fears and impulses, lingering in excluded zones, concocting evidence of Satanic cult activity, and occasionally becoming the focus of missionary or police persecution.[81]

Conclusions

For many, the reality of evil emerges in the disaster, the atrocity, or the horrific crime. Yet the term alone can only serve to comment on the effect those horrors have on us. How does evil become elaborated and situated as a realm—a myth of conspiracy? How do we move from declaring something "evil" to imagining its evilness? Myths of evil, we have seen throughout this book, provide the notion of evil with structure and coherence and, indeed, a creeping, immanent danger personified in this world by conspirators, their direct victims, and their opponents. This chapter has thus examined the variety of ways that such myths, and the realms they conjure of witches or demons or predacious Satanists, can become real for people—visible and tangible in society itself. I have focused on public performances of evil, in which an individual either plays the witch or demon directly and according to roles latent in the mythic imagination, or acts "as if" she were a victim or opponent of the witch or demon, indirectly conjuring evil as an immanent threat. They are both kinds of dramatic mimesis—the representation and interpretation of reality or of a myth with the capacity to seem real through some kind of public performance. We may speak of mimesis here despite the fact that the realm of evil these performances make tangible is one that lacks historical or forensic credibility. But in those cultures and subcultures whose awareness of evil forces comes out of genuine convictions, mimetic performances undergird—even in some cases constitute—the experience of those forces. They corroborate, in Lévi-Strauss's terms, a system and its spiritual coherence in situations where the denial of that system is all but impossible.

Mimetic performances of evil inevitably involve interpretation, even parody in some cases. Indeed, the mimetic performance of evil is always parody—critique or caricature—in some sense, because it must operate at a critical distance from the mythic roles it brings into public presence. Distortion, exaggeration, and sometimes even comedy occur in the space of that distance. Evil is articulated in sexual, infanticidal, carnivalesque, or bestial terms. Performances invite voyeurism or rage or protectiveness or cool-minded ritual combat. Deep or dusty images of the demonic emerge as relevant, active, and modern: the demon of heroin, the Satanic cult with abortion training, the Satanic youth romanticizing suicide, the diabolical version of a popular water spirit, the witch who steals Eucharists. Even if tradition and circumstances compel the performer to express the demonic in a particular way—as a foul-mouthed, angry Beelzebub, for example—ultimately it is her own sense of the audience's expectations, and even more, her own subjective experience of the demonic, that will shape her performance.

In this sense I have argued that the performances of evil under discussion, in contrast to that of the child in Halloween costume, have usually involved conviction in the role. The confessing witch, the demoniac, the SRA survivor, and even the youth Satanist are not actors in the popular sense of maintaining a pretense to a temporary role. In these cases the role—the experience of or identity with the demonic—engulfs the person and calls on the deepest level of psychological engagement, involving transgressive or regressive displays and all the elements of dark fantasy discussed in chapter 5. The term "performance," as I have pointed out, pertains not so much to the performer's own sensibility as to the impact that a certain sequence of behaviors, gestures, and speech, circumscribed by tradition and rumor, exerts on observers. Moreover, the term as I have used it pertains also to the impact those observers will have on the performer. For the audience itself stands in a ritually or socially circumscribed situation—an exorcism, a therapy session, a ritual-murder investigation—and has its own traditional notions of demonic roles, its own everyday anxieties for children, and its own, often inchoate fears of absolute evil that demand embodiment through the performer. From this standpoint the audience interacts with the performer sometimes verbally (as in popular responses to youth Satanists), sometimes physically (as in the torture of accused witches and Jews).

Through the course of these interactions between actor and audience—witch and crowd, SRA survivor and support group, and so forth—the actor becomes the very manifestation of an evil realm and its insidious effects. She affirms a worldview in the presence of those anxious to preserve it or expand it. And as an example of this *manifesting* function of the performance of evil, we might consider a type of indirect mimesis not broached earlier: the publication of illustrations of witches' Sabbats and ritual murders through broadsides and posters. Such media served as a popular means of disseminating rumors of "real" witches and "real" ritual murders over the early modern period, especially in Germany. The broadsides and posters depict the crimes, they situate those crimes in the larger context of some depraved cult, and they celebrate the resulting executions of the monstrous witches or Jews (See figure 9). In this way cheap pictures of legendary acts of evil reflected performances already past and resolved.[82] And yet they also served to manifest, to validate the existence of, a realm of evil—to demonstrate its immediate and current threat.

Depictions of witches' Sabbats included in witch-finding manuals like Pierre de Lancre's (See figure 5) certainly contributed to the demonstration of its existence in early modern Europe. But perhaps no greater example of the graphic mimesis of evil exists than the large mural of the abused body of little St. Simon of Trent that was painted next to the busiest gate of the city of Frankfurt in the decades following his alleged 1474 ritual murder at the hands of Jews. (The mural was even restored in 1678.) (See figure 10.) There he lay, the archetypal child, naked, prone, and bleeding from multiple stab-wounds, in enormous scale, until the late eighteenth century, accompanied by a legend describing the Jews' crime. The historical impact of this mural was considerable, for it kept the Simon of Trent legend alive before Jews, Christians, and civic leaders. Moreover, Simon's posture invited

1475 am Grünen-Donnerstag war das Kindlein Simon 2½ Jahr alt von den Juden umbracht

Au Weyh Rabb Anfch au au maufchi au weyh au au.

FIGURE 10   Simon of Trent portrayed on seventeenth-century mural on
Frankfurt Brückenturm. Detail of broadsheet *Judensau Brückenturm* (1678), C 11363. Frankfurt, Germany, Historisches Museum
Frankfurt/Main. Photograph: Ursula Seitz-Gray. The reproduction of the mural accompanied a caricature of Jews riding and
suckling a pig and conversing with the Devil, all crowning a series
of mocking verses. The broadsheet served to commemorate the
1678 renovation of the Brückenturm and its mural.

parallels: not only of the innocent Christ child, here polluted, but
also the corpse of the crucified Jesus that had so often inflamed German communities with its ancient injustice. The victim of covert
atrocities thus emerged as public spectacle, Frankfurt's (although actually Trent's) own little Christ-figure. Indeed, more than simply re-
calling the legend of Simon's quasi-martyrdom, the mural's design
promoted the rumor of Jewish ritual cravings as a real and visible
threat, a realm of evil implicit and tangible through the enlarged image of a horribly abused Everychild.[83] "Performance" in the sense of
active representation can then also emerge in iconography, which in
this case realizes and excites the communities' anxieties about children, Jews, and evil.[84]

I have suggested a distinct division between roles of indirect and of
direct mimesis—that is, representing the presence of evil by dramatic
implication or in one's very body and being. Certainly the formulation
of one or the other role reflects boundaries that society itself imposes
on those situations that call forth the performance of evil. To "be" a Satanic witch is usually unsafe, the result of coercion or psychopathology;
while to "be" a demon or to suffer a demon's or Satanic cult's afflictions

challenges society to purify and avenge the victim. Today we can usually cope with the provocation of direct mimesis in the form of youth Satanists. Lévi-Strauss's story of the Zuni witch-boy resulted in popular satisfaction and acquittal. Yet in the Renaissance the direct mimesis of diabolical witchcraft usually demanded execution. Demoniacs, in contrast, would invite pity and protective rage, even when they presented themselves in lewd and rebellious ways (as in the famous case of the nuns of Loudun), or as repeatedly invited to join the Devil's company of witches (as at Salem), or even as covenanted servants of the Devil, like Elizabeth Knapp in 1671 in Groton, Massachussetts.[85]

But sometimes audiences' responses to possession behavior could switch to suspicion, leading to executions of demoniacs.[86] So also those specialists in indirect mimetic performance—the professional discerners of evil like witch-finders and witch-cleansers and exorcists—might come to be regarded as witches themselves.[87] In these ways there has always existed occasional slippage between direct and indirect mimesis, where the one who demonstrates evil by implication comes to embody evil himself, or the one who embodies evil comes to seem like its victim. Yet a realm of evil, whether of demons, witches, Satanists, or other monsters, is not frivolously called into presence in societies. It makes a difference to our capacity to resolve it whether that realm approaches our territory through its victims, its monstrous denizens, or simply through our own gestures against it, as in exorcisms or hunts.

In the end, these forms of mimesis reaffirm in dramatic, interactive ways the myths of evil that lie deep in cultures, emerging repeatedly in social anxieties, rumors, and collective panics. Far from wanting them to disappear or be disproven, cultures seek their verification—even their revitalization in modern terms. When historical and social circumstances decree, roles for the mimetic performance of evil open up and invite actors.

7 Mobilizing against Evil

Contemplating Evil, Chasing Evil

THE COMPONENTS of a myth of evil conspiracy lie deep in culture—"hard-wired," as it were, to society and self, rather than produced independently at every discrete point in history. However, the *activation* of those components, to mobilize people to purge evil from their midst, is a process embedded in social and historical context. It is here that I want to discuss the interaction of these latent components and the contexts in which they arise and provoke.

Let us consider first the "depth" of those components that articulate evil in terms of inversion and perversion and yet allow a transgressive thrill in their contemplation: sexual excess, incest and cannibalism, a disorder of bodily fluids and orifices, nocturnal and secret behavior, and ritual states. In chapter 5 I explored various psychoanalytic understandings of this symbolism, especially its reflection of a primary-process realm of bodily sensation, and I furthermore used these psychoanalytic models to understand the emergence of SRA motifs as a kind of feminist and evangelical Christian pornography. Yet psychoanalytic models have tended to emphasize the individual self as the principal site for the negotiation of this kind of symbolism, while I have taken the view throughout this book that the tableaux of inversion and perversion that so preoccupy people as to inflame mass-panics should be considered primarily as products of *social* thinking. The long trajectory of literature about the Other from antiquity, discussed in chapter 4, should support this view: the construction of the *social* Other as cannibal-savage, demon, sorcerer, vampire, or an amalgam of them all, draws on a consistent repertoire of symbols of inversion. The stories we tell about people out on the periphery play with their savagery, libertine customs, and monstrosity. At the same time, the combined horror and pleasure we derive from contemplating this Otherness—sentiments that have influenced the brutality of colonists, missionaries, and armies entering the lands of those Others—certainly affect us at the level of individual fantasy, as well. Thus, as much as psychoanalytic theory of primary-process fantasy may explain *why* horrors of cannibalism and perversion might have an allure for the viewer or listener, we must attribute the symbolism and the sentiments they produce to social thinking equally. Their activation in culture certainly occurs in both collective and individual dimensions: the pornographic obsessions of an Epiphanius of Salamis or Henry Institoris (author of the *Malleus Maleficarum*), for example, as well as the revulsed anxiety for details among modern communities convinced of Satanic child abusers in their midst.

This interprenetration of psychology and social symbolism in the conjuring of monstrosity and inversion is perhaps even more vividly apparent in the image of the night-witch, that universal figure of a predacious, child-eating, part-animal, and sexually ravenous female. It is a total picture of terror, of monstrous danger, constructed through a series of inversions of both custom (we are clothed; witch dances naked) and maternal intimacy (mother protects babies; witch eats them).[1] And here again, if generations of Western psychologists (most notably Bruno Bettelheim) have demonstrated the active function of such an image for the individual psyche (even that of children), we must not forget that for many historical peoples this witch posed a community danger; and discussions of her tendencies and modes of aversion took place collectively, not in some pristine children's story-time. The night-witch has, indeed, challenged anthropologists, often averse to speaking of "universals," to come up with an explanation of nearly identical figures in North American, Asian, South American, European, and African indigenous cultures. Is it that the inversion of social propriety, appetite, and maternity can only be symbolized in a limited number of ways? Is it that underneath the night-witch lies not so much the bad mother as the idea that evil may come from another person? Any way one analyzes this figure of evil, so fundamental to the Sabbat of the witch-hunts, for example, one finds oneself at the intersection of society and individual psyche. It is perhaps best to conclude that such a figure, by her characteristics, has the capacity to activate terror and excitement in both individual and collective dimensions.[2]

The imaginative roots of the myth of evil conspiracy, then, lie between the most basic structures of social thinking—about Otherness,
about impropriety, about order and inversion—and the most basic features of individual psychology and fantasy, from the terrors and allures of
primary-process imagery to the developing ego's various constructions of
moralizing force (superego), dangerous insatiability (id), passivity, rage,
maternity, and phallic power. In that sense we can speak of the symbols
of evil, such as they have emerged in the real, conspiratorial forms conjured in historical panics, to be "hard-wired" to self and society.

And yet their activation in history has occurred through patterns of
social interaction and within particular historical contexts. If a repertoire of demonic images and symbols is latent in society and in the individual imagination, mapped onto landscape and social topography in
ever fluctuating ways, the emergence of these symbols in the form of a
coordinated threat, a myth of evil conspiracy, occurs through two types
of social performance. Initially, as chapter 3 described, we see in every
such mobilization the active leadership of experts in the discernment of
evil. They will integrate latent fears and symbols in a locally coherent
picture of organized evil, and thus immanent danger; they will make
themselves or their institutions indispensable to public safety—uniquely
capable of discerning, combatting, and cleansing evil. Through their
gestures and rituals—their indirect mimetic performances, as I classify
them in chapter 6—they can demonstrate the real presence of evil before audiences. A transformation takes place; what was latent or inchoate becomes coordinated and subversive. The community must
act—or allow others to act on its behalf. Soon the community, now
anxious in the face of coordinated conspiracy, requires a second type of
social performance. Representatives of that conspiracy—direct mimetic
performers—emerge voluntarily (such as the possessed) or by the coercive force of the experts (such as alleged witches or Satanists). It also
requires conspiracy be reified in the guise of victims, through whose
dramatic affliction an evil conspiracy becomes a grave and tangible
threat—as well as a source of voyeuristic fascination, as we also saw in
chapter 6.

If expert leadership and mimetic performances constitute the evil
conspiracy—integrate latent images of terror and atrocity in tangible

local terms—what situations allow these roles to emerge in the first place? I suggested in chapter 1 that the most general historical context for all the cases examined in this book would be the encounter between, on the one hand, the local world, the village or traditional social enclave, with its relatively flexible, improvised constructions of misfortune and malign powers (discussed in the beginning of chapter 2), and, on the other hand, a geographically broad, totalizing discourse of authority, power, and evil that compels those local systems to reframe experience according to its more far-reaching terms. We find examples of these "global" or totalizing systems not only in missionary Christianity and postcolonial capitalist modernity, with their deep influence on witch-cleansing movements and evangelical Christian crusades in Africa and elswhere, but also in the antiheresy preaching crusades and inquisitions of the fifteenth- and sixteenth-century European Church, and even in the ideology of the Roman Empire as an ordering force against foreign and secret religious activity. Often the flourishing or diminishment of witch-cleansing movements can be linked to the rise or fall or character of such a broad discourse of evil. Evil becomes a function of broad networks (of Jews, Satanists, witches, Christians) rather than local divisions and enmities. In the modern West (and increasingly throughout the contemporary world), the erosion of local worlds and frameworks for misfortune have led communities to think almost exclusively in global terms and to seek anxiously for one or another system through which to frame social problems like youth deviance, brutal crimes, and family instability. Hence the ascendancy in the United States and United Kingdom of moral crusades and conspiracy theories over the last century.[3] A panic like SRA is then ignited not by catastrophe (as in the Indian massacres that lay behind the Salem witch-purge) or by the coercive force of some outside crusade (as in the early modern European witch-hunts or many Jewish blood-libel inquisitions), but by an anxious culture's discovery of a new social problem and its immediate framing in terms of conspiracy and evil.

Such encounters between local and global discourses actually provide new opportunities for individuals to emerge as experts, to concoct roles for the discernment of evil and impurity, and to frame local anxieties in the captivating new terms—and often with the captivating new accoutrements—of the global ideology. The most charismatic witch-finders in Africa and Europe were those who stood *between* systems and worldviews. Such cultural encounters likewise have provided opportunities for those alternative roles of the disenfranchised and powerless: demonic possession and the indirect mimetic performance of victim. Through the agency of their actors these roles have had the striking capacity to articulate new dimensions of cosmic threat and thus to spark purges of evil. In every case, what terrifies people is the immanent, lurking threat of monstrous atrocities—acts that are utterly horrible, that no proper person would commit, that are done for some "cultic" cravings, that call forth our deepest revulsion and yet, at some level, our *recognition*: something clearly evil. In the end, the scope of a people's response to the perceived threat of organized evil—that is, whether panic, inquisition, or pogrom—depends on the means available to mobilize, the nature of the institutions behind the dissemination of that threat, and, in recent times, legal or political barriers.

Matters of Fact and Fantasy

Fears of an evil realm and mobilizations to purge its partisans from the landscape condense primal images of inversion and perversion. In panics, a myth of evil conspiracy builds on those images, ramifying them and situating them in the real world through the performances of experts, victims, and alleged perpetrators. This theory of the emergence of myths of evil conspiracy, that is, begins with the premise that the allegations of witches, Satanists, blood-thirsty Jews, and cannibalistic Christians have *never* been justified—that there was never fire within the smoke. Yet through history scholars have certainly debated whether Gnostic perversions, witches' Sabbats, SRA, and even Jewish ritual murder had some measure of historical factuality.

This book, as should be clear, eschews such debates altogether, taking the position not only that no evidence has ever been found to verify the atrocities as historical events, but also that more productive and incisive work on these materials will rest on a new positivism about rituals in history—a confidence in the *ahistoricity* of certain extreme scenes of ritual. What can we find if, instead of imagining that

religion and the sacred might give rise to *every* conceivable act—
a rather self-indulgent line of speculation encouraged by the writings
of René Girard and Mircea Eliade—we start from the proposition that
ritual itself can function as an organizing theme, a myth, for *contemplating* Otherness, inversion, and evil? Having demonstrated the utility
of this position in the preceding chapters, it is now time to defend its
historical, forensic, and ethnographic bases by addressing some types
of evidence that seem to challenge it.

While I will qualify in more detail shortly the differences between
evil atrocities imagined and the strange ritual acts and "Satanic" phenomena reliably documented, it is worth asking what it means to establish the nonexistence of the evil conspiracies and their alleged
atrocities discussed in this book in such a positivistic manner, especially in a field—religious studies—given to bracketing questions of
historical truth. We may consider the matter in its plainest historical
terms in regard to SRA. No forensic or archaeological evidence for Satanic cult atrocities as alleged by SRA experts has ever been found: no
bodies, crime sites, burials, or even past pregnancies of those claiming
to have been sacrificial "breeders."[4] Research and clinical psychologists alike have shown that the patients' memories of abusive Satanic
ceremonies upon which the SRA conspiracy was based were so con-
taminated by media, improper and unethical therapy techniques, and
SRA subcultures that, whatever psychological or traumatic truths they
revealed about the patients, they could never stand as eyewitness or
historical documentation of real religious practices.[5] The question
then follows, if there is no reliable evidence for SRA, and if indeed
simpler explanations for the claims can be found in their social and
psychological circumstances, on what basis can we assume that it
should exist, especially on the scale alleged by its revealers?

This question is remarkably similar to one raised in the beginning of
the twentieth century by the scholar of Judaism Hermann Strack: if
there is no reliable evidence for *Jewish ritual murder*, on what basis
could scholars in his time presume that *it* existed? The scholars imput-
ing historicity to ritual-murder accusations, whom Strack was opposing, relied for their image of covert, violent cabals of Jews on uncritical
readings of Rabbinic and Kabbalistic texts.[6] Yet, the occasional anti-
Semitic web page notwithstanding, Jews never drank Christian blood

or abducted Christian children for sacrifice. Here was clearly a case of smoke without the merest glint of fire.

In the case of SRA, or for that matter diabolical Sabbats or heretics' perverse rites, scholarly credulity usually derives from preconceived theories about "antinomian" or "libertine" cults: that certain religious groups in history have sought not cosmic order and morality but transcendence through disorder, immorality, and perversion. The hypothesis contends that they believe that through meticulously perverting morality—even to the point of engaging in orgies and eating babies—they will break through the confines of this world, which were set by the Devil or meant only for the simple-minded, and gain cosmic release. In the mid-twentieth century, such luminaries as Gershom Scholem and Mircea Eliade celebrated this idea as a key dynamic in religion and mysticism. However, the historical evidence for real antinomian practices consists entirely of rumor, innuendo, and accusations (such as those made against Christian heretics).[7] Still, this preoccupation with the very possibility of antinomian ritual has informed even contemporary speculations on rationales for alleged Satanic cult abuse: for example, that individuals who truly embrace postmodern nihilism *might* logically want to practice antinomian rituals, that there *must* be deviants on the margins of mainstream religion who customarily pervert traditional teachings, that there *must* be people who seek the primitive sorts of power that could be released through human sacrifice and incestuous orgy.[8]

In these various cases of supposed antinomian and murderous rituals, a certain intellectual sophistry has been employed to argue the possibility or even likelihood that somewhere, someone must have committed the imagined deviant acts. It is a sophistry that coincidentally reverts quite quickly to comments on the current state of culture and morality. For example, the philosopher Ian Hacking reasons thus:

> I think it is possible that there have been and will be ongoing satanic rituals by organized sects in which children are viciously abused. I know that in my hometown, which has an undeserved reputation for being the most decent, safe, urbane, and dull large city in North America, goats are sacrificed to Satan on the roofs of warehouses only a few streets from my home. I fear that once any idea, no matter how depraved, is in general circulation,

then someone will act it out. Even if a decade ago no goat-sacrificing satanists tortured children, my lack of faith in human nature leads me to think it possible that some do so now. When vile stories are rampant, minds that are sufficiently confused, angry, and cruel will try to turn fiction into fact. It is possible that some local secret society, with loose relationships to other groups in other places, has gone completely off the deep end. Perhaps somebody, somewhere, has used an adolescent to breed a baby for human sacrifice. I sadly do not think it is impossible for such things to happen—or even terribly unlikely. Hence in my view a person could in principle have rather accurate memories of such events.[9]

This reliance on possibility and supposition, as if the range of historical religious expressions were so unbounded as to reflect all one's conjurations, resembles the intellectual speculations of those turn-of-the-century anthropologists Edward Tylor and James Frazer on how primitive mankind first thought up the idea of supernatural beings—a tactic Edward Evans-Pritchard dubbed the "If I Were a Horse" way of thinking.[10] "If I were a primitive, how would I deal with departed ancestors (or natural laws)" now becomes "If I were a dedicated libertine, how would I celebrate or act out my beliefs?"—or even, as in Hacking, "If I were an impressionable and angry individual, or group of angry individuals, how would I draw on Satanic rumors to act out my feelings?"

One is entitled to one's sociological speculations, of course, but it is essential to check them against historical and ethnographic *realia* if they are to serve as any more than pessimistic opinions—lest they become the kind of a priori assertions about the state of the world that have preoccupied the pages of SRA manuals. Hence we must ask, has there ever existed any religious group or rites sufficiently similar to myths of evil conspiracy and ritual atrocity that they might either be enacting such myths, lend historical credibility to such myths, or otherwise lend credence to Hacking's candid sentiments? And what evidence might there be to assure the historian that actual practices might lie beneath outsiders' fantasies of ritual atrocity?

In the case of Jewish ritual murder and early Christian cannibalistic orgies, scholars no longer allow that grains of truth might lie behind the monstrous allegations. In the case of witches' Sabbats there has been, from Jules Michelet to Margaret Murray and Carlo Ginzburg, perhaps somewhat more inclination to impute plausibility to the general scheme of nocturnal, orgiastic rendezvous, even if not Satanic.[11] Yet this inclination lies on fundamentally a priori grounds—that such repeated confessions, even under torture, *must* have some basis in historical reality—not a historically critical skepticism toward polemical topoi and judicial context. In the case of SRA there has unfortunately been considerable credulity among psychiatrists, social workers, police, and even some scholars toward the notion of organized Satanic cults. But most social scientists have now begun to approach the SRA panic in the same way as the earlier ones—not as a controversy but as the reemergence of similar motifs and fears from a similar mythic reservoir.[12] In this way we can appreciate the religious, symbolic, and polemical imagination—of demonic witches or Jews or Satanists as much as classic tableaux of heaven and hell—*as* imagination, as the construction and projection of myths of organized evil, not simply as evidence of weird rituals.

There have been, to be sure, religious and criminal phenomena of rather bizarre character (to the modern Western observer) that have often been linked to or confused with images of organized evil and rites of evil: heterodox religious sects with arcane practices; carnivalesque religious parody and "antistructure"; anthropophagy and ritualized murder; malign ritual and sorcery; and certainly sexual abuse committed under the most coercive and authoritarian of social environments. I want here to note some of the differences between the documented occurrences of these phenomena and the mythic tableaux in which they are represented as monstrous inversions.

We might look first at those heterodox Christian, Jewish, and Muslim groups in history whose primary writings suggest—and outsiders' polemical writings luridly accuse—the insiders' sense of superiority to, or transcendence of, basic religious law and morality. Early Christian so-called Gnostics and early modern Jewish Sabbataeans have been said to have thus systematically inverted moral law to express a quasi-angelic or apocalyptic transcendence. Such inversions, some scholars have suggested, *would* emerge as orgies, eating of impurities, parodies of proper ritual or law, much as opponents describe.[13] However, no insiders' texts actually outline such abominations, and moral transcendence itself is understood subtly and metaphorically, not literally. Indeed, the literature of these Gnostic sects of early Christianity specifically advocates ascetic practices and sexual renunciation, hardly the orgiastic perversions imagined by heresiographers. The same is true of the medieval renunciant movement of the Cathars. One might infer, of course, that simply in raising the issue of sexuality, even as something to be renounced, these groups might have inspired opponents to imagine the worst.[14]

Likewise, the idea of a sect of Jewish mystics who sought "Redemption through Sin," as in the title of Gershom Scholem's famous essay, has been little more than a fantasy of the Other's perversity, here in rational form. We do find in the literature of the eighteenth-century messianic sect around Jacob Frank some startling realignments and symbolic reinterpretations of the sexual relationships among believers, although it is unclear which practices meant to invert the Torah and which reflected the kind of realignment of sexual relations typical to sectarian movements with strongly charismatic leaders (as in the early Mormon movement). These realignments (of wives and husbands, girls and Frank himself) amount to quite systematic sexual exchanges, in no way resembling the orgiastic debauchery imputed to such sects and always reflecting back on the sacred omnipotence of the leader.[15]

Anthropologists from Émile Durkheim to Victor Turner held up the ecstasy and disorder of collective gatherings as both paradigmatic for religious experience and prone to acts of moral excess. The *communitas*, in Turner's terminology, of a carnival or a revolution represents a moment of disowning, even repudiating, order in every aspect of social life—gender roles, authority and hierarchy, the reverence for sacred objects, sexual propriety, the demarcation of space—before reestablishing that order at the end of this liminal period.[16] Would this concept, observable in many situations in the modern and premodern worlds, lend some authenticity to the images of perversity and inversion imputed to organized evil? Certainly there is an element of carnival in reports of the ancient Bacchanale and those of the witches' Sabbat, but are the carnivalesque elements part of their reality or part of a reservoir of disturbing scenes projected into a fictional tableau? The historical Bacchanale may well have had such a character; however, the rumors of orgies and human sacrifice, all taking place in darkness amidst a scene of cacaphonous frenzy, in an account written some hundred years after the events, suggest a conglomeration of horrors well beyond the typical extremes of festival *communitas*. The details amount to a systematic portrait of cult subversion.[17]

As for depictions of the witches' Sabbat, scholars have shown clear links between alleged Sabbat inversions and clerical condemnations of festival behavior in early modern Europe.[18] Sometimes peasant fantasies of fairy dances are discernible in constructions of the Sabbat, yet these supernatural festivities are quite ordered: elegant, full of ordinary delights, proceeding stage by stage. Indeed, Turner's very idea of pure *communitas*—temporary chaos, egalitarianism, sexual libertinism, and ecstasy—has been criticized as unrepresentative of real liminal behavior, whether in festivals or elsewhere. Often hierarchies are reinforced, gender roles caricatured but not inverted or equalized, space reordered strictly, sexuality controlled. Thus societies do have the occasional propensity to shift into a festival mode—a public, not covert, mode, and for a brief period—but that mode does not involve complete moral inversion.[19]

Even if not in *communitas*, there are recorded cases of ritualized transgression: that is, temporary and focused acts that transgress specific cultural mores. They are all highly specific and in no case involve complete or permanent amorality or immorality, even if some examples are quite lurid. Studies of the violence inflicted by the Mozambican rebel army Renamo, for example, reveal degrees of attention to things destroyed, to the killling of the helpless, and even to the treatment of victims' bodies that can certainly be labelled "ritualized," but with what aim did they take place? "Their purpose," observes an anthropologist close to the events, "is to instill a paralysing and incapacitating fear into the wider population. They do this by conjuring a vision of inhumanity and maniacal devotion to the infliction of suffering that sets them outside of the realm of social beings and hence beyond social control and even resistance." And yet, Renamo's extreme, ritual transgression itself has limits, as the soldiers cleave to numerous traditions of power-definition and rules of social hierarchy (such as avoiding the rape of prepubescent girls).[20]

In a much more ancient and culturally controlled context, Hindu Tantric practices involve the deliberate use of impure substances, like menstrual blood, semen, and wild animals, to demonstrate the specialist's "own super-human power to transcend the boundaries of pure and impure, clean and unclean, to overstep the limitations of the social order and physical universe alike." And yet, Tantric rites, rare as they are, are always performed in the context of a highly articulated moral and religious system, often to assert the specialist's eminence in that system rather than to destroy it.[21]

Even recent attempts to enact transgression in a ritualized form have resulted in quite limited inversions of morality. The theatrical attempts at obscenity by the early twentieth-century esotericist Aleister Crowley, for example, occurred no more than a couple of times with little dramatic success. Figures like Crowley and Anton LaVey, author of the *Satanic Bible*, and their nineteenth-century forebears, were in explicit reaction to what they viewed as Victorian or Catholic shame cultures, and their notions of sexual rites, staged profanations, and indeed their public roles were all meant to create a space for mutual eroticism and sexual freedom at a time when such ideas were deemed obscene. Yet the celebrated sexual transgressions were quite tame and nonexploitative compared to pornography of the time. Abuse of children and human sacrifices were never even considered.[22]

Of course, in these last two cases of Tantra and modern esoteric groups, immediate outsiders to the practices (not to speak of distant Westerners reading their tabloids) deemed them monstrous, subversive to society, and of a much more organized type of perversity. It is important for us, weighing various kinds of reliable evidence for organized evil, Satanic atrocities, and ritualized abuse, to recognize how limited, particular, and even moralizing these transgressive rites can be.

Anthropophagy—a preferable term to "cannibalism" for its reservation of judgment and of imputations of monstrosity—has certainly been part of many cultures in history as an open, collective, rather than secret and transgressive, act. Ethnographers who have addressed this act have broken it down into such a diversity of approaches to consumption of the human body that one can hardly speak of a uniform "cannibalism": what parts are eaten, by whom, and under what circumstances? War? Famine? Hunting rites? Ritual anthropophagy can signify the assimilation of the Other's power, the obliteration of the Other's presence, mourning, or cosmic notions of predator and prey.[23] These various features emerged in a quite gruesome *New York*

Times Magazine article on ritual anthropophagy by militias in the Congo. The acts were public, both demonstrating military superiority and reflecting a hunger—literally—for the potency and resilience that their victims' body parts could offer. That pygmies were the favored victims revealed the allure of the Other: rather than as monsters, as chapter 4 discussed, militias viewed the unusual pygmies as sources of magical power.[24]

But cannibalism has also, cross-culturally, been *imputed* to the Other, signifying his nature as disorderly, bestial, and basically threatening. This monstrous anthropophagy has particularly informed Western concepts of cannibalism. W. Arens is doubtless correct that these fantasies of the cannibal Other, a monstrous or titillating folklore topos, are far more common than actual incidences of ritual anthropophagy.[25] But even in acknowledging the existence of anthropophagy, we can propose that the individual cases (a) differ enormously among each other; (b) differ significantly from Western depictions of monstrous or savage cannibalism in being overt (not secret) and meticulously ritualized (not frenzied) acts; and (c) refer not to primal, subhuman violent instincts but to subtle cosmological and social concepts of personhood, ingestion, and body. It is not always possible to distinguish monstrous cannibalism from ritual anthropophagy, and most early modern European reports of the latter deliberately recast it as the former. Nevertheless, images of monstrous cannibalism generally are constructed to demarcate us as human and orderly, them as bestial, chaotic, and even predatory.

Are there forms of ritual aggression—sorcery and malign ritual—meant to disable, bind, and kill people? Again, the reality of sorcery is easily confused with the caricature of sorcery as the intrinsically dangerous magic of the Other: "Those people down in that village—they are all sorcerers and eat children"; "Stay away from Monsieur Joseph who lives by the swamp—he is a sorcerer and can kill you." The magic of the Other is predatory and dangerous, while the magic of our ritual experts, our local wise women and cunning men and saints, is beneficial and protective. Yet research on local ritual expertise cross-culturally shows that these experts are typically known *both* for healing-protection *and* for binding, cursing, even attempted homicide. One expert may be known more for healing and protection than for harm,

of course, and may characterize (or even invent) a rival as an evil sorcerer. Or she may enjoy a reputation as frightening sorceress, charac-
terizing her more village-based rivals as weak and limited (but then at-
tracting clients for her peerless love potions). An indigenous term, like
bòkò in Haiti, might exist to denote a "class" of evil sorcerers, but this
is simply a label with flexible subjects. Malign and beneficial rituals
and reputations extend from (and against) personalities, in such cases,
not offices or guilds. And historically, innumerable self-defined experts
in ritual healing have found themselves hauled off as malicious sorcerers and witches.[26]

That being said, there are isolated and often ambiguous cases of a
malign, homicidal sorcery maintained as a craft, even occasionally
with a kind of subculture. Sometimes, as in the Philippines in the
1960s, it was a craft cultivated alongside healing and divination, and
its threats expressed an alternative (subjudicial) form of social pres-
sure.[27] Other times, as in the Kanaimà sorcerers of modern highland
Guyana and Brazil, the sorcerers' subculture channels a complex aggression from older warrior traditions and colonial experience.[28] Such
ethnographic accounts certainly might fulfill our deepest negative
fantasies of savage ritual, yet in neither case can we infer from such
historically and culturally particular types of ritual aggression that
something similar might lie behind allegations of early modern witchcraft or modern Satanic cults. Indeed, the closest example of such ritual
aggression in modern times, a Mexican drug gang's attempt to create
supernatural protection for itself through the murders and mutilations
of several people in Matamoros in 1989, shows not a resemblance to
common notions of organized evil but rather the exceedingly idiosyncratic ways that *criminals* assemble their own ritual traditions for protection and power.[29]

One feature distinctive of the nineteenth- and twentieth-century
West, as I discussed in chapter 6, is the appropriation of Satanic conspiracy motifs by small groups: at one point to frame fictional fantasies
of erotic transgression, as in French Decadent novels (with extremely
rare cases of theatrical enactment), and then as a contemporary youth
"deviant style," meant to provoke shock publicly, to express feelings of
marginality, and to parody cultural anxieties about evil. The existence
of these roles and "Satanic" groups does not make the myths they try

to embody somehow historically real, but rather points to an awareness among some in society that the myths have great power, great danger, even an oppressiveness, and that one can play with the symbols, imaginatively and theatrically, if one is willing to accept some ostracism. Yet some believers in a modern Satanic conspiracy have pointed to these contemporary youth enactments of Satanism as evidence of a more extensive Satanism in society, even as a symptom of a deeper nihilism that might conceivably be expressed in ritual atrocities. Much as readers of Nietzsche were once thought to be capable of any atrocity conceivable, so youth who adopted such a vivid identification with evil were imagined as opening themselves up to ritual indulgence in bloody crimes—that by engaging with Satanic motifs, they might well come to enact the very evil that society itself conjured.[30]

I have suggested in chapter 6 that this appraisal would be a gross misunderstanding of this deviant style. In fact, given the elaborateness of Satanic roles and materials available to youth, it is important to note how seldom crimes actually take place in this guise. Still, it is not at all surprising that such an ostentatious appropriation of evil identities among adolescents and deviant individuals might occasionally *coincide* with acts of pathological violence, so that someone (or a group) espousing some form of Satanic devotion mutilates or kills. Newspapers celebrate these acts—as well as unrelated acts, like the Manson and Columbine murders—as "Satanic cult murders," conveying the popular belief that only "Satanic" deviance could lead youth to commit such atrocities.[31] Yet the correlation between Satanic self-definition and extreme violence may not be causal, for at least as many (and as gory) youth atrocities are committed with no Satanic accoutrements at all.[32] Close study of adolescents' motivations for assuming Satanic identities, at least in modern America, would suggest that feelings of deviance and powerlessness are common, that Satanic symbols provide powerful boundary markers in Christian environments, and that pathologically violent individuals and groups will *also* exploit these same symbols for more aggressive acts. There is no basis, then, for regarding contemporary Satanic regalia or even Satanic killings as suggestive of a more pernicious Satanic cult conspiracy or of some incipient danger in Satanic styles.

Finally, the panic about SRA in the 1980s and 1990s obscured the matter of real intrafamilial sexual abuse, but it did raise the question, if real sexual abuse is so rampant, is not Satanic cult abuse likely? And another question followed: if one denies Satanic cult abuse, is one implicitly denying the high incidence of sexual abuse itself? Intrafamilial sexual abuse can certainly take quite horrendous forms (invariably with abundant physical and direct eyewitness evidence).[33] Yet it is often committed under quite ambiguous circumstances, merging loyalty, domination, parental love, terror, and even an incipient eroticism in the victim. Indeed, some feminist critics of SRA diagnoses and therapies have pointed out that the search for Satanic ritual motifs, in their semblance of pure evil, actually diminished the significance of the more complex, intimate, non-Satanic sexual abuse. "It is as though the ugly reality of fathers sexually violating children in their care and trust," the author Louise Armstrong observed at the crest of the SRA panic,

> had become unbearably meaningless. It required a larger canvas, bolder strokes, a more apocalyptic message of menace, to give it impact and point. . . . Once the experience [of parental sexual abuse] had been robbed of larger significance, once the stories had become no more than stories, then grander stories became the only vehicle for both gaining attention and finding coherence.[34]

SRA conspiracy theories arose as the combined construction of police, mental health professionals, patients, and trauma-recovery groups, partially as a response to the rediscovery of intrafamilial sexual abuse. The terrifying myth of a realm of pure evil linking countless women's memories posited one kind of sexual abuse as utterly beyond this moral world, involving Satanic rituals and parental devotion to the Devil. Unfortunately, as most psychologists came to recognize, intrafamilial sexual abuse is very much part of this world, committed within the normative moral structures of family and religion.

In fact, as researchers for the National Center for Abuse and Neglect found in the mid-1990s, the focus on unfounded atrocities by Satanic cults against children obscured the numerous and well-documented ritual atrocities against children committed in the course of mainstream religious ceremonies. Gail Goodman and her team had

to develop a separate category, "religious abuse," to describe the burnings, beheadings, dismemberments, drownings, and poisonings done to
purify or exorcise children from demons—a decade's rough sampling of
which I have documented in the note.[35] Recent, documented disclo-
sures of sexual abuse by Catholic priests and as part of Mormon polyg-
amous fundamentalism add to the verifiable scope of this religious
abuse. And the case of exorcisms reminds us again of the need in religious studies to attend to real evidence—in this case, emergency room
admissions and corpses—rather than conjuring ritual activities that
"might be" or that emerge from coerced memories. Many such cases of
exorcistic abuse of children (and adults) are committed by the men-
tally ill, to be sure, yet their techniques usually follow those sanctioned
in various deliverance ministries.[36] More importantly, these cases do
exhibit a kind of "ritual" murder: assaults and homicides performed in
a ceremonial, traditionalized context that articulates basic Christian
beliefs.

What is particularly ironic in acknowledging this kind of ritual
crime is that it is performed, not out of *devotion* to organized evil
(demons, Satan, witchcraft), but rather to *expel* it. We see it also in the
attention to the bodies of lynching victims in early-twentieth-century
America, or of the Jews of Jedwabne, Poland, who had to march while
chanting ignominious slogans and bearing statue parts out to the place
of their mass-incineration.[37] In the meticulous attention to the body
and place of these individuals, we see ritual in its most basic and real
sense: a group has invested itself in some object whose transformation
will bring about public renewal and stability. But the performers, the
participants, understand themselves not to be doing evil but rather to
be cleansing their communities from evil: monstrous, pernicious evil.

I close this book by returning to a point I made in the introduction: that historically verifiable atrocities take place not in the ceremonies of some evil realm or as expressions of some ontological evil
force, but rather in the course of *purging* evil and its alleged devotees
from the world. From the most localized witch-finding movement to
the most broad-scale attempts at genocide, it is the discourse of evil
and monstrosity and of their *annihilation* that most consistently moti-
vates participants—in moods of determination and ebullience—to
unspeakable violence, evil.

Notes

PREFACE

1. Debbie Nathan, "The Making of a Modern Witch Trial," *Village Voice*, Sept. 29, 1987, 19–32.

CHAPTER I
Introduction

1. Cf. Baroja 1965:143–98; Henningsen 1980:125–42, 206–16.

2. Cohn 1993; Levack 1995; Clark 2003; Briggs 1996; Monter 1993.

3. Minucius Felix, *Octavius* 9–10; Tertullian, *Apol.* 8; Tatian, *Or.* 25.3; Justin, *Apol.* 2.12; Athenagoras, *Embassy for the Christians* 3.34–35. On the nature of these rumors, see Edwards 1992, McGowan 1994, Rives 1995, Nagy 2002.

4. Cf. Tammerlin Drummond, "Kenyan Villagers' Suspicions, Fears, Spark Deadly Witch Hunt," *Los Angeles Times* August 3, 1993; "Kenya 'Witch Hunters' Lynch 10 People," Reuters, September 5, 1998; and especially Ogembo 2001. Compare Robert A. LeVine, "Witchcraft and Sorcery in a Gusii Community," in Middleton and Winter 1963: 221–55.

5. Joan Baez, *Play Me Backwards* (Virgin Records, 1992). Articles in professional journals: e.g., Young, Sachs, Braun, and Watkins 1991; Kent 1993; reviews of Noblitt and Perskin 2000 by John Schmuttermaier, *Contemporary Psychology* 46, no. 6 (2001): 615–17, and by Adelheid Herrmann-Pfandt, *Numen* 49 (2002): 103–4.

6. On the evangelical and charismatic Christian context of Satanic conspiracy panics in particular, see Cuneo 2001; Dyrendal 2003; Luhrmann 2004. For the broader cultural context see note 10, below.

7. Beard, North, and Price 1998: 211–44; Rives 1995; Nagy 2002.

8. Inter alia, Boyer and Nissenbaum 1974; Demos 1982; Norton 2002.

9. See, e.g., Comaroff 1997; Geschiere 1997; Moore and Sanders 2001.

10. On the historical and cultural context of the Satanic Abuse panic, see Richardson, Best, and Bromley 1991; Victor 1993; Nathan and Snedeker 1995; La Fontaine 1998; Ellis 2000; Medway 2001.

11. Needham 1978: 33–41 on witch as symbol of inversion (quotation from p. 45); Cohn 1975: 258–63. The present book is indebted to the bold combination of historical, psychological, and folklore studies that distinguishes Cohn's *Europe's Inner Demons*, but it is his 1975 "Postscript: Psycho-Historical Speculations," albeit rather dated and excised for the second edition, that lies closest to the interests of this book.

12. Pierre de Lancre (1611) writes that the demons that Basque witches celebrate come from India and Japan (*Tableau . . . des mauvais anges* 1.2, de Lancre 1982: 80); Emmanuel Eni reveals that instructions to the Satanic witch-cult in Nigeria came from "an Occult Society in India" (Eni 1987: 12–15). Satanic Ritual Abuse specialists James Noblitt and Pamela Perskin relate Satanic rituals to primitive and secret ritual traditions over a vast geographical and temporal range (Noblitt and Perskin 2000: 89–144).

13. See esp. Comaroff and Comaroff, eds., 1993; Geschiere 1997.

14. See esp. Bromley 1991; Philip Jenkins, *Intimate Enemies: Moral Panics in Contemporary Great Britain* (New York: De Gruyter, 1992); Goode and Ben-Yehuda 1994; West and Sanders 2003; Barkun 2003. Cf. Ashforth 2005: 128–30—urban South Africans no longer have the ancestral ritual traditions to maintain personal safety.

15. William Ian Miller, *The Anatomy of Disgust* (Cambridge, Mass.: Harvard University Press, 1997), xiii.

16. On the satisfactions and certainty of using a discourse of evil, see Pocock 1985 and Delbanco 1995, with Lance Morrow's *Evil: An Investigation* (New York: Basic Books, 2003) a paragon example, asserting an authentic evil although only through the piling up of anecdotes. On "evil" in contemporary culture, see Ellis 2000 and Clark 2003. On the *Left Behind* series, see Melani McAlister, "Prophecy, Politics, and the Popular: The *Left Behind* Series and Christian Fundamentalism's New World Order," *South Atlantic Quarterly* 102, no. 4 (2003): 773–98; Glenn W. Shuck, "Marks of the Beast: The *Left Behind* Novels, Identity, and the Internalization of Evil," *Nova Religio* 8, no. 2 (2004): 48–63; and Amy Johnson Frykholm, *Rapture Culture: Left Behind in Evangelical America* (New York: Oxford University Press, 2004).

17. I am inspired here by Stanley Fish's response to post-9/11 rhetoric, "Condemnation without Absolutes," *New York Times* October 15, 2001. This book thus stands apart from the contemporary psychological and philosophical discussions of evil, such as took place at the widely covered "Conference on Evil: A Two-day Dialogue Among Psychoanalysts, Philosophers and

Theologians," Metropolitan Center for Mental Health, New York, May 1–2, 2005, and in the pages of *Hedgehog Review* 2, no. 2 (Summer, 2000).

CHAPTER 2
An Architecture for Chaos

1. Smith 1978: 437.

2. See, e.g., on Asian cultures: James C. Scott, "Protest and Profanation: Agrarian Revolt and the Little Tradition." *Theory and Society* 4 (1977): 22–25; Caplan 1985: 110–16; and Richard von Glahn, *The Sinister Way: The Divine and the Demonic in Chinese Religious Culture* (Berkeley: University of California Press, 2004). On European culture: Stewart 1991. On Africa: Van Beek 1994; Meyer 1999: 88–94; Westerlund 2000.

3. See in general Douglas 1966: 94–113. As applied in recent historical-anthropological studies, see Stewart 1991: 15, 98, 107–8, 114–15, 172–73, 189–90, and Flint 1991: 102, 147–57 (esp. 153–54).

4. William Brashear, "Zauberformular: Exkurs," *Archiv für Papyrusforschung* 36 (1990): 61–73; Stewart 1991: 102–4, 156–57, 164–69, 217–18; Flint 1991: 204–13, 262–68; Campbell Bonner, "Demons of the Bath," *Studies Presented to F. Ll. Griffith* (London: Egypt Exploration Society, 1932), 203–8; L. Keimer, "L'horreur des égyptiens pour les démons du désert," *Bulletin de l'Institut d'Égypte* 26 (1944): 135–47; Aufrère 1998; Horden 1993: 182–83.

5. Greece: Christopher A. Faraone, *Talismans and Trojan Horses: Guardian Statues in Ancient Greek Myth and Ritual* (New York: Oxford University Press, 1992), 36–53; Roy Kotansky, "Greek Exorcistic Amulets," *Ancient Magic and Ritual Power*, ed. Marvin Meyer and Paul Mirecki (Leiden: Brill, 1995), 243–78, esp. 253–54. Egypt: Herman Te Velde, *Seth, God of Confusion: A Study of His Role in Egyptian Mythology and Religion* (Leiden: Brill, 1977), 13–26.

6. Israel: Lev. 17:7; Isa. 13:21, 34:14; Jer. 9:11, 10:22; Lam. 5:18; and note the Azazel tradition in Lev. 16:20–22, 26. Azande: E. E. Evans-Pritchard, *Witchcraft, Oracles, and Magic among the Azande* (Oxford: Clarendon, 1937), 50–62.

7. Philippe Borgeaud, "L'animal comme opérateur symbolique," *L'Animal, l'Homme, le Dieu dans le proche-orient ancien*, Cahiers du CEPOA 2 (Leuven: Peeters, 1984), 13–19; Gilbert Dagron, "Image de bête ou image de Dieu: La physiognomie animale dans la tradition grecque et ses avatars byzantins,"

Poikilia: Études offertes à Jean-Pierre Vernant (Paris: Éditions de l'École des hautes études en sciences sociales, 1987), 69–80; Romm 1992: 77–81 (on the "race" of dog-headed people); Ruth Padel, *In and Out of the Mind: Greek Images of the Tragic Self* (Princeton: Princeton University Press, 1992), 120–25, 130–33, 141–52; and especially on demonology: Stewart 1991: 104–5, 182–83, 187–89, and Johnston 1995: 370–75. See also Barbara Allen Woods, *The Devil in Dog Form*, Folklore Studies 11 (Berkeley and Los Angeles: University of California Press, 1959).

8. Claude Lévi-Strauss, *Totemism*, trans. Rodney Needham (Boston: Beacon Press, 1963), 89. The principle as applied to animals has been further developed in Edmund Leach, "Anthropological Aspects of Language: Animal Categories and Verbal Abuse," *New Directions in the Study of Language*, ed. Eric H. Lenneberg (Cambridge, Mass.: MIT Press, 1964), 23–63; Andrew and Marilyn Strathern, "Marsupials and Magic: A Study of Spell Symbolism among the Mbowamb," *Dialectic in Practical Religion*, Cambridge Papers in Social Anthropology 5, ed. E. R. Leach (Cambridge: Cambridge University Press, 1968),179–202; and Stanley J. Tambiah, "Animals are Good to Think and Good to Prohibit," *Ethnology* 8 (1969): 423–59.

9. Stewart 1991: 76–115, esp. 87–91.

10. Elite context of demonological synthesis: cf. Parkin, in Parkin 1985: 10–11. On the role of writing in facilitating this shift from situational speculation to abstract speculation, see Walter J. Ong, *Orality and Literacy: The Technologizing of the Word* (London and New York: Methuen, 1982), 49–57; and especially on the role of the list in this process: Jack Goody, *The Domestication of the Savage Mind* (Cambridge: Cambridge University Press, 1977), 74–111. Cf. John Baines, "Egyptian Myth and Discourse: Myth, Gods, and the Early Written and Iconographic Record," *Journal of Near Eastern Studies* 50 (1991): 101–4.

11. Abusch 1989

12. Cf. Wash Edward Hale, *Ásura in early Vedic Religion* (Delhi: Motilal Banarsidass, 1986). *Asura/ahura* means human "lord" at earliest stage of both Vedic Indian and Avestan Iranian religion.

13. Marijan Molé, *Culte, mythe et cosmologie dans l'Iran ancien* (Paris: Presses universitaires, 1963), 14–24; Martin Schwartz, "The Religion of Achaemenian Iran," in *The Cambridge History of Iran 2*, ed. Ilya Gershevitch (Cambridge: Cambridge University Press, 1985), 678–84 (quotation from Schwartz, 680); Dale Bishop, "When Gods Become Demons," *Monsters and Demons in the Ancient and Medieval Worlds*, ed. Ann E. Farkas, Prudence Oliver Harper, Evelyn B. Harrison (Mainz: Philipp von Zabern, 1987), 95–100.

Compare Mary Boyce, A History of Zoroastrianism, 1: The Early Period, 2nd ed. (Leiden: Brill, 1989), 197–203.

14. Vendidad 21.4, trans. James Darmesteter, The Zend-Avesta 1, Sacred Books of the East 4 (Oxford: Clarendon, 1880), 228.

15. See Shaul Shaked, "Qumran and Iran: Further Considerations," Israel Oriental Studies 2 (1972): 438–40; Schwarz, "Religion of Achaemenian Iran," 681–84. See also Louis Herbert Gray, "The Foundations of the Iranian Religions," Journal of the K. R. Cama Institute 15 (1929): 175–219. On ancient Zoroastrian rituals of protection, see Pierfrancesco Callieri, "In the Land of the Magi: Demons and Magic in the Everyday Life of Pre-Islamic Iran," Démons et merveilles d'orient, Res Orientales 13, ed. Rika Gyselen (Bures-sur-Yvette: Groupe pour l'Étude de la Civilisation du Moyen-Orient, 2001), 12–19.

16. Bundahishn 34, trans. Boyce, in Textual Sources for the Study of Zoroastrianism (Totowa, N.J.: Barnes and Noble, 1984), 52. See Geo Widengren, "Leitende Ideen und Quellen der iranischen Apokalyptik," Apocalypticism in the Mediterranean World and the Near East, 2nd ed., ed. David Hellholm (Tübingen: Mohr/Siebeck, 1989), 148–51.

17. Boyce, History of Zoroastrianism, 1:201; M. J. Dresden, "Mythology of Ancient Iran," Mythologies of the Ancient World, ed. Samuel Noah Kramer (Garden City, N.Y.: Doubleday, 1961), 357.

18. On lists in oral priestly culture, See Wendy Doniger, "Rationality and Authority in The Laws of Manu," in The Notion of 'Religion' in Comparative Research, ed. Ugo Bianchi (Rome: Bretschneider, 1994), 43–47, and in general Jan Vansina, Oral Tradition as History (Madison: University of Wisconsin Press, 1985), 179–82. Compare on ritual listing John L. McCreery, "Negotiating with Demons: The Uses of Magical Language," American Ethnologist 22 (1995): 144–64, and Richard Gordon, " 'What's in a List?' Listing in Greek and Graeco-Roman Malign Magical Texts," The World of Ancient Magic, Papers from the Norwegian Institute at Athens 4, ed. David R. Jordan, Hugo Montgomery, and Einar Thomassen (Bergen: Norwegian Institute at Athens, 1999), 239–78, esp. 242, 246–50.

19. I.E.S. Edwards, Hieratic Papyri in the British Museum, Fourth Series: Oracular Amuletic Decrees of the Late New Kingdom (London: British Museum, 1960), 4–5, 10, 25, 53.

20. Edwards, Oracular Amuletic Decrees, xvi–xxiii.

21. Frankfurter 2002.

22. Ramsay MacMullen, Christianizing the Roman Empire (New Haven: Yale University Press, 1984), 17–42, 59–67; Flint 1991.

23. Horden 1993.

24. Celsus, *apud* Origen, *Contra Celsum* 1.68.

25. Luke 11:24–26, from the lost Synoptic Sayings Source (// MT 12:43–45). Cf. Marcus 1999, esp. 273.

26. Roy Kotansky, *Greek Magical Amulets*, Papyrologica Coloniensia 22, 1 (Opladen: Westdeutscher Verlag, 1994), ##67; 33, ll. 13–14; 24.

27. Kotansky, *Greek Magical Amulets*, #52.

28. 4Q560, Douglas L. Penney and Michael O. Wise, ed., "By the Power of Beelzebub: An Aramaic Incantation Formula from Qumran," *Journal of Biblical Literature* 113, no. 4 (1994): 627–50. On "shrine-spirit [*prky'*]," see ibid., 643–44. Cf. Émile Puech, "*11QPsAp*ᵃ: Un rituel d'exorcismes. Essai de reconstruction," *Revue de Qumran* 14 (1990): 377–408, and Philip S. Alexander, "'Wrestling Against Wickedness in High Places': Magic in the Worldview of the Qumran Community," *The Scrolls and the Scriptures: Qumran Fifty Years After*, ed. Stanley E. Porter and Craig A. Evans (Sheffield: Sheffield Academic Press, 1997), 319–30.

29. Cairo Geniza TS K1.18+30, ed. and trans. Schiffman and Swartz 1992: 69–82 (translation p. 73).

30. On the demonology of these amulets, see Schiffman and Swartz 1992: 34–36.

31. Joseph Naveh and Shaul Shaked, *Amulets and Magic Bowls: Aramaic Incantations of Late Antiquity* (Jerusalem: Magnes, 1985), Bowl 1 (trans. 125), Bowl 8 (trans. 173). "Demon" in Bowl 1 similarly translates Aramaeic *dyv* (124, l.4).

32. On Lilith, see *Anchor Bible Dictionary* 4:324–25, s.v. Moses Gaster, "Two Thousand Years of a Charm Against the Child-Stealing Witch," in Gaster, *Studies and Texts* (New York: Ktav, 1971 [1925]), 2:1005–38; and Paul Perdrizet, *Negotium Perambulans in Tenebris: Études de démonologie gréco-orientale* (Strasbourg: Istra, 1922), 19–25.

33. On demonological nomenclature, see Schiffman and Swartz 1992: 35–36. On the nature of the combination of Jewish and Zoroastrian demonology, see Naveh and Shaked, *Amulets and Magic Bowls*, 18 (with Bowl 13), and Shaul Shaked, "Bagdāna, King of the Demons, and Other Iranian Terms in Babylonian Aramaic Magic," *Papers in Honour of Professor Mary Boyce*, Acta Iranica 25 (Leiden: Brill, 1985), 511–25. Anders Hultgard offers a useful historical background to such Jewish-Zoroastrian syntheses in "Prêtres juifs et mages zoroastriens—influences religieuses à l'époque hellénistique," *Revue d'histoire et de philosophie religieuses* 68 (1988): 415–28.

34. Gordon, "'What's in a List?'" 248–50, 263–64.

35. *T.Reub* 3:3–7, trans. H. W. Hollander and M. De Jonge, *The Testaments of the Twelve Patriarchs: A Commentary* (Leiden: Brill, 1985), 91–92.

36. 1QS III.13–IV.26; 1QM XIII, XVII.5. See Shaked, "Qumran and Iran," 438–42.

37. Trans. M. A. Knibb, *The Apocryphal Old Testament*, ed. H.F.D. Sparks (Oxford: Clarendon, 1984), 189, 191. See discussions of these lists in Devorah Dimant, "*1 Enoch* 6–11: A Methodological Perspective," *SBL Seminar Papers 1978*, ed. Paul J. Achtemeier (Missoula: Scholars Press, 1978), 323–24; Matthew Black, "The Twenty Angel Dekadarchs at I Enoch 6.7 and 69.2," *Journal of Jewish Studies* 33 (1982): 227–35; George W. E. Nickelsburg, *1 Enoch 1*, ed. Klaus Baltzer (Minneapolis: Fortress, 2001), 178–81, 197–201; and Annette Yoshiko Reed, *Fallen Angels and the History of Judaism and Christianity* (Cambridge: Cambridge University Press, 2005).

38. Peter Brown, *The Making of Late Antiquity* (Cambridge, Mass.: Harvard University Press, 1978), 75.

39. See discussions in Dennis C. Duling, "Testament of Solomon," *The Old Testament Pseudepigrapha 2*, ed. James H. Charlesworth (Garden City, N.Y.: Doubleday, 1987), 937–51; and Richard P. H. Greenfield, *Traditions of Belief in Late Byzantine Demonology* (Amsterdam: Hakkert, 1988), 158–63.

40. Pablo Torijano argues that a single exorcistic formula has determined the structure of *Test. Sol.*'s demon list: *Solomon the Esoteric King: From King to Magus, Development of a Tradition* (Leiden: Brill, 2002), 58–68. On the influence of *Test. Sol.* on the composition of protective amulets, see Kotansky, *Greek Magical Amulets*, 174–80, and David R. Jordan and Roy D. Kotansky, "A Solomonic Exorcism," *Kölner Papryi* 8, Papyrologica Coloniensia 7, 8 (Opladen: Westdeutscher Verlag, 1997), 53–69.

41. Cf. Sarah Iles Johnston, "The *Testament of Solomon* from Late Antiquity to the Renaissance," in *The Metamorphosis of Magic from Late Antiquity to the Early Modern Period*, ed. Jan N. Bremmer and Jan R. Veenstra (Leuven: Peeters, 2002), 42–48.

42. One might compare the story of Jesus's exorcism of the Gerasene demoniac, in which the "legion" of demons inhabiting a man are transferred to a herd of pigs, which then hurl themselves into the sea (Mark 5:1–13).

43. On attempts to systematize the demons of monastic experience, see J. van der Vliet, "Demons in Early Coptic Monasticism: Image and Reality," in *Coptic Art and Culture*, ed. H. Hondelink (Cairo: Shouhdy, 1990), 135–56; and Brakke 2006.

44. Stewart 1991.

45. De Certeau 1996: 93.

46. Hunt 1998; Cuneo 2001, chaps. 10, 14.

47. Hammond and Hammond 1973: 47–48.

48. Hammond and Hammond 1973: 113–15.

49. Cf. Lewis 1989: 59–119, Stirrat 1977, 1992: 78–98.

50. The historical analysis of demonology in this chapter differs fundamentally from the more theological and sensationalist history of the devil produced by Jeffrey Burton Russell: *The Devil* (Ithaca: Cornell University Press, 1987); *Satan* (Ithaca, 1981); *Lucifer* (Ithaca, 1984); *Mephistopheles* (Ithaca, 1986); and *The Prince of Darkness* (Ithaca, 1988).

CHAPTER 3
Professionals in the Identification of Evil

1. Spirit-affliction and the hegemony of new prophets: Lewis 1989: 116–18. Demonization of local deities in Christianization: Van Beek 1994; Douglas 1999; Meyer 1994; 1996; 1999 (esp. chaps. 4, 6).

2. See Yonina Talmon, "Pursuit of the Millennium: The Relation between Religious and Social Change," *Archives européennes de sociologie* 3 (1962): 125–48; Kenelm Burridge, *New Heaven, New Earth: A Study of Millenarian Activities* (Oxford: Blackwell, 1969); Bryan R. Wilson, *Magic and the Millennium* (New York: Harper and Row, 1973).

3. Ngundeng: Douglas H. Johnson, *Nuer Prophets: A History of Prophecy from the Upper Nile in the Nineteenth and Twentieth Centuries* (Oxford: Clarendon, 1994), 96–99 (quotation from 96); Handsome Lake and Melanesian shaman: Thomas W. Overholt, *Prophecy in Cross-Cultural Perspective* (Atlanta: Scholars Press, 1986), 105, 112, 117, and 285–95, esp. 292–93.

4. Cf. Marcus 1999, and further, Forsyth 1987: 285–97.

5. A.-J. Festugière, *Les moines d'Orient 1: Culture ou sainteté* (Paris: Éditions du Cerf, 1961), chap. 1; Aufrère 1998; and Frankfurter 2003: 351–64.

6. Hymn "On Apa Antony," ed. and trans. K. H. Kuhn and W. J. Tait, *Thirteen Coptic Acrostic Hymns* (Oxford: Ashmolean, 1996), 128–29.

7. *Testament of Jacob*, in James H. Charlesworth, ed., *Old Testament Pseudepigrapha*, vol. 1 (Garden City, N.Y.: Doubleday, 1983).

8. Flint 1999; Frankfurter 2003.

9. Douglas 1999; see also Meyer 1994, 1999; and Frankfurter 2000.

10. Stirrat 1992: 87.

11. Cf. Caplan 1985.

12. Stirrat 1992: 89.

13. Stirrat 1992: 95, 97.

14. Comaroff 1997: 13.

15. See esp. Willis 1970, with specific discussions in Green 1997; Auslander 1993; Redmayne 1970; Richards 1982; Chakanza 1985; Yamba 1997.

16. Auslander 1993: 171.

17. Comaroff and Comaroff 1993; Moore and Sanders 2001. See now Meyer 2003: 27–28, 36, on the analogous role of contemporary Ghanaian popular films in discerning Satan's presence in the world.

18. On local witch-finders in early modern Europe: Thomas 1970; Klaniczay 1990: 236–43; de Blécourt 1994; Simpson 1996; Briggs 1996, chap. 5; MacFarlane 1999, chap. 8; Gijswijt-Hofstra 1999. Cf. Favret-Saada 1980.

19. Thomas 1970: 61, See also Thomas 1971: 185–86, 548–50.

20. John Gaule, *Select Cases of Conscience Touching Witches and Witchcrafts* (1646), 7, quoted in Clark 1997: 518. On the larger social function of witchcraft, as opposed to other explanations for misfortune, see Thomas 1970: 57; 1971: 542–46.

21. Lancashire 1612: Notestein 1968: 149 and chap. 7. Sixteenth-century Lorraine: Briggs 1996: 177–79. Seventeenth-century Basque: Henningsen 1980: 216, 326.

22. Bernardino of Siena, Sermon (1427), trans. in Kors and Peters 2001: 136–37. See Kieckhefer 1998 and Franco Mormando, *The Preacher's Demons: Bernardino of Siena and the Social Underworld of Early Renaissance Italy* (Chicago: University of Chicago Press, 1999), 52–108, esp. 52–72.

23. Simpson 1996: 15.

24. On the social status and claims of cunning men, see Briggs 1996: 182–87, and, on claims of supernatural clairvoyance in witch-finding, MacFarlane 1999: 126.

25. Briggs 1996: 187–208. On the rounding-up of local clairvoyants/witch-finders as witches, see also Ginzburg 1983 and Henningsen 1990.

26. Cohn 1993, chap. 9.

27. Ibid., chaps. 11–12; Levack 1995

28. Cohn 1993, chaps. 3–4, 11. The early witch-finders' appeal to heresiographical models to develop the notion of diabolical witchcraft is now explicit in early fifteenth-century documents from Switzerland: see Ostorero et al. 1999.

29. Ostorero et al. 1999; Bailey 2003; Jacques-Chaquin 1987. On manuals, see Anglo 1977; Cohn 1993: 68–73, 209–10; Levack 1995: 50–59; Broedel 2003, esp. 7–8.

30. Larner 1984: 4.

31. On extraction of testimony to complement or elaborate official models, see Trevor-Roper 1969: 101–2; Jacques-Chaquin 1978: 147–59; 1987: 78; Levack 1995: 53–59.

32. See Trevor-Roper 1969: 136–39, and Anglo 1977 on the *Malleus Maleficarum*'s warnings to civic officials.

33. Baroja 1965: 148, and chap. 11 in general. Cf. *Malleus Maleficarum* 3.15 and 2.12 on the dangers that witches are supposed to pose to inquisitors.

34. Monter 1976: 81–85.

35. Larner 1984: 14.

36. Baroja 1965, chap. 12; McGowan 1977; Jacques-Chaquin in De Lancre 1982: 10–15.

37. Kors and Peters 2001: 173–74.

38. De Lancre, *Tableau* 5.1, 3.2; Baroja 1965: 168–69.

39. Sharpe 1996: 237–38. See further Hopkins 1928 and Notestein 1968, chap. 8. On the unusual nature of the Hopkins witch-panic, see also Thomas 1970: 58; 1971: 451, 457–58; and MacFarlane 1999: 135–44.

40. On the circulation of such self-promotional tracts around English witch-finders, see Gibson 1999, who shows that some had actually read and learned from continental witch-finders.

41. Gaule, *Select Cases of Conscience*, p. 93, quoted in MacFarlane 1999: 141. On apocalyptic features of witch-finding, see Clark 1997: 321–62.

42. *Report of the Presidential Commission of Inquiry into the Cult of Devil Worship in Kenya.* (Nairobi: Kenya, 2000), http://www.lawafrica.com/reports/go.asp?file=devilworship.xml. See also Droz 1997.

43. Sweden (1668–1670): Ankarloo 1990: 295, 302–4, 309–10. Normandy (1670): Briggs 1996: 52, 195. Switzerland: Monter 1976: 59–60, 100, 138–40. In general, see Henningsen 1980: 208–16; Briggs 1996: 233–35; Sluhovsky 1996; and Clark 1997, chaps. 26–27. On the use of possession among women and disenfranchised classes, see Lewis 1989.

44. Clark 1997, chap. 28.

45. Thomas 1971: 483–89.

46. See Clark 1997: 426 on Lille (1613).

47. Boyer and Nissenbaum 1974: 1–21, 146–51.

48. Cotton Mather, "A Further Account of the Tryals of the New-England Witches, Sent in a Letter from Thence, to a Gentleman in London" (1693), repr. in *Cotton Mather: On Witchcraft* (New York: Bell, n.d.), 170.

49. Robert Calef, "More Wonders of the Invisible World" (1700), in Burr 1914: 344.

50. Calef, "More Wonders," in Burr 1914: 350.

51. Testimony of Nathaniel Cary, in ibid., 351.

52. On these features of the trials of Rebecca Nurse and Rev. Burroughs, see Boyer and Nissenbaum 1974: 14, 17, 148.

53. Calef, "More Wonders," in Burr 1914: 372.

54. Ibid., 373.

55. See esp. Sluhovsky 1996 on the coaching of the possessed.

56. On childrens' facility in these roles, see Ankarloo 1990: 303–4, 309; La Fontaine 1998: 113–18; and Boyer and Nissenbaum 1974: 23–30 for the performative aspects of the Salem trials.

57. Although cf. Roper 2000 on a case in 1723 Germany in which parents appealed to the state to imprison their children as witches.

58. Lewis 1989. On Salem, see Norton 2002. On cultural pressures and possession, see also Karen McCarthy Brown, *Mama Lola: A Vodou Priestess in Brooklyn* (Berkeley: University of California Press, 1991), 252–57.

59. Delbanco 1995. Works of Hal Lindsey: e.g., *Satan Is Alive and Well on Planet Earth* (Grand Rapids: Zondervan, 1972), and *Planet Earth, 2000 A.D.: Will Mankind Survive?* (Palos Verdes Calif.: Western Front, 1996). Works of Tim LaHaye: *Left Behind* series (12 volumes; Wheaton Ill.: Tyndale House, 1996–2004). Media and evil: Cuneo 1998; McAlister 2003. Evangelical influence: Passantino and Passantino 1992; Clark 2003, chaps. 1–2; Dyrendal 2003.

60; Luhrmann 2004.

61. Hunt 1998; Ellis 2000, chaps. 1–2; Cuneo 2001; cf. Hammond and Hammond 1973.

62. Hicks 1991a, 1991b; Ellis 1991: 288–90; Crouch and Damphousse 1991.

63. Nathan 1991.

64. See, on these cultural developments, Nathan 1991: 80–81; Armstrong 1994, chap. 11; Haaken 1998.

65. In general, see Nathan and Snedeker 1995: 53–106.

66. Core and Harrison 1991: 150, emphasis added.

67. Luhrmann 2004.

68. Smith and Pazder 1980.

69. Victor 1998: 203.

70. On Kee MacFarlane's background and interview methods, see Nathan and Snedeker 1995: 15–16, 50, 77–85, with critical remarks on 140–59.

71. Kee MacFarlane, testimony in "Child Abuse and Day Care: Joint hearing before the Subcommittee on Oversight of the Committee of Ways and Means, and Select Committee on Children, Youth, and Families" (September 17, 1984), 45.

72. Ibid., 46.

73. On Roland Summit: Nathan and Snedeker 1995: 20–21, 129. On the Darlings: ibid., 95–96, 99, 102–3.

74. Ibid., 129, 281n 112.

75. Transcript of presentation by Lieutenant Brad Darling, Santa Clara, California (April 1986), provided by Michael Snedeker. See Nathan and Snedeker 1995: 103.

76. Ibid., 102.

77. Ibid., 99–103, with transcript of April 1986 presentation.

78. On the metamorphosis to crusader, see ibid., 57, 146; La Fontaine 1998: 141. On other cases of zealous social workers, see Mark Smith, "Objectivity questioned in abuse probe at Gilmer," *Houston Chronicle* (May 22, 1994), regarding social workers Debbie Minshew and Ann Goar in Gilmer, Texas; and Bikel 1995, regarding Little Rascals nursery school (North Carolina). Cf. Holgerson 1995 on such techniques used in Sweden. The hybrid (MFA, Ph.D.) expert in "ritual crime" Dawn Perlmutter has assembled her own "Institute for the Research of Organized and Ritual Violence" (www .ritualviolence.com), published a handbook (*Investigating Religious Terrorism and Ritualistic Crimes* [CRC Press, 2003]), and consults with police departments (October 2005: Utah Division of the International Association for Identification).

79. Sandi Gallant: see Nathan and Snedeker 1995: 113, 129–30.

80. American influence on U.K. panic: Jenkins 1992: 158–61; La Fontaine 1998: 106–10; Medway 2001: 219–41.

81. Core and Harrison 1991, jacket cover; cf. Jenkins 1992: 167–69; John Parker, *At the Heart of Darkness: Witchcraft, Black Magic, and Satanism Today* (London: Sidgwick & Jackson, 1993), 305–7.

82. On general on the importation of SRA ideas to the United Kingdom, see Jenkins 1992, chaps. 7–8; La Fontaine 1998: 163–67 (with 173–74 on Coleman); and Medway 2001: 221–31 On Coleman's view of Satanic conspiracy, see Coleman 1994.

83. On the relative frequency of social workers (vs. psychiatrists and clinical psychologists) seeing SRA patients, see Goodman et al. 1994: 25, 40–41, 48.

84. Smith and Pazder 1980: 117.

85. Nathan and Snedeker 1995: 89; see 89–90, 113.

86. See esp. Matt Keenan, "The Devil and Dr. Braun," *New City* (June 22–28, 1995), 9–11; Bikel and Dretzin 1995.

87. See Ganaway 1992; Loftus 1993; D. Stephen Lindsay and J. Don Read, "Psychotherapy and Memories of Childhood Sexual Abuse: A Cognitive Perspective," *Applied Cognitive Psychology* 8 (1994): 281–338; Coons 1994; Spanos, Burgess, and Burgess 1994; Mulhern 1994; Ofshe and Watters 1994; Bikel and Dretzin 1995; Bikel 1995; Stroup 1996, chap. 3; Pope 1996; Lynn et al. 1998; Haaken 1998.

88. See Nathan 1991: 80–81 and Armstrong 1994, chap. 11.

89. Friesen 1992.

90. E.g., Sakheim and Devine 1992; *Journal for Theology and the Church* 20, no. 3 (1992); *Journal of Psychohistory* 21, no. 4 (1994); and the appreciative comments by Noblitt and Perskin (2000: 51, nn.48–50) on the work of Friesen.

91. Gould 1995: 335, 336, emphasis added (referring at the end to Lanning 1991).

92. Hill and Goodwin 1989; Katchen and Sakheim 1992; Kent 1993; Kahr 1994; DeMause 1994; Noblitt and Perskin 2000. See in general Frankfurter 2001.

93. Cory Hammond, taped lecture at the Fourth Annual Eastern Regional Meeting on Abuse and Multiple Personality, June 25–29, 1992, quoted in Ofshe and Watters 1994: 187. See esp. Mulhern 1991, 1994.

94. See now American Psychiatric Association Board of Trustees, "Statement on Memories of Sexual Abuse," *IJCEH* 42, no. 4 (1994): 261–64, and Samuel J. Knapp and Leon VandeCreek, *Treating Patients with Memories of Abuse: Legal Risk Management* (Washington, D.C.: APA, 1997), 102–5.

95. Bennett Braun, taped presentation given at the Midwestern Conference on Child Sexual Abuse and Incest, University of Wisconsin, Madison, October 12, 1992, quoted in Ofshe and Watters 1994: 248.

96. See Passantino and Passantino 1992; Victor 1993: 230–32; and equally in England: La Fontaine 1998: 28–29, 38–40, 121–22; Medway 2001: 159–61, 226–28, 368–72. McMinn and Wade 1995 find Christian therapists have a slightly higher likelihood of receiving SRA patients and finding SRA indicators in patients.

97. See Harding 1987; La Fontaine 1998: 38–39.

98. Victor 1993: 338. On Warnke and other born-again "ex-Satanists," see in general Mulhern 1994: 274–75; Medway 2001: 163–74, and Dyrendal 2003.

99. Ellis 2000, chaps. 1–2, 4.

100. Cuneo 2001: 95, 133–34, 151, 159.

101. Cf. Hunt 1998; Ellis 2000: 10–23, 32–40, 87–89; Cuneo 2001: 203.

102. MacNutt 1995, chap. 17; Cuneo 2001: 196–97, 210–11; Medway 2001: 251; Luhrmann 2004.

103. Wright 1994: 24–25.

104. Bromley 1994: 55–61.

105. See, e.g., the broad scope of misfortunes deemed Satanic in Raschke 1990.

CHAPTER 4
Rites of Evil

1. Minucius Felix, *Octavius* 9.5–7, ed. and trans. Gerald H. Rendall, Loeb Classical Library (London: Heinemann, 1931), 336–39. Athenagoras (*Legatio* 3.1; 31.1, early second century) and Tertullian (*Ad uxorem* 2.4–5, late second century) also refer to such rumors.

2. Pierre de Lancre, *Tableau de l'Inconstance des mauvais anges et démons* [1612], 6.2 (De Lancre 1982: 288–89).

3. Sharon J. Ireland and Murray J. Ireland, "A Case History of Family and Cult Abuse," *Journal of Psychohistory* 21, no. 4 (1994): 425–26.

4. Hsia 1988: 30.

5. Cf. Smith 1978: 427–28; 2004: 230–50.

6. Strabo 4.5.4, ed. Jones, Loeb Classical Library 2:258; Tacitus 5.5, ed. Moore, Loeb Classical Library 2:182. Further on ritual atrocities imputed to Jews in antiquity, see esp. Bickerman 1980.

7. On Scythians, see Strabo 7.3.6–9. In general on the sacrifices and perverse customs of the barbarian Other, see Hartog 1988: 180–92; Graf 1997: 26–27; Nippel 2002; Baraz 2003, chaps. 1–2.

8. *Acts of Andrew and Matthias* 1, ed and trans. Dennis Ronald MacDonald, *The Acts of Andrew and The Acts of Andrew and Matthias in the City of the Cannibals* (Atlanta: Scholars Press, 1990), 70–73.

9. Nock 1972: 170–71; Winkler 1980.

10. Achilles Tatius, *Leucippe and Clitophon* 3.15.1–5, trans. S. Gaselee, Loeb Classical Library (Cambridge, Mass.: Harvard University Press, 1969), 164–67.

11. Lollianos, *Phoinikika* B.1v, ed. Susan A. Stephens and John J. Winkler, *Ancient Greek Novels: The Fragments* (Princeton: Princeton University Press, 1995), 342–43.

12. See Brent D. Shaw, "'Eaters of Flesh, Drinkers of Milk': The Ancient Mediterranean Ideology of the Pastoral Nomad," *Ancient Society* 13–14 (1982–1983): 5–31; Rives 1995: 73–74; Beard, North, and Price 1998: 233–34.

13. Cassius Dio 68.32; 71.4.

14. Pseudo-Nilus of Ancyra, *Narratio* 3.3, ed. F. Conca (Leipzig: Teubner, 1983), 12–13, translation (with emphasis) mine.

15. Cf. W. Robertson Smith, *Lectures on the Religion of the Semites* (New York: Appleton, 1889), 319–33; Sigmund Freud, *Totem and Taboo*, trans. James Strachey (New York: Norton, 1950), 132–61; with critiques by Eliade 1976: 6–8; Bell 1997: 260–62; and Frankfurter 2001: 365–80. On the literary

nature of the Pseudo-Nilus text, see Daniel Caner, "Sinai Pilgrimage and Ascetic Romance: Pseudo-Nilus' *Narrationes* in Context," *Travel, Communication and Geography in Late Antiquity: Sacred and Profane*, ed. Linda Ellis and Frank L. Kidner (Aldershot: Ashgate, 2004), 135–47.

16. Bucher 1981; Zika 2003, chap. 10; Lestringant 1997: 24–25, 56–57; Jahoda 1999: 97–104.

17. Lestringant 1997: 29, quoting *Sensuyt le Nouveau Monde et Navigations*, f. 73v.

18. Cervantes 1994: 25–39.

19. See, e.g., Bronislaw Malinowski, *Argonauts of the Western Pacific* (New York: Dutton, 1961), 77, 237–44; Benson Saler, "Nagual, Witch, and Sorcerer in a Quiché Village," in *Magic, Witchcraft, and Curing*, ed. John Middleton (Austin: University of Texas Press, 1967), 86–87; Smith 1978: 427; Stewart 1991: 38–42.

20. João Manoel de Macedo, *Pai Royal-Feiticeiro*, trans. in Lindsay Hale (Rio de Janeiro: Typográfico Americain, 1869), 127–29; "Mama Oxum: Reflections of Gender and Sexuality in Brazilian Umbanda," in *Òsun Across the Waters: A Yoruba Goddess in Africa and the Americas*, ed. Joseph M. Murphy and Mei-Mei Sanford (Bloomington: Indiana University Press, 2001), 223.

21. See Hurbon 1995: 185–93.

22. On images of monstrous inversion in African witch-beliefs, see La Fontaine 1963: 196–97, 214–15; Mair 1969: 36–42; Chilver 1990: 233; Niehaus 2002; and among the Navaho, see Kluckholn 1944: 26-30, 138–48.

23. See Cohn 1993, chap. 9; cf. Kluckholn 1944: 27.

24. Muchembled 1990: 146–53; Bailey 1996; Broedel 2003.

25. *Errores Gazariorum*, trans. E. Peters, in Kors and Peters 2001: 161.

26. Ostorero, in Ostorero, Bagliania, and Utz Tremp 1999, 308–9.

27. See Stephens 2002: 32–124.

28. Remy 1974: 61 (1.17).

29. Bronislaw Malinowski, *Coral Gardens and Their Magic* (New York: American Books, 1935; repr. New York: Dover, 1978), 2:218–23.

30. Cf. Zika 2003, chaps. 6–7, 10–12.

31. McGowan 1977: 191, 192. Cf. De Lancre, *Tableau de l'Inconstance*, bk. 2, disc. 4, plus "Description et figure de Sabbat des Sorciers," in De Lancre 1982: 56.

32. Cf. Ginzburg 1983; Henningsen 1990; Klaniczay 1990.

33. Cf. Meyer 2003, and further on Mami Wata as emblem of a fruitful Otherness, see Kramer 1993: 217–39.

34. Meyer 1995; Ogembo 2001.

35. Cf. Meyer 2003; Bastian 2001.

36. Meeting of National Council of Churches of Kenya, January 30, 1998: "Devil Worship Probe Reveals Differing Opinions," Africa News Service, February 16, 1998. Witch-cleansing movements: Ogembo 2001, plus "Kenya 'Witch Hunters' Lynch 10 People," Reuters September 5, 1998.

37. Droz 1997.

38. *Report of the Presidential Commission of Inquiry into the Cult of Devil-Worship in Kenya* (Nairobi: Kenya, 2000), http://www.lawafrica.com/reports/go.asp?file=devilworship.xml, §§93, 91bis, p. 43.

39. Ibid., §96, p. 45. §95 alleges animal metamorphoses of devotees.

40. Cf. Meyer 1995; Ogembo 2001: 17–18.

41. Cf. Meyer 1995; Shaw 1996; Bastian 2002, 2003; O'Brien 2000: 520–25.

42. Brown 1970; Kippenberg 1997; Gordon 1999: 253–66.

43. Gordon 1987 and Johnston 1995 on ancient images of the night-witch.

44. Lucan, *Pharsalia* 6.507–9, 553–59, trans. Georg Luck, in *Arcana Mundi* (Baltimore: Johns Hopkins University Press, 1985), 197, 198. Cf. Horace, *Epode* 5, in which a group of witches prepare to extract the organs of a boy.

45. Philostratus, *V. Apollonii* 7.11, ed. and trans. Conybeare, Loeb Classical Library (Cambridge, Mass.: Harvard University Press, 1912), 2:168–69.

46. Beard, North, and Price 1998: 228–44.

47. Bacchanalia: Livy, *Ab urbe condita* 39.8–14, with discussions in Pailler 1988: 523–96 (and 21–24, 214–18, on Bacchanalia as a "cult conspiracy"); Beard, North, and Price 1998: 95–96; Nagy 2002:

48. Minucius Felix, *Octavius* 9.5–7, ed. and trans. Rendall, etc.

49. Rives 1995: 77–80.

50. Zika 2003: 458.

51. Henrichs 1970: 33. Cf. E. R. Dodds, *The Greeks and the Irrational* (Berkeley: University of California Press, 1951), esp. 270–82; Eliade 1976: 87–93; Benko 1984, chap. 3; and Wilken 1984: 19–21.

52. See further Frankfurter 2001.

53. Edwards 1992; McGowan 1994; Rives 1995; Williams 1996, chap. 8; and esp. Cohn 1993: 1–15

54. Tertullian, *Apologia* 40.1.

55. Georg Simmel, *Conflict and the Web of Group-Affiliations*, trans. Kurt H. Wolff and Reinhard Bendix (New York: Free Press, 1955); Lewis A. Coser, *The Functions of Social Conflict* (New York: Free Press, 1956); and Smith 2004:251–302, esp. 274–76. On such rhetoric in early Christianity, see Pagels

1991 and David Frankfurter, "Jews or Not? Reconstructing the 'Other' in Rev. 2:9 and 3:9," *Harvard Theological Review* 94, no. 4 (2001): 403–25.

56. Cf. Coser, *Functions of Social Conflict*, 70.

57. Epiphanius of Salamis, *Panarion* 26.3.3–5.7, trans. Philip R. Amidon, *The Panarion of St. Epiphanius, Bishop of Salamis: Selected Passages* (New York: Oxford University Press, 1990), 76–77.

58. I am, of course, indebted in this discussion to Douglas 1966.

59. Pseudo-Dioscorus, *Panegyric on Macarios*, 5.1–2, trans. in Johnson 1980: 22–23. See also Frankfurter 2000: 287–89.

60. Cohn 1975, chaps. 2–3; 1993, chaps. 3–4.

61. Paul of Chartres, *Narrative of Heretics of Orléans*, trans. in Wakefield and Evans 1991: 78–79, emphasis mine.

62. Cf. Adémar of Chabannes, *Chronicle* 3.59, trans. in Wakefield and Evans 1991: 75.

63. Cohn 1993, chap. 9.

64. *Errores Gazariorum*, trans. in Kors and Peters 2001: 160–61. Cf. Utz Tremp, in Ostorero, Bagliania, and Utz Tremp 1999: 290–91.

65. Cf. Hans Fründ (1428), ed. and trans. Catherine Chène, in Ostorero Bagliania, and Utz Tremp 1999: 36–37.

66. On these aspects of the *Errores Gazariorum*, see Bailey 1996 and Ostorero in Ostorero, Bagliania, and Utz Tremp 1999: 308–9, 314–21, 327–28.

67. Boguet 1929: xliv; cf. Briggs 1996:161.

68. Haliczer 1987; Hsia 1988: 7–12; Langmuir 1990: 271–77; Rubin 1999: 72–78.

69. Euripides, *Bacchae*, 751–54, 122–31, trans. William Arrowsmith, *Euripides 5*, The Complete Greek Tragedies (Chicago: University of Chicago Press, 1959), 187, 204.

70. Cf. Dirk Obbink, "Dionysus Poured Out: Ancient and Modern Theories of Sacrifice and Cultural Formation," in *Masks of Dionysus*, ed. Thomas H. Carpenter and Christopher A. Faraone (Ithaca: Cornell University Press, 1993), 65–86.

71. Thomas 1971, chap. 3; Clark 1997: 360–62.

72. One must reckon with some negative potency in Protestant responses to Catholic ritual objects: see Natalie Zemon Davis, "The Rites of Violence," in *Society and Culture in Early Modern France* (Stanford: Stanford University Press, 1975), 152–87, 315–26.

73. Barnett 1999: 107.

74. On this caricature of ritual, see Mary Douglas, *Natural Symbols* (New York: Pantheon, 1982), chap. 1; Peter Burke, "The Repudiation of Ritual in

Early Modern Europe," in *The Historical Anthropology of Early Modern Italy* (Cambridge: Cambridge University Press, 1987), 223–38; Jonathan Z.Smith, *Drudgery Divine: On the Comparison of Early Christianities and the Religions of Late Antiquity* (Chicago: University of Chicago Press, 1990), esp. 44–46; Bell 1997: 253–67; Barnett 1999, chap. 6. On scatological and demonological characterizations of Catholic cult in early Protestantism, see Philip M. Soergel, *Wondrous in His Saints: Counter-Reformation Propaganda in Bavaria* (Berkeley: University of California Press, 1993), 60–69, 152–58.

75. Increase Mather, *An Essay for the Recording of Illustrious Providences* (1684), chap. 4, p. 127. John Wesley, *Concise Ecclesiastical History* (London, 1781), 1:262, quoted in Barnett 1999: 115.

76. Joseph Jacobs, "Little St. Hugh of Lincoln: Researches in History, Archaeology, and Legend," in Dundes 1991: 44. See also Hsia 1988: 38 and Baraz 2003: 79–80.

77. Medway 2001: 3–6, 79–99, 142–43, and Introvigne 1997.

78. Bataille 1962.

79. Jules Michelet, *La Sorcière*, trans. A. R. Allison (Paris: Carrington, 1904; in French with van Maele engravings, Paris: Chevrel, 1911). Interestingly, G. Christopher Hudson's illustrations accompanying Michelet's 1939 English translation (New York: Walden) clearly stress the savage-orgiastic interpretation of ritual, with naked and nubile women frolicking wildly and lasciviously with devils.

80. J.-K. Huysman, *Là-Bas*, trans. Brendan King (Sawtry: Dedalus, 2001), 254. On Huysman's Black Mass fantasy, see Praz 1970: 320–41; Introvigne 1997: 100–42, esp. 135–37.

81. Smith and Pazder 1980: 117.

82. Frankfurter 2001: 357–59.

83. Kent 1993: 234, 236.

84. See Bullard 1989, Whitmore 1995, Partridge 2004. Cf. Spanos, Burgess, and Burgess 1994.

85. Kent 1993: 229–41.

86. Hill and Goodwin 1989: 43; Kahr 1994: 53; Katchen and Sakheim 1992: 21–43; Noblitt and Perskin 2000, chap. 8.

87. Kieckhefer 1998.

88. While the category "religion" is most certainly a modern Western construction with a discernable post-Reformation character, local cultures have long developed their own constructions of areas of meaningful action, even if used to differentiate themselves from others. See on these categories Talal Asad, *Genealogies of Religion: Discipline and Reasons of Power in Christianity and*

Islam (Baltimore: Johns Hopkins University Press, 1993), 27–79, and Smith 2004: 179–96.

89. Cohn 1993: 7.

90. Rowland 1990: 163–68.

91. Stephens 2002: 197–240, 249–56.

92. Hsia 1988, chaps. 1–2; Haliczer 1987; Rubin 1999: 59–60, 87.

93. Lucan, *Pharsalia* 6.554–58, trans. Luck, in *Arcana Mundi* 198

94. Campion-Vincent 1990; cf. Scheper-Hughes 1996, 2000. In 1985 Ann Landers addressed rumors that aborted babies were being processed into cosmetic collagen creams (July 16, 1985). This discussion is not to deny that in some contemporary cases maverick ritual experts in Africa have killed for body-parts to use in some rituals: see discussion in chapter 7, below.

95. Cf. Frankfurter 2001: 365–80, and on new understandings of the nature of sacrifice, Smith 1987 and McClymond 2002, 2004.

96. Katchen and Sakheim 1992: 25–26.

97. DeMause 1994: 510, 511; cf. 512, where the author asserts that trance states and group-merging with the leader are typical of SRA.

98. Cf. Jacques-Chaquin 1987; Kieckhefer 1998: 105–7.

99. Kieckhefer 1998: 105.

100. See Moscovici 1987, Bromley 1994.

101. Jacques-Chaquin 1987: 76–80.

102. Hualde, *The Bishop's Report*, f. 8, SD Text 8, trans. in Henningsen 1980: 209.

103. Noblitt and Perskin 2000: 159.

104. Gould 1995, quoted above (p. 63).

105. Jacques-Chaquin 1987: 82.

106. Moore 1987: 100.

CHAPTER 5
Imputations of Perversion

1. E.g., Louis Cozolino, "Some Questions Come to Mind: A Response to Ganaway," *Journal for Theology and the Church* 20, no. 3 (1992): 206–7; Stephen A. Kent, "Diabolic Debates: A Reply to David Frankfurter and J. S. La Fontaine," *Religion* 24 (1994): 361–78.

2. Early Christians: e.g., Benko 1984: 54–78. Jewish ritual murder: see Strack 1971 [1909]: vi–xvi, 206–35. Witches' Sabbats: Murray 1921; Ginzburg 1991; see in general Cohn 1993.

3. Cf. Praz 1970: 320–41; Bataille 1986: 108.

4. See, e.g., Arens 1979: 27–28; Lestringant 1997: 27–31; Jahoda 1999: 101–4.

5. See esp. Rives 1995.

6. See Smith 1978: 425–30; 2004: 230–50.

7. Geschiere 1997: 40. Further on the "society" of witches, see Evans-Pritchard in Marwick 1982: 31 (Azande); Parsons in Marwick 1982: 235 (Pueblo); and cf. Stewart 1991: 175–77 on the "society" of demons in Greek imagination.

8. Nock 1972: 170; Winkler 1980: 166–75.

9. Baraz 2003.

10. New World cannibals: Arens 1979, Bucher 1981, Lestringant 1997, Jahoda 1999. Influence of images on witch-cult illustrations: Zika 2003, chaps. 10–12.

11. See Briggs 1996: 384–92.

12. Haaken 1998.

13. Rubin 1999.

14. Stephens 2002, chaps. 1–4.

15. Cf. Jacques-Chaquin in De Lancre 1982: 36–37.

16. Gilmore 2003, chaps. 5–8.

17. Rachel L. Swarns, "Not Your Usual Vampires, but Scary Nonetheless," *New York Times*, January 14, 2003.

18. On local fascination with the nature of demons and night-witches, see Stewart 1991, esp. 12–16, 99–108, 162–91; Johnston 1995; Cohn 1993, chap. 9; Mair 1969: 36–42.

19. See esp. Cohn 1993.

20. Cohn 1975: 258–63; cf. Briggs 1996: 163–68, 373–74, 384–88; Twitchell 1985, chap. 2; Gilmore 2003. Both "recovered memory" therapists and their antipsychoanalytic critics, like Frederick Crews ("The Revenge of the Repressed," *New York Review of Books* [November 17, 1994]: 54–60; [December 1, 1994]: 49–58) distorted an originally subtle notion of repression, which concerned repudiated impulses that became distanced, yet intrinsic to the self, over the course of development. It is a pity that the same term "repression" came to legitimize a simplistic theory of traumatic memory that itself paved the way for uncritical acceptance of SRA claims.

21. Epiphanius, *Panarion* 26.

22. A. McGowan 1994, Rives 1995, Cohn 1993, chap.3. Use of Epiphanius: Boguet 1929, chap. 21.

23. *Malleus Maleficarum* 1.6, 8–9; 2.1.4, with Stephens 2002, chaps. 1–4 and Broedel 2003.

24. Genital mutilation in Jewish ritual murder: Hsia 1988: 29, 74, with images of Simon of Trent (1493), 49, and Regensburg children (1615), 221. Orléans 1969: Morin 1971, esp. 44–48, 55–66; cf. Roger Cohen, "Calais Rumormongers Mirror a Demonic Time for Europe," *New York Times* October 30, 1992: A1, 4.

25. Anne Hart, "A Survivor's Account," in Patricia L. Pike and Richard J. Mohline, "Ritual Abuse and Recovery: Survivors' Personal Accounts," *Journal of Psychology and Theology* 23, no. 1 (1995): 47.

26. Peter Williamson, *French and Indian Cruelty: Exemplified in the Life and Various Vicissitudes of Fortune of Peter Williamson* (5th ed., Edinburgh, 1762; facsimile edition, Bristol: Thoemmes Press, 1996); see Pauline Turner Strong, *Captive Selves, Captivating Others: The Politics and Poetics of Colonial American Captivity Narratives* (Boulder, Colo.: Westview, 1999), esp. 195–200.

27. Bucher 1981, Jahoda 1999: 15–25; Lestringant 1997; Zika 2003: 427–44.

28. Further on secrecy and transgression, see Urban 2003: 302–3.

29. Bataille 1962.

30. Haaken 1998, esp. chaps. 4, 10; De Certeau 1996, chaps. 3, 7; and on erotic imagination in cloistered environments, Elliott 1999.

31. Elliott 1999: 8–9.

32. On female nakedness and witchcraft, see remarks on Hans Baldung Grien's "Three Witches" (1514) in Margaret Miles, *Carnal Knowing: Female Nakedness and Religious Meaning in the Christian West* (New York: Vintage, 1989), 136–38; Clark 1997: 11–13; and Zika 2003, chaps. 6–7. Female nakedness and cannibalistic savagery in the Americas: Bucher 1981, chap. 5.

33. Roper 1994: 206. See in general idem, 1994: 203–6; Jacques-Chaquin 1978: 154–56.

34. See esp. Stewart 1991: 106–8, 176–77.

35. See Levack 1995: 137–38, 143–44, and Rebecca Lesses' important discussion of the demoness Lilith, "Exe(o)rcising Power: Women as Sorceresses, Exorcists, and Demonesses in Babylonian Jewish Society of Late Antiquity," *Journal of the American Academy of Religion* 69, no. 2 (2001): 354–59.

36. Stephens 2002: 54.

37. Cf. Shaffer and Cozolino 1992: 191; Rose 1996: 44.

38. See Haaken 1998: 188–89. The foundational essay on this type of imaginative identification with a victim is Freud 1955 [1919].

39. Bullard 1989, Spanos, Burgess, and Burgess 1994: 437–38; Whitmore 1995: 70–72; with primary sources including Gwen L. Dean, "Comparison of Abduction Accounts with Ritual Maltreatment," in *Alien Discussions: Proceedings of the Abduction Study Conference*, ed. Andrea Pritchard et al.

(Cambridge, Mass.: North Cambridge Press, 1994), 354–66; and David M. Jacobs, *The Threat: Revealing the Secret Alien Agenda* (New York: Simon and Schuster, 1998), 185–207. Cf. Partridge 2004.

40. Haaken 1998, chap. 4 (quotation, 100).

41. Mock-wedding dress: Hart, in Patricia L. Pike and Richard S. Moline, "Ritual Abuse and Recovery: Survivors' Personal Accounts," *Journal of Psychology & Theology* 23, no. 1 (1995): 47. Drawing of ritual abuse: Fraser, "Visions of Memories: A Patient's Visual Representation of Ritual Abuse Ceremonies," in Fraser 1997: 193–96.

42. Zika 2003, chap. 6. On oral-genital themes in monster legends, see Twitchell 1985.

43. Haaken 1998: 93–95, 231; Gilmore 2003: 180–84. The foundational essays are Melanie Klein's "Criminal Tendencies in Normal Children" [1927], "Personification in the Play of Children" [1929], and "The Early Development of Conscience in the Child" [1933], in *Love, Guilt and Reparation and Other Works, 1921–1945* (New York: Delacorte, 1975), 170–85, 199–209, 248–57.

44. In Kent 1993: 237

45. Henri Boguet, 1929: 56–57, chap. 21.

46. E.g., Guazzo, *Compendium* 1.12; De Lancre, *Tableaux* 3.5. In general, Jacques-Chaquin in De Lancre 1982: 34–35, Briggs 1996: 382–84, 390–92; and Pócs 1999, chap. 5.

47. Ofshe 1992, esp. 142–49; Wright 1994, chap. 11.

48. Cf. F. Janker and P. Janker-Bakker, "Experiences with Ritualistic Child Sexual Abuse: A Case Study from the Netherlands," *Child Abuse & Neglect* 15: 191–96; Nathan and Snedeker: 114–15; La Fontaine 1998, chap. 7.

49. Roper 2000.

50. Cf. Kieckhefer 1998.

51. Minucius Felix, *Octavius* 9.5.

52. Epiphanius, *Panarion* 26.5.5.

53. Zika 2003, chap. 12; Stephens 2002: 249–56.

54. See De Lancre, *Tableau* 3.3. See Jacques-Chaquin 1978: 142–44 and, on fifteenth-century Swiss depictions of witches' cannibalism, Utz Tremp and Ostorero, in Ostorero Bagliania, and Utz Tremp 1999: 57–58, 320–21.

55. Hsia 1988, chap. 1; cf. Bynum 1987: 48–69.

56. Rubin 1999.

57. See Hsia 1988: 75, 204 (on Regensburg case); Trachtenberg 1943: 134–39; Langmuir 1990: 271–77; and Zika 2003: 473–79.

58. Cassius Dio, *History* 68.32; *Corpus Papyrorum Judaicarum* 437 (papyrus letter in which a mother prays that her son might not be "roasted" by the

Jews); Apion, apud Josephus, c. *Apionem*, 2.91–96. See in general, Bickerman 1980; and Peter Schäfer, *Judaeophobia: Attitudes Toward the Jews in the Ancient World* (Cambridge, Mass.: Harvard University Press, 1997), 62–65.

59. McGowan 1994; Rives 1995; Zika 2003, chap. 12.

60. Augé 1982: 229–33; Twitchell 1985, chap. 2; Gilmore 2003: 176–84.

61. Twitchell 1985, chap. 3.

62. See Freud 1955 [1919] and Devereux 1980 [1966]. On the symbolism of the fetus among antiabortion protesters, see Faye D. Ginsburg, *Contested Lives: The Abortion Debate in an American Community* (Berkeley: University of California Press, 1989), 104–7.

63. Sanday 1986, chap. 5.

64. Lewis 1986; Shaw 1996; cf. Whitehead 2002: 193–94 on similar understandings of cannibalism in Guyana.

65. Cervantes 1994, chap. 1.

66. Hsia 1988, chap.1, and Camporesi 1995: 53–76; Alan Dundes, "The Ritual Murder or Blood Libel Legend: A Study of Anti-Semitic Victimization through Projective Inversion," in Dundes 1991, 336–76.

67. Winter 1963; La Fontaine 1963; Needham 1978: 33–42; Pocock 1985.

68. Needham 1978: 35–50.

69. Lesourd 1973; McGowan 1977; Clark 1997: 90–91, chap. 2; and Pócs 1999: 88–91.

70. Eni 1987: 18.

71. Meyer 1995:248. Cf. Meyer 2003 and more broadly Thoden van Velzen and Van Wetering 2001.

72. Bastian 2001: 82–88 (quotation, 82).

73. See Lewis 1989.

74. Stirrat 1977; Cuneo 2001: 225.

75. De Certeau 1996, chaps. 4, 7; Sluhovsky 2002.

76. Sr. Jeanne des Anges, *Autobiographie*, ed. Gabriel Legué and Gilles de la Tourette (Paris: Delahaye and Lecrasmier, 1886; 2nd ed. Montbonnet-St. Martin: Millon, 1985), 76, trans. in De Certeau 1996: 29.

77. Ibid., 79, trans. in De Certeau 1996: 31.

78. De Certeau 1996: 104–6; see also Walker and Dickerman 2001: 4–9 (contemporaneous French case, also expressing sexual desire in demonized form), and Sluhovsky 2002: 1396–1405 on wider context of sexual discourse. Cf. Haaken 1998: 235–37, on SRA fantasies.

79. Taussig 1987: 104–21; cf. Shaw 1996: 46–51.

80. Taussig 1987: 105.

81. Roger Casement, "Correspondence respecting the Treatment of British Colonial Subjects and Native Indians Employed in the Collection of

Rubber in the Putumayo District," *House of Commons Sessional Papers* (February 14, 1912–March 1913), 68: 103, 104, quoted in Taussig 1987: 125–26.

82. Taussig 1987: 133; cf. Taussig 1993: 63–68.

83. Haaken 1998.

84. Haaken 1998, esp. chap. 4.

85. See esp. Zika 2003: 456–58, 473–79.

86. Chaucer, "The Prioress's Tale," ll. 548–57, trans. Nevill Coghill (London, 1977), in Dundes 1991: p. 94. Original:

Twies a day it passed thurgh his throte,

To scoleward and homward whan he wente,

On cristes mooder set was his entente.

As I have seyd, thurghout the juerie,

This litel child, as he cam to and fro,

Ful murily than wolde he synge and crie

O alma redemptoris everemo.

The swetnesse hath his herte perced so

Of cristes mooder that, to hire to preye,

He kan nat stynte of syngyng by the weye.

87. Philip de Vier, *Blood Ritual* (Hillsboro, W.V.: National Vanguard Books, 2001), 106.

88. Hsia 1988: 50–56, 204; Rubin 1999: 77–78. On children in European witch-panics, see Monter 1993: 383–85 and Ankarloo 1990: 302–5, 309–10 (1675 Sweden). Cf. Sarah Iles Johnston, "Charming Children: The Use of the Child in Ancient Divination," *Arethusa* 34 (2001): 97–117.

89. Boguet 1929: 7–8, chap. 4.

90. Rubin 1999: 24.

91. Nathan and Snedeker 1995; Holgerson 1995; La Fontaine 1998, chap. 7.

92. See Bettelheim 1976: 8–9, 74–75, 120–23, 144–50.

93. Remy, *Demonolatry*, 2.2. See Monter 1993.

94. Roper 2000: 127.

95. European witch-hunts: Cohn 1975, 258–63; De Certeau 1996; Briggs 1996, chap. 10; Roper 1994, chap. 9; Elliott 1999. Fantasy in SRA "memories": Ganaway 1989; Spanos, Burgess, and Burgess 1994; Haaken 1998; Lynn et al. 1998; and Night-witch: Needham 1978: 23–50; cf. Stewart 1991, Gilmore 2003.

CHAPTER 6
The Performance of Evil

1. "Safety Management for Conference Attendees" (2002), http: // members.aol.com/smartnews/conference_safety.htm, accessed May 24, 2005; "Ritual Abuse Hot-Line Training: Material for a Training Session on Ritual Abuse for Crisis Counselors and Hot-line Workers" (1995), http: //www .rainfo.org/resources/ra_hotl.shtml, accessed May 24, 2005. See also "Psychiatric Patients Thought Police Officers Were a Satanic Cult [Houston]" (Associated Press, September 23, 1998): "One former patient has testified that therapists told them cult members joined professions beginning with the letter 'P.' That included priests, police, politicians, physicians, and plumbers."

2. Lévi-Strauss 1963 (quotation, 174).

3. See Carol Laderman and Marina Roseman, eds., *The Performance of Healing* (New York: Routledge, 1996), esp. articles by Schieffelin, Laderman, and Desjarlais.

4. Hammond and Hammond 1973: 49, 50

5. Cuneo 2001: 224–25.

6. Cf. Cuneo 2001: 218–20; Hunt 1998. Further on the diverse functions of demon-possession: Lewis 1989; Stirrat 1977; Ferber 1993; Briggs 1996: 388–89; Sluhovsky 1996; and De Certeau 2000, chap. 7.

7. Anson D. Shupe Jr. and David G. Bromley, "Apostates and Atrocity Stories," in *The Social Impact of New Religious Movements*, ed. Bryan Wilson (New York: Rose of Sharon, 1981), 179–215.

8. On the nature of real Satanist groups, see Moody 1974; William Sims Bainbridge, "Social Construction from Within: Satan's Process," in Richardson, Best, and Bromley 1991: 297–310; La Fontaine 1999: 94–114; pace Raschke 1990: 81–157.

9. On evangelical contexts for ex-Satanists: Passantino and Passantino 1992; Medway 2001, chap. 7; Dyrendal 2003.

10. On evangelical deliverance ideology: Susan F. Harding, "Convicted by the Holy Spirit: The Rhetoric of Fundamental Baptist Conversion," *American Ethnologist* 14 (1987): 167–81.

11. Jenkins and Maier-Katkin 1991; Lowney 1997: 108–11.

12. Cf. Walker and Dickerman 2001 on a French *possédée* later tried as a witch, and Sluhovsky 1996 on the performative agency of the possessed.

13. Linda Dégh and Andrew Vázsonyi, "Does the Word 'Dog' Bite? Ostensive Action: A Means of Legend-Telling," *Journal of Folklore Research* 20 (1983): 5–34; Ellis 1989, 1990, 1991.

14. Ellis 1989; Victor 1993, chap. 7. An additional form of enacting evil that ought properly to be brought into consideration of the full range would be Devil-masquing in Latin-American festivals: sometimes meant to intimidate, sometimes to amuse.

15. Kramer 1993, esp. 240–53; Taussig 1993.

16. Cf. Fraser 1993 on exorcism narratives as articulations of Multiple Personality Disorder.

17. Briggs 1996: 388–82.

18. Cf. studies of the "creation" of Satanic abusers in Ofshe and Watters 1994, chaps. 8, 11.

19. Bastian 2002.

20. See Willis 1970: 130–31; Bourdillon 2000: 191–93.

21. Modernity and witchcraft idioms: Geschiere 1997, 2001; Moore and Sanders 2001. Witch-cleansing as revolt against seniors: Willis 1968: 10–13; Auslander 1993; Douglas 1999; Ogembo 2001; Geschiere 2001: 64–65.

22. Auslander 1993 (quotation, 173). On increasing brutality of witch-finding since 1950s, see also Green 1997 (Tanzania); Yamba 1997 (Zambia); Geschiere 1997: 183–87 and 2001 (Cameroon); and Ogembo 2001 (Kenya).

23. Bastian 2001: 82–88.

24. For what follows, Henningsen 1980: 30–36.

25. Henningsen 1980: 52–54.

26. Cf. Favret-Saada 1980 on European witchcraft accusations in their local context.

27. Jacques-Chaquin 1978: 157–58; Clark 1997: 513.

28. De Lancre, *Tableau* 3.4, in De Lancre 1982: 193.

29. Stephens 2002: 196. See in general Jacques-Chaquin 1978: 146–59. Carrying the accused above the ground: *Malleus Maleficarum* 3.8 (Kramer 1971: 215). On the dramatic effects (and misogynist implications) of stripping the accused: Roper 1994: 205–8; Levack 1995: 137–38; Rowlands 2001: 57–60.

30. Stephens 2002: 36.

31. Jacques-Chaquin 1978: 158–60.

32. Joseph Jacobs, "Little St. Hugh of Lincoln: Researches in History, Archaeology, and Legend," in Jacobs, ed., *Jewish Ideals and Other Essays* (New York: Macmillan, 1896), 192–224, repr. in Dundes 1991: 41–71, esp. 43–45.

33. Langmuir 1984: 835.

34. Ibid., 835–36.

35. Note that in 1238, converts assembled from around Europe by the German emperor Frederick II to judge a case of Jewish ritual murder explained that the charges did not fit in any way with Jewish law or tradition: Langmuir 1990: 264–65.

36. Hsia 1988: 29–30, cf. 75.

37. Ibid., 30.

38. See Frankfurter 2004.

39. See Ginzburg 1983; Henningsen 1990; Cohn 1993: 162–80, 211–33; and Pócs 1999: 73–105.

40. See Hunt 1998; Cuneo 2001: 151, 159.

41. Chakanza 1985: 232–33 (Malawi, 1953); cf. Yamba 1997: 213–14. The technique is an extension of what Ellis has called "quasi-ostension" (Ellis 1991: 289–91).

42. Mather, *Memorable Providences*, §§12–22, in Hall 1999: 267–75, and Burr 1914: 107–19.

43. See esp. Lewis 1989; Sluhovsky 1996; De Certeau 1996, chap. 7.

44. E.g., cases in Hartford, Connecticut, in 1662 (in Hall 1999: 149–54) and Groton, Massachusetts, in 1671 (in Hall 1999: 197–212).

45. *Apud* Deodat Lawson, *A Brief and True Narrative of Some Remarkable Passages* . . . (1692), in Hall 1999: 285–88.

46. Lowney 1997: 108–10.

47. Sally Jesse Raphael Show, February 28, 1989: "Baby Breeders," quoted in Victor 1993: 84–85.

48. See Haaken 1998: 88–102, esp. 90, 92.

49. See Armstrong 1994, chap. 11.

50. See MacNutt 1995, chap. 17; Cuneo 2001: 209–12.

51. Goodman et al. observe that "a very small group of clinicians, each claiming to have treated scores of cases, accounted for most of the reports of ritualistic child abuse" (1994: 63).

52. Glass 1993: 103–6; Johnson 1994; Brenner 1994; Youngson 1994; Fraser 1997: 125–26.

53. Mollon 1994: 139.

54. See Stroup 1996: 148–55.

55. Cozolino 1990: 226; Mollon 1994: 147.

56. See esp. Haaken 1998: 211–21.

57. Casement 1994: 23–24.

58. Therapists' recantations of this worldview are thus extraordinarily rare, testifying to the permanence of these conversions. The most reflective

recantation (of a sort) is George A. Fraser, "Ritual Abuse: Lessons Learned as a Therapist," in Fraser 1997: 119–35.

59. Pearlman and Saakvitne 1995: 146. See further 144–46 and passim on countertransference and vicarious traumatization in trauma therapy.

60. Stroup 1996: 162–70, 195–96; cf. Bloom 1994: 462–69. Columbia University psychiatrist Michael Stone is reportedly proposing the incorporation of the category "evil" in forensic psychology (*New York Times*, February 8, 2005).

61. Glass 1993: 103.

62. Mollon 1994: 139.

63. Bastian 2003: 78.

64. See Ellis 1990, 1991.

65. Rubin 1999: 54; cf. 88–89.

66. See Rubin 1999: 91, 108.

67. Ibid., 24–28, 77–78.

68. On historical prototypes to modern Satanic-Goth self-presentations, see Praz 1970, chap. 5; Introvigne 1997; and Medway 2001: 9–21.

69. See Ellis 1991: 281 on "folk groups," and Introvigne 2000 on historical relationships among these groups.

70. L. Clark 2003, chap. 1, and Lowney 1995. On the impact of religious attitudes on deviant self-definition, see also L. Clark 2003: 79–81, 89.

71. Bourget, Gagnon, and Bradford 1988.

72. Moody 1974; Lowney 1995. Compare Dresser 1989 and Keyworth 2002 on self-defined Vampires.

73. Lewis 2001, 2002.

74. Levine and Strumpf 1983; Williams, "For More Youths, It's Always Halloween," *New York Times*, October 25, 1989; Lewis 2001: 8.

75. B. Friesen 1990; Ellis 1990; Lowney 1995: 463–65, 478.

76. Note that mimesis of the Devil has often invited parody as part of performance, such as in Devil-masquing in Europe and Latin America.

77. See Ellis 1990, 1991.

78. Langone and Blood 1990: 44–72; Raschke 1990; Passantino and Passantino 1992. Self-proclaimed police Satanism expert Don Rimer still (2005) offers his seminar "Satanism and the Occult: The New Youth Subculture" to police and community groups around Virginia and further afield: see, e.g., *The Virginian Pilot* (May 14, 2001): B1 and *The Roanoke Times* (February 22, 2002): B1, and promotional brochures kindly provided to me by Robert Hicks, Virginia Dept. of Criminal Justice, Richmond, Virginia, in March 2003).

79. "Satanic" crimes by individuals with prior sociopathy: Douglas Belkin and Chris Frates, "Suspected Satanism Frightens Neighbors," *Boston Globe*, July 12, 2001, B1, 4; Victor 1993: 141–46. Adoption of "Satanic context" ex post facto: Lowney 1997: 110–11.

80. "Court Jails 'Satanist' Heavy Metal Fans," Reuters, March 7, 2003; cf. "Sentences Cut for Metal Rockers," Reuters, April 5, 2003.

81. On self-professed Satanic "churches," usually populated by young adults in conscious reaction against Christian hegemony, see Introvigne 1997, La Fontaine 1999, and Lewis 2002.

82. See, e.g., Roper 1994: 200; Hsia 1988: 57–65; Gibson 1999. On the dissemination and effects of illustrated broadsheets promoting Jewish ritual crimes in sixteenth-century Germany, see Christine Mittlmeier, *Publizistik im Dienste anti-jüdischer Polemik*, Mikrokosmos 56 (Frankfurt: Peter Lang, 2000), 43–100.

83. Hsia 1988: 61–62, 210–17.

84. In a modern form of these murals, popular Ghanaian films about Satanic cults and Christianity are understood by audience and actors alike to reveal truths about Devil-worship and conspiracy: Meyer 2002, 2003.

85. Loudun: De Certeau 1996: 104–5. Salem witches invited to join Devil: Lawson (1692) in Hall 1999: 288; Mather (1693) in Hall 1999: 291–92. Elizabeth Knapp: Hall 1999: 197–212.

86. See, e.g., Clark 1997: 426.

87. E.g., Caleb Powell (Massachussetts, 1680), in Hall 1999: 235–39.

CHAPTER 7
Mobilizing against Evil

1. Principal bibliography includes Mair 1969: 36–42; Gordon 1987; Stewart 1991:162–91; La Fontaine 1992; Cohn 1993: 162–80; Johnston 1995.

2. See especially Needham 1978: 23–50, on probing the implications for society and psychology of the night-witch archetype.

3. In general, Moscovici 1987, Goode and Ben-Yehuda 1994, West and Sanders 2003, and Barkun 2003. Cf. Jon P. Mitchell, "The Devil, Satanism and the Evil Eye in Contemporary Malta," in Clough and Mitchell 2001: 77–103; cf. also encounters between local and radically systematized demonologies discussed in Caplan 1985 and Meyer 1999.

4. See in general Lanning 1991, 1992; Victor 1993; Earl 1995.

5. See, e.g., Ganaway 1989; Ceci and Bruck 1993; Loftus 1993; Coons 1994; DeYoung 1994; Spanos, Burgess, and Burgess 1994; Pressley and

Grossman 1994; Ofshe and Watters 1994; Pope 1996; Bottoms, Shaver, and Goodman 1996; De Rivera and Sarbin 1998; Haaken 1998; cf. Mulhern 1994; Nathan and Snedeker 1995; La Fontaine 1998.

6. Strack 1971 [1909].

7. Gershom Scholem, "Redemption through Sin" and "The Crypto-Jewish Sect of the Dönmeh (Sabbataians) in Turkey," in Scholem, *The Messianic Idea in Judaism* (New York: Schocken, 1971), 78–141, 142–66; Eliade 1976: 85–92. Cf. Frankfurter 2001: 368–73.

8. Cf. Raschke 1990; Kent 1993; Noblitt and Perskin 2000. See in general Frankfurter 2001: 373–80.

9. Ian Hacking, *Rewriting the Soul: Multiple Personality and the Sciences of Memory* (Princeton: Princeton University Press, 1995), 284n21.

10. Edward E. Evans-Pritchard, *Theories of Primitive Religion* (Oxford: Clarendon, 1965), 24, 43, 47.

11. Jules Michelet, *Satanism and Witchcraft: A Study in Medieval Superstition* [1862], trans. A. R. Allison (New York: Walden, 1939); Margaret Alice Murray, *The Witch-Cult in Western Europe* (Oxford: Clarendon, 1921); Jeffrey Burton Russell, *Witchcraft in the Middle Ages* (Secaucus, N.J.: Citadel, 1972); Ginzburg 1991, with astute criticisms by Cohn 1975, chap. 6 and 1993, chap. 8.

12. Cf. Stevens 1991, Victor 1993, Frankfurter 1994, La Fontaine 1998, Ellis 2000.

13. E.g., Benko 1984: 54–78, and Jorunn Jacobsen Buckley, "Libertines or Not: Fruit, Bread, Semen, and Other Bodily Fluids in Gnosticism," *Journal of Early Christian Studies* 2, no. 1 (1994): 16–21.

14. Peter Brown, *The Body and Society: Men, Women, and Sexual Renunciation in Early Christianity* (New York: Columbia University Press, 1988), 116–21; Williams 1996, chap. 8.

15. I refer here to primary materials in Harris Lenowitz, ed. *The Collection of the Words of the Lord [Jacob Frank]*, <http://www.languages.utah.edu/kabbalah/protected/dicta_frank_lenowitz.pdf> (18 January 2005). See Ada Rapaport-Albert, *Female Bodies—Male Souls: Asceticism and Gender in the Jewish Mystical Tradition* (Oxford: Littman Library of Jewish Civilization, 2007), and Elliot Wolfson, "Beyond Good and Evil: Hypernomianism, Trans-morality, and Kabbalistic Ethics, " in *Crossing Boundaries: Ethics, Antinomianism and the History of Mysticism*, ed. J. J. Kripal and W. Barnard (New York and London: Routledge, 2002), 103–56. On similar phenomena around sexuality and charismatic leadership in Mormonism, Jon Krakauer's work is unparalleled: *Under the Banner of Heaven* (New York: Random House, 2003).

16. Émile Durkheim, *The Elementary Forms of the Religious Life*, trans. Karen E. Fields (New York: Free Press, 1995 [1912]), 218; Victor Turner,

"Passages, Margins, and Poverty," in Turner, *Dramas, Fields, and Metaphors: Symbolic Action in Human Society* (Ithaca: Cornell University Press, 1974), 257. Cf. Frankfurter 2001: 367–68.

17. Cf. Beard, North, and Price 1998: 91–96.

18. Lesourd 1973; Clark 1997: 11–30.

19. Cf. John D. Kelly and Martha Kaplan, "History, Structure, and Ritual," *Annual Review of Anthropology* 19 (1990): 119–50, esp. 136–39.

20. Wilson 1992 (quotation, 531).

21. Urban 2003 (quotation, 287). The processional use of exhumed corpse-parts (of naturally deceased people) by Shiva-devotees in contemporary Bengal Indo-Asian News Service, April 14, 2005, belongs to such an articulated moral tradition, too, even if the processions shock outsiders (and the families of the deceased).

22. Urban 2003: 288–99; idem, "*Magia Sexualis*: Sex, Secrecy, and Liberation in Modern Western Esotericism," *Journal of the American Academy of Religion* 72, no. 3 (2004): 713–14. On LaVey, see Introvigne 1997: 257–81.

23. Augé 1982: 233–43; Lewis 1986; Sanday 1986; Whitehead 2002: 193–94; and Aparecida Vilaça, "Relations between Funerary Cannibalism and Warfare Cannibalism: The Question of Predation," *Ethnos* 65, no. 1 (2000): 83–106.

24. Daniel Bergner, "The Most Unconventional Weapon," *New York Times Magazine* October 26, 2003.

25. Arens 1979; cf. Bucher 1981; Lestringant 1997; Gilmore 2003: 176–87.

26. See, e.g., Alfred Métraux, *Voodoo in Haiti*, trans. Hugo Charteris (New York: Schocken, 1972), 266–322; Saler 1967; Ginzburg 1983; Briggs 1996: 171–218; David Frankfurter in "Panel Discussion," *Numen* 46 (1999): 313–17; Frankfurter 2002: 163–64, 173–77.

27. Richard W. Lieban, *Cebuano Sorcery: Malign Magic in the Philippines* (Berkeley: University of California Press, 1967).

28. Whitehead 2002.

29. Cf. Thomas A. Green, "Accusations of Satanism and Racial Tensions in the Matamoros Cult Murders," in Richardson, Best, and Bromley 1991: 237–48; cf. Ronald Smothers, "2 Accused of Storing Stolen Remains for Rituals," *New York Times*, October 9, 2002. Recent reports of so-called *muti*-killings in South Africa and the United Kingdom may in some cases reflect the hybrid ritual instructions of individual sorcerers: Paul Vallely, "Torso in the Thames—Muti: The Story of Adam," *Independent on Sunday*, August 3, 2003: 16; Sharon LaFraniere, "Toddler's Killing Exposes Ghoulish South African Practice," *New York Times*, September 28, 2003: A3; Michael Dynes, "'Magic Medicine' Murders Bedevil South Africa," *The Times*, October 4,

2003: 20. Yet it is often unclear what the circumstances might be for an incident of homicide-mutilation *before* the sensationalist interpretations of indigenous ritual-killing experts, to whom police tend to give limitless authority. See Ashforth 2005: 41–42, 72, 133–46 on *muti* (whose meaning in South Africa is equivalent to our term "potion"); Bastian 2003 on the typically obscure nature of violent crimes interpreted as ritual; and on the politics of linking of violent crimes to African religion, Afe Adogame, "Engaging the Rhetoric of Spiritual Warfare: The Public Face of Aladura in Diaspora," *Journal of Religion in Africa* 34, no. 4 (2004): 511–16.

30. E.g., Raschke 1990, Langone and Blood 1990. Dangers imputed to Nietzsche: Sander L. Gilman, "The Nietzsche Murder Case," in Gilman, *Difference and Pathology: Stereotypes of Sexuality, Race, and Madness* (Ithaca: Cornell University Press, 1985), 59–75.

31. E.g., " 'Satanic' Gang Beating," West Palm Beach, Florida, March 24, 1990; homicidal "Vampire Cult" of five Kentucky teenagers, Eustis, Florida, November 1996; high-school "Satanic cult" with charismatic leader planning school killing spree, several students shot, Pearl, Mississippi, September 1997. See also Geraldo Rivera, "Devil Worship: Exploring Satan's Underground" (TV talkshow, October 25, 1988); Bob Larson, *Satanism: The Seduction of America's Youth* (Nashville: Nelson, 1989); Raschke 1990: 111–17; and, on Columbine as Satanic in motivation, Bob Larson, *Extreme Evil: Kids Killing Kids* (Nashville: Nelson 1999), 8–12.

32. E.g., teen girls kill mother, Gulfport, Mississippi, July 1992; three teens lure and beat to death another in their circle, Philadelphia, Pennsylvania, June 2003.

33. So also in the exceedingly rare cases of mass sexual abuse: e.g., a day care worker in Reno, Nevada, who had both sexually assaulted more than twenty-five toddlers *and videotaped it* (Tom Gardner, Associated Press, March 1, 2001).

34. Armstrong 1994: 257, 259 (and chap. 11 more generally). See further Haaken 1998.

35. Goodman et al. 1994: 99–114; cf. Ellis 2000: 112–15. Further examples: Kira Canhoto (2 yrs.), forced to drink water, Ontario, January 1995; Eric Smith Jr. (14 yrs.), stabbed/beheaded, New Mexico, July, 1995; Tiffany Lopez (2 yrs.), drowned in tub, Quebec, September 1995; Xayomar Geigel (6 yrs.), stabbed with sword, New Hampshire, May 1996; boy (8 yrs.), beaten with paddle, New York, May 1997; Jessica Helm (7 yrs.), shot, Arizona, May 1998; Saimani Amete (4 yrs.), forced to drink water, Sydney, Australia June 1999; Signifagance Oliver (4 yrs.), drowned in tub, New York, November 2001; Terrence Cottrell Jr. (8 yrs.), suffocated, Milwaukee, August 2003; and

unnamed Angolan immigrant girl (8yrs.), tortured/attempted drowning for witchcraft, London, May 2005.

36. See, e.g., Hammond and Hammond 1973, chap. 14 ("Ministry to Children").

37. See Frankfurter 2004 (with bibliography and analysis of lynching ritual). Jedwabne: Jan Gross, *Neighbors: The Destruction of the Jewish Community in Jedwabne, Poland* (Princeton: Princeton University Press, 2001), 20, 98.

Select Bibliography

NOTE: sources cited here appear more than once in the notes or are considered essential to the subject. All other sources receive full entries in the notes.

Abusch, Tzvi. 1989. "The Demonic Image of the Witch in Standard Babylonian Literature: The Reworking of Popular Conceptions by Learned Exorcists." In *Religion, Science, and Magic in Concert and in Conflict*, ed. Jacob Neusner, Ernest S. Frerichs, and Paul Virgil McCracken Flesher, 27–58. New York: Oxford University Press.

Anglo, Sydney. 1977a, "Evident Authority and Authoritative Evidence: The *Malleus Maleficarum*." In Anglo 1977b. 1–31.

———, ed. 1977b. *The Damned Art: Essays in the Literature of Witchcraft*. London, Henley, and Boston: Routledge, Kegan & Paul.

Ankarloo, Bengt. 1990. "Sweden: The Mass Burnings (1668–76)." In Ankarloo and Henningsen 1990, 285–317.

Ankarloo, Bengt, and Stuart Clark, eds. 1999a. *Witchcraft and Magic in Europe: Ancient Greece and Rome*. Philadelphia: University of Pennsylvania Press.

———, ed. 1999b. *Witchcraft and Magic in Europe: The Eighteenth and Nineteenth Centuries*. Philadelphia: University of Pennsylvania Press.

———, ed. 1999c. *Witchcraft and Magic in Europe: The Twentieth Century*. Philadelphia: University of Pennsylvania Press.

———, ed. 2002. *Witchcraft and Magic in Europe: The Period of the Witch Trials*. Philadelphia: University of Pennsylvania Press.

Ankarloo, Bengt, and Gustav Henningsen, eds. 1990. *Early Modern European Witchcraft: Centres and Peripheries*. Oxford: Clarendon Press.

Arens, W. 1979. *The Man-Eating Myth: Anthropology and Anthropophagy*. New York: Oxford University Press.

Armstrong, Louise. 1994. *Rocking the Cradle of Sexual Politics*. Reading, Mass.: Addison-Wesley.

Ashforth, Adam. 2005. *Witchcraft, Violence, and Democracy in South Africa*. Chicago: University of Chicago Press.

Aufrère, Sydney. 1998. "L'Égypte traditionnelle, ses démons vus par les premiers chrétiens," *Études Coptes* V, Cahiers de la Bibliothèque copte 10, ed. M. Rassart-Debergh. Paris: Peeters, 63–92.

Augé, Marc. 1982. *Génie du paganisme*. Paris: Gallimard.

Auslander, Mark. 1993. "'Open the Wombs!': The Symbolic Politics of Modern Ngoni Witchfinding," in Comaroff and Comaroff 1993, 167–92.

Bailey, Michael. 1996. "The Medieval Concept of the Witches' Sabbath." *Exemplaria* 8, no. 2: 419–39.

———. 2003. *Battling Demons: Witchcraft, Heresy, and Reform in the Late Middle Ages*. University Park: Penn State University Press.

Baraz, Daniel. 2003. *Medieval Cruelty: Changing Perceptions, Late Antiquity to the Early Modern Period*. Ithaca: Cornell University Press.

Barkun, Michael. 2003. *A Culture of Conspiracy: Apocalyptic Visions in Contemporary America*. Berkeley: University of California Press.

Barnett, S. J. 1999. *Idol Temples and Crafty Priests: The Origins of Enlightenment Anticlericalism*. Houndmills & London: Macmillan.

Baroja, Julio Caro. 1965. *The World of the Witches*. Trans. O.N.V. Glendinning. Chicago: University of Chicago Press.

Bastian, Misty L. 2001. "Vulture Men, Campus Cultists, and Teenaged Witches: Modern Magics in Nigerian Popular Media." In *Magical Interpretations, Material Realities: Modernity, Witchcraft and the Occult in Postcolonial Africa*, ed. Henrietta L. Moore and Todd Sanders. London and New York: Routledge, 71–96.

———. 2002. "'The Daughter She Will Eat Agousie in the World of the Spirits': Witchcraft Confessions in Missionised Onitsha, Nigeria." *Africa* 72, no. 1: 84–111.

———. 2003. "'Diabolic Realities': Narratives of Conspiracy, Transparency, and 'Ritual Murder' in the Nigerian Popular Print and Electronic Media." In West and Sanders 2003, 65–91.

Bataille, Georges. 1962. *Erotism: Death and Sensuality*. Trans. by Mary Dalwood. New York: Walker and Co. [Reprint edition: San Francisco: City Lights, 1986.]

Beard, Mary, John North, and Simon Price. 1998. *Religions of Rome 1: A History*. Cambridge: Cambridge University Press.

Behringer, Wolfgang. 2004. *Witches and Witch-Hunts*. Cambridge: Polity.

Bell, Catherine. 1997. *Ritual: Perspectives and Dimensions*. New York: Oxford University Press.

Benko, Stephen. 1984. *Pagan Rome and the Early Christians*. Bloomington: Indiana University Press.

Bennetts, Leslie. 1993. "Nightmares on Main Street." *Vanity Fair* (June): 42–62.

Bettelheim, Bruno. 1976. *The Uses of Enchantment: The Meaning and Importance of Fairy Tales*. New York: Vintage.

Bickerman, Elias. 1980. "Ritualmord und Eselskult: Ein Beitrag zur Geschichte antiker Publicistik." In Bickerman, *Studies in Jewish and Christian History*, Part 2, Leiden: Brill, 225–55.

Bikel, Ofra. 1995. "Divided Memories" [Documentary]. PBS *Frontline* (April 4, April 11).

Bikel, Ofra, and Rachel Dretzin. 1995. "The Search for Satan" [Documentary]. PBS *Frontline* (October 24).

Blécourt, Willem de. 1999. "The Witch, Her Victim, The Unwitcher, and the Researcher: The Continued Existence of Traditional Witchcraft." In Ankarloo and Clark 1999c, 141–214.

Bloom, Sandra L. 1994. "Hearing the Survivor's Voice: Sundering the Wall of Denial." *Journal of Psychohistory* 21, no. 4: 461–77.

Boguet, Henri. 1929. *An Examen of Witches* [1602], tr. E. Allen Ashwin and ed. Montague Summers. London: Rodker.

Bottoms, Bette L., Phillip R. Shaver, and Gail S. Goodman. 1996. "An Analysis of Ritualistic and Religion-Related Child Abuse Allegations." *Law and Human Behavior* 20, no. 1: 1–34.

Bourdillon, M.F.C. 2000. "Witchcraft and Society." In *African Spirituality: Forms, Meanings, and Expressions*. Ed. Jacob K. Olupona. New York: Crossroad, 176–97.

Bourget, Dominique, André Gagnon, and John M. W. Bradford. 1988. "Satanism in a Psychiatric Adolescent Population." *Canadian Journal of Psychiatry* 33: 197–201.

Boyd, Andrew. 1991. *Blasphemous Rumours: Is Satanic Ritual Abuse Fact or Fantasy? An Investigation*. London: Fount.

Boyer, Paul, and Stephen Nissenbaum. 1974. *Salem Possessed: The Social Origins of Witchcraft*. Cambridge: Harvard University Press.

Brakke, David. 2006. *Demons and the Making of the Monk: Spiritual Combat in Early Christian Egypt*. Cambridge, Mass.: Harvard University Press.

Brenner, Ira. 1994. "A Twentieth-Century Demonologic Neurosis?" *Journal of Psychohistory* 21, no. 4: 501–4.

Briggs, Robin. 1996. *Witches and Neighbors: The Social and Cultural Context of European Witchcraft*. New York: Viking.

Broedel, Hans Peter. 2003. *The Malleus Maleficarum and the Construction of Witchcraft: Theology and Popular Belief*. Manchester and New York: Manchester University Press.

Bromley, David G. 1991. "Satanism: The New Cult Scare." In Richardson 1991, 49–72.

———. 1994a. "The Satanism Scare in the United States." In Jean-Baptiste Martin, ed. *Le Défi magique 2: Satanisme, sorcellerie*, 49–64. Lyon: Presses universitaires de Lyon.

————. 1994b. "The Social Construction of Subversion: A Comparison of Anti-Religious and Anti-Satanic Cult Narratives." In Anson Shupe and David G. Bromley, eds. *Anti-Cult Movements in Cross-Cultural Perspective*, New York and London: Garland, 49–69.

Brown, Peter. 1970. "Sorcery, Demons, and the Rise of Christianity from Late Antiquity into the Middle Ages." In Douglas 1970, 17–45.

Bucher, Bernadette. 1981. *Icon and Conquest: A Structural Analysis of the Illustrations of deBry's GREAT VOYAGES*. Trans. Basia Miller Gulati. Chicago: University of Chicago Press.

Bullard, Thomas E. 1989. "UFO Abduction Reports: The Supernatural Kidnap Narrative Returns in Technological Guise" *Journal of American Folklore* 102 (1989): 147–70.

Burket, Roger C., Wade C. Myers, W. Bradford Lyles, and Frank Carrera III. 1994. "Emotional and Behavioral Disturbances in Adolescents Involved in Witchcraft and Satanism." *Journal of Adolescence* 17: 41–52.

Burr, George Lincoln. 1914. *Narratives of the Witchcraft Cases, 1648–1706*. New York: Scribner's.

Bynum, Caroline Walker. 1987. *Holy Feast and Holy Fast: The Religious Significance of Food to Medieval Women*. Berkeley: University of California Press.

Campion-Vincent, Véronique. 1990. "The Baby-Parts Story: A New Latin American Legend." *Western Folklore* 49, no. 1: 9–25.

Camporesi, Piero. 1995. *Juice of Life: The Symbolic and Magic Significance of Blood*. Trans. Robert R. Barr. New York: Continuum.

Caplan, Lionel. 1985. "The Popular Culture of Evil in Urban South India." In Parkin 1985, 110–27.

Casement, Patrick. 1994. "The Wish Not to Know." In Sinason 1994, 22–25.

Ceci, Stephen J., and Maggie Bruck. 1993. "Suggestibility of the Child Witness: A Historical Review and Synthesis." *Psychological Bulletin* 113, no. 3: 403–39.

Cervantes, Fernando. 1994. *The Devil in the New World: The Impact of Diabolism in New Spain*. New Haven: Yale University Press.

Chakanza, J. C. 1985. "Provisional Annotated Chronological List of Witch-Finding Movements in Malawi, 1850–1980." *Journal of Religion in Africa* 15, no. 3: 227–43.

Chilver, E. M. 1990. "Thaumaturgy in Contemporary Traditional Religion: The case of Nso' in Mid-Century." *Journal of Religion in Africa* 20, no. 3: 226–47.

Clark, Lynn Schofield. 2003. *From Angels to Aliens: Teenagers, the Media, and the Supernatural*. New York: Oxford University Press.

Clark, Stuart. 1997. *Thinking with Demons: The Idea of Witchcraft in Early Modern Europe*. Oxford: Oxford University Press.

Clough, Paul, and Jon P. Mitchell, eds. 2001. *Powers of Good and Evil: Social Transformation and Popular Belief*. New York and Oxford: Berghahn.

Cohn, Norman. 1975. *Europe's Inner Demons*. New York: Basic Books.

———. 1993. *Europe's Inner Demons*, rev. ed. Chicago: University of Chicago Press.

Coleman, Joan. 1994. "Satanic Cult Practices." In Sinason 1994, 242–53.

Comaroff, Jean. 1997. "Consuming Passions: Child Abuse, Fetishism, and 'The New World Order.'" *Culture* 17, nos. 1–2: 7–19.

Comaroff, Jean, and John Comaroff, eds. 1993. *Modernity and Its Malcontents: Ritual and Power in Postcolonial Africa*. Chicago: University of Chicago Press.

Coons, Philip M. 1994. "Reports of Satanic Ritual Abuse: Further Implications about Pseudomemories." *Perceptual and Motor Skills* 78: 1376–78.

Core, Dianne, and Fred Harrison. 1991. *Chasing Satan: An Investigation into Satanic Crimes against Children*. London: Gunter.

Cozolino, Louis J. 1990. "Ritualistic Child Abuse, Psychopathology, and Evil." *Journal of Psychology and Theology* 18, no. 3: 218–27.

Crouch, Ben M., and Kelly R. Damphousse. 1991. "Law Enforcement and the Satanic Crime Connection: A Survey of 'Cult Cops.'" In Richardson, Best, and Bromley 1991, 191–204.

Cuneo, Michael W. 1998. "Of Demons and Hollywood: Exorcism in American Culture." *Studies in Religion* 27: 455–65.

———. 2001. *American Exorcism: Expelling Demons in the Land of Plenty*. New York: Doubleday.

Damphousse, Kelly R., and Ben M. Crouch. 1992. "Did the Devil Make Them Do It? An Examination of the Etiology of Satanism Among Juvenile Delinquents." *Youth and Society* 24, no. 2: 204–27.

de Blécourt, Willem. 1994. "Witch Doctors, Soothsayers, and Priests: On Cunning Folk in European Historiography and Tradition." *Social History* 19: 285–303.

de Certeau, Michel. 1996. *The Possession at Loudun*. Trans. Michael B. Smith. Chicago: University of Chicago Press.

de Lancre, Pierre. 1982 [1610]. *Tableau de l'Inconstance des Mauvais Anges et Démons*. Ed. Nicole Jacques-Chaquin. Paris: Aubier.

Delbanco, Andrew. 1995. *The Death of Satan: How Americans Have Lost the Sense of Evil*. New York: Farrar, Straus, and Giroux.

DeMause, Lloyd. 1994. "Why Cults Terrorize and Kill Children." *Journal of Psychohistory* 21, no. 4: 505–18.

Demos, John Putnam. 1982. *Entertaining Satan: Witchcraft and the Culture of Early New England*. Oxford: Oxford University Press.

De Rivera, Joseph, and Theodore R. Sarbin, eds. 1998. *Believed-In Imaginings: The Narrative Construction of Reality*. Washington, D.C.: American Psychological Association.

Devereux, George. [1966] 1980. "The Cannibalistic Impulses of Parents." In *Basic Problems of Ethnopsychiatry*. Trans. Basia Miller Gulati and George Devereux. Chicago: University of Chicago Press, 122–37.

DeYoung, M. 1994. "One Face of the Devil: The Satanic Ritual Abuse Moral Crusade and the Law." *Behavioral Sciences and the Law* 12: 389–407.

———. 1996. "Speak of the Devil: Rhetoric in Claims-Making About the Satanic Ritual Abuse Problem." *Journal of Sociology and Social Welfare* 23: 55–74.

Douglas, Mary. 1966. *Purity and Danger: An Analysis of Concepts of Pollution and Taboo*. London: RKP.

———. ed. 1970. *Witchcraft Confessions and Accusations*. London and New York: Tavistock.

———. 1999. "Sorcery Accusations Unleashed: The Lele Revisited, 1987." *Africa* 69, no. 2: 177–93.

Dresser, Norine. 1989. *American Vampires: Fans, Victims, Practitioners*. New York: Random House.

Droz, Yvan. 1997. "Si Dieu veut . . . ou suppôts de Satan? Incertitudes, millénarisme et sorcellerie chez les migrants kikuyu." *Cahiers d'Études africaines* 38, no. 1: 85–117.

Dundes, Alan, ed. 1991. *The Blood Libel Legend: A Casebook in Anti-Semitic Folklore*. Madison: University of Wisconsin Press.

Dyrendal, Asbjørn. 2003. "True Religion versus Cannibal Others? Rhetorical Constructions of Satanism among American Evangelicals." Ph.D. dissertation, University of Oslo.

Earl, John. 1995. "The Dark Truth About the Dark Tunnels of McMartin." *Issues in Child Abuse Accusations* 7, no. 2.

Edwards, M. J. 1992. "Some Early Christian Immoralities." *Ancient Society* 23: 71–82.

Eliade, Mircea. 1976. *Occultism, Witchcraft, and Cultural Fashions: Essays in Comparative Religions*. Chicago: University of Chicago Press.

Elliott, Dyan. 1999. *Fallen Bodies: Pollution, Sexuality, and Demonology in the Middle Ages*. Philadelphia: University of Pennsylvania Press.

Ellis, Bill. 1989. "Death by Folklore: Ostension, Contemporary Legend, and Murder." *Western Folklore* 48: 201–20.

———. 1990. "The Devil-Worshippers at the Prom: Rumor-Panic as Therapeutic Magic." *Western Folklore* 49, no. 1: 27–49.

———. 1991. "Legend-Trips and Satanism: Adolescents' Ostensive Traditions as 'Cult' Activity." In Richardson, Best, and Bromley 1991, 279–95.

————. 2000. *Raising the Devil: Satanism, New Religions, and the Media.* Lexington: University Press of Kentucky.

Eni, Emmanuel. 1987. *Delivered from the Powers of Darkness.* Ibadan: Scripture Union Press.

Epiphanius of Salamis. 1990. *Panarion.* Trans. Philip R. Amidon. New York: Oxford University Press.

Evans-Pritchard, Edward E. 1937. *Witchcraft, Oracles, and Magic among the Azande.* Oxford: Clarendon.

————. 1982. "Witchcraft among the Azande." In Marwick 1982, 29–37.

Favret-Saada, Jeanne. 1980. *Deadly Words: Witchcraft in the Bocage.* Trans. Catherine Cullen. Cambridge: Cambridge University Press.

Ferber, Sarah. 1993. "Le sabbat et son double." In Jacques-Chaquin and Préaud 1993, 101–9.

Finkelhor, David, Linda Williams, and N. Burns. 1988. *Nursery Crimes: Sexual Abuse in Daycare.* Newburg Park, Calif.: Sage Publications.

Flint, Valerie. 1991. *The Rise of Magic in Early Medieval Europe.* Princeton: Princeton University Press.

————. 1999. "The Demonisation of Magic and Sorcery in Late Antiquity: Christian Redefinitions of Pagan Religions." In Ankarloo and Clark 1999a, 279–348.

Forsyth, Neil. 1987. *The Old Enemy: Satan and the Combat Myth.* Princeton: University Press.

Frankfurter, David 1993. *Elijah in Upper Egypt: The Apocalypse of Elijah and Early Egyptian Christianity.* Minneapolis: Fortress.

————. 1994. "Religious Studies and Claims of Satanic Ritual Abuse." *Religion* 24: 353–60.

————. 2000. "'Things Unbefitting Christians': Violence and Christianization in Fifth-Century Panopolis." *Journal of Early Christian Studies* 8, no. 2: 273–95.

————. 2001. "Ritual as Accusation and Atrocity: Satanic Ritual Abuse, Gnostic Libertinism, and Primal Murders." *History of Religions* 40, no. 4: 352–80.

————. 2002. "Dynamics of Ritual Expertise in Antiquity and Beyond: Towards a New Taxonomy of 'Magicians.'" In *Magic and Ritual in the Ancient World,* Ed. Marvin Meyer and Paul Mirecki. Leiden: Brill, 159–78.

————. 2003. "Syncretism and the Holy Man in Late Antique Egypt." *Journal of Early Christian Studies* 11, no. 3: 339–85.

————. 2004. "On Sacrifice and Residues: Processing the Potent Body." In *Religion in Cultural Discourse: Essays in Honor of Hans G. Kippenberg on the Occasion of his 65th Birthday.* Ed. by Brigitte Luchesi and Kocku von Stuckrad

Religionsgeschichtliche Versuche und Vorarbeiten 52. Berlin and New York: De Gruyter, 511–33.

Fraser, George A. 1993. "Exorcism Rituals: Effects on Multiple Personality Disorder Patients." *Dissociation* 6, no. 4: 239–44.

———, ed. 1997. *The Dilemma of Ritual Abuse*. Washington D.C.: American Psychiatric Press.

Freud, Sigmund. [1919] 1955. "'A Child is Being Beaten': A Contribution to the Study of the Origin of Sexual Perversions." In *Standard Edition of the Complete Psychological Works of Sigmund Freud*, vol. 17. Ed. James Strachey. London: Hogarth Press, 175–204.

Friesen, Bruce K. 1990. "Powerlessness in Adolescence: Exploiting Heavy Metal Listeners." In *Marginal Conventions: Popular Culture, Mass Media, and Social Deviance*. Ed. Clinton R. Sanders. Bowling Green, Ohio: Bowling Green State University Popular Press, 65–77.

Friesen, James G., Jr. 1992. "Ego-Dystonic or Ego-Alien: Alternate Personality or Evil Spirit?" *Journal of Psychology and Theology* 20, no. 3: 197–200.

Frijhoff, Willem. 2000. "Sorcellerie et possession du moyen-âge aux lumières," *Revue d'histoire ecclésiastique* 95, no. 3: 112–42.

Ganaway, George K. 1989. "Historical Truth versus Narrative Truth: Clarifying the Role of Exogenous Trauma in the Etiology of MPD and its Variants." *Dissociation* 2, no. 4: 205–20.

———. 1991. "Alternative Hypothesis Regarding Satanic Ritual Abuse Memories." Unpublished paper delivered at the American Psychological Association Annual Meeting, San Francisco, California, August.

———. 1992. "Some Additional Questions: A Response." *Journal of Psychology and Theology* 20, no. 3: 201–5.

Gaster, Moses. 1971. "Two Thousand Years of a Charm against the Child-Stealing Witch." In *Studies and Texts*, vol. 2, New York: Ktav, 1005–38.

Geschiere, Peter. 1997. *The Modernity of Witchcraft: Politics and the Occult in Postcolonial Africa*. Trans. Peter Geschiere and Janet Roitman. Charlottesville: University Press of Virginia.

———. 2001. "Witchcraft and New Forms of Wealth: Regional Variations in South and West Cameroon." In Clough and Mitchell 2001, 43–76.

Gibson, Marion. 1999. *Reading Witchcraft: Stories of Early English Witches*. London and New York: Routledge.

Gijswijt-Hofstra, Marijke. 1999. "Witchcraft after the Witch-Trials." In Ankarloo and Clark 1999b, 95–189.

Gilhus, Ingvild Salid. 1990. "Carnival in Religion: The Feast of Fools in France." *Numen* 37, no. 1: 24–52.

Gilmore, David D. 2003. *Monsters: Evil Beings, Mythical Beasts, and All Manner of Imaginary Terrors*. Philadelphia: University of Pennsylvania Press.

Ginzburg, Carlo. 1983. *The Night Battles: Witchcraft and Agrarian Cults in the Sixteenth and Seventeenth Centuries*. Trans. John and Anne Tedeschi. Baltimore: Johns Hopkins University Press.

———. 1991. *Ecstasies: Deciphering the Witches' Sabbath*. Trans. Raymond Rosenthal. New York: Pantheon.

Glass, James M. 1993. *Shattered Selves: Multiple Personality in a Postmodern World*. Ithaca: Cornell University Press.

Goode, Erich, and Nachman Ben-Yehuda. 1994. *Moral Panics: The Social Construction of Deviance*. Oxford: Blackwell.

Goodman, Gail S., Jianjian Qin, Bette L. Bottoms, and Phillip R. Shaver. 1994. *Characteristics and Sources of Allegations of Ritualistic Child Abuse*. Washington, D.C.: Center for Child Abuse and Neglect.

Gordon, Richard. 1987. "Lucan's Erictho." In *Homo Viator: Classical Essays for John Bramble*. Ed. M. Whitby and P. Hardie. Bristol: Bristol Classical Press, 231–41.

———. 1999. "Imagining Greek and Roman Magic." In Ankarloo and Clark 1999a, 159–275.

Gould, Catherine. 1995. "Denying Ritual Abuse of Children." *Journal of Psychohistory* 22, no. 3: 329–39.

Graf, Fritz. 1997. "Medea, the Enchantress from Afar: Remarks on a Well-Known Myth." In *Medea: Essays on Medea in Myth, Literature, Philosophy, and Art*. Ed. James J. Clauss and Sarah Iles Johnston, Princeton: Princeton University Press, 21–43.

Grant, Robert M. 1983. "Charges of 'Immorality' Against Various Religious Groups in Antiquity." In Grant, *Christian Beginnings: Apocalypse to History*. London: Variorum, 161–70 (§ V).

Green, Maia. 1997. "Witchcraft Suppression Practices and Movements: Public Politics and the Logic of Purification." *Comparative Studies in Society and History* 39, no. 2: 319–45.

Guazzo, Francesco Maria. [1608] 1988. *Compendium Maleficarum*. Trans. E. A. Ashwin. Ed. Montague Summers. New York: Dover.

Haaken, Janice. 1998. *Pillar of Salt: Gender, Memory, and the Perils of Looking Back*. New Brunswick N.J.: Rutgers University Press.

Haliczer, Stephen. 1987. "The Jew as a Witch: Displaced Aggression and the Myth of the Santo Niño de La Guardia." In *Cultural Encounters: The Impact of the Inquisition in Spain and the New World*. Ed. Mary Elizabeth Perry and Anne J. Cruz. Berkeley: University of California Press, 146–56.

Hall, David D. 1999. *Witch-Hunting in Seventeenth-Century New England: A Documentary History 1658–1693.* 2nd ed. Boston: Northeastern University Press.

Hammerton-Kelley, Robert G., ed. 1987. *Violent Origins: Ritual Killing and Cultural Formation.* Stanford: Stanford University Press.

Hammond, Frank, and Ida Mae Hammond. 1973. *Pigs in the Parlor: A Practical Guide to Deliverance.* Kirkwood, Mo.: Impact Christian Books.

Harding, Susan F. 1987. "Convicted by the Holy Spirit: The Rhetoric of Fundamental Baptist Conversion." *American Ethnologist* 14: 167–81.

Hartog, François. 1988. *The Mirror of Herodotus: The Representation of the Other in the Writing of History.* Trans. Janet Lloyd. Berkeley: University of California Press.

———. 2001. *Memories of Odysseus: Frontier Tales from Ancient Greece.* Trans. Janet Lloyd. Chicago: University of Chicago Press.

Henningsen, Gustav. 1980. *The Witches' Advocate: Basque Witchcraft and the Spanish Inquisition (1609–1614).* Reno: University of Nevada Press.

———. 1991. "'The Ladies from Outside': An Archaic Pattern of the Witches' Sabbath." In Ankarloo and Henningsen 1990, 191–215.

———. 1991–1992. "The White Sabbath and other Archaic Patterns of Witchcraft," *Acta Ethnographica . . . Hungaricae* 37: 293–304.

Henrichs, Albert. 1970. "Pagan Ritual and the Alleged Crimes of the Early Christians." *Kyriakon* I. Ed. Patrick Granfield and Josef A. Jungmann. Münster: Aschendorff, 18–35.

Hicks, Robert D. 1991a. "The Police Model of Satanic Crime." In Richardson, Best, and Bromley 1991, 175–189.

———. 1991b. *In Pursuit of Satan: The Police and the Occult.* Buffalo: Prometheus.

Hill, Sally, and Jean Goodwin. 1989. "Satanism: Similarities Between Patient Accounts and Pre-Inquisition Historical Sources." *Dissociation* 2, no. 1: 39–44.

Holgerson, Astrid. 1995. "Professionals as Evaluators or Indoctinators in Sex Abuse Cases." *Issues in Child Abuse Accusations* 7.

Hopkins, Matthew. [1647] 1928. *The Discovery of Witches.* Ed. Montague Summers. London: Cayme Press.

Horden, Peregrine. 1993. "Responses to Possession and Insanity in the Earlier Byzantine World." *Social History of Medicine* 6: 177–94.

Hsia, R. Po-chia. 1988. *The Myth of Ritual Murder: Jews and Magic in Reformation Germany.* New Haven: Yale University Press.

Hunt, Stephen. 1998. "Managing the Demonic: Some Aspects of the Neo-Pentecostal Deliverance Ministry." *Journal of Contemporary Religion* 13, no. 2: 215–30.

Hurbon, Laënnec. 1995. "American Fantasy and Haitian Vodou." *Sacred Arts of Haitian Vodou.* Ed. Donald J. Cosentino. Los Angeles: UCLA Press/Fowler Museum, 181–97.

Introvigne, Massimo. 1997. *Enquête sur le satanisme: Satanistes et antisatanistes du XVIIè siècle à nos jours.* Trans. Philippe Baillet. Paris: Dervy.

———. 2000. "The Gothic Milieu: Black Metal, Satanism, and Vampires." *CESNUR* Homepage <http://www.cesnur.org/testi/gothic.htm>.

Jacques-Chaquin, Nicole. 1978. "Le malefice de taciturnité: Esquisse d'une étude du mythe de la sorcière." *Cahiers de Fontenay* 9–10: 137–69.

———. 1987. "Demoniac Conspiracy." In *Changing Conceptions of Conspiracy.* Ed. Carl F. Graumann and Serge Moscovici. New York: Springer-Verlag, 71–85.

Jacques-Chaquin, Nicole, and Maxime Préaud, eds. 1993. *Le Sabbat des sorciers en Europe (XVè-XVIIIè siècles).* Grenoble: Millon.

Jahoda, Gustav. 1999. *Images of Savages: Ancient Roots of Modern Prejudice in Western Culture.* London and New York: Routledge.

Jenkins, Philip. 1992. *Intimate Enemies: Moral Panics in Contemporary Great Britain.* New York: Walter De Gruyter.

Jenkins, Philip, and Daniel Maier-Katkin. 1991. "Occult Survivors: The Making of a Myth." In Richardson, Best, and Bromley 1991, 127–44.

Johnson, D. W. 1980. *A Panegyric on Macarius, Bishop of Tkôw, Attributed to Dioscorus of Alexandria.* 2 vols. CSCO 415–16, S. Coptici 41–42. Louvain: Sécretariat du CSCO.

Johnson, Matt. 1994. "Fear and Power: From Naivete to a Believer in Cult Abuse." *Journal of Psychohistory* 21, no. 4: 435–41.

Johnston, Sarah Iles. 1995. "Defining the Dreadful: Remarks on the Greek Child-Killing Demon." In Meyer and Mirecki 1995, 361–87.

———. 1999. *Restless Dead.* Berkeley: University of California Press.

Kahr, Brett. 1994. "The Historical Foundations of Ritual Abuse: An Excavation of Ancient Infanticide." In Sinason 1994, 45–56.

Katchen, Martin H., and David K. Sakheim. 1992. "Satanic Beliefs and Practices." In Sakheim and Devine 1992, 21–43.

Kent, Stephen A. 1993. "Deviant Scripturalism and Ritual Satanic Abuse." *Religion* 23: 229–41, 355–67.

Keyworth, David. 2002. "The Socio-Religious Beliefs and Nature of the Contemporary Vampire Subculture." *Journal of Contemporary Religion* 17, no. 3: 355–70.

Kieckhefer, Richard. 1998. "Avenging the Blood of Children: Anxiety over Child Victims and the Origins of the European Witch Trials." In *The Devil, Heresy and Witchcraft in the Middle Ages: Essays in Honor of Jeffrey B. Russell.* Ed. Alberto Ferreiro. Leiden: Brill, 91–109.

Kippenberg, Hans G. 1997. "Magic in Roman Civil Discourse: Why Rituals could be Illegal." In *Envisioning Magic: A Princeton Seminar and Symposium*, Ed. Peter Schäfer and Hans G. Kippenberg. Leiden: Brill, 137–63.

Klaniczay, Gábor. 1990. "Hungary: the Accusations and the Universe of Popular Magic." In Ankarloo and Henningsen 1990, 219–55.

Kluckholn, Clyde. 1944. *Navaho Witchcraft*. Cambridge, Mass.: Harvard University Press.

Kors, Alan Charles, and Edward Peters. 2001. *Witchcraft in Europe, 400–1700: A Documentary History*. 2nd ed. Philadelphia: University of Pennsylvania Press.

Kotansky, Roy. 1995. "Greek Exorcistic Amulets." In Meyer and Mirecki 1995, 243–77.

Kramer, Fritz. 1993. *The Red Fez: Art and Spirit Possession in Africa*. Trans. Malcolm R. Green. London: Verso.

Kramer [Institoris], Heinrich, and James Sprenger. [1484] 1971. *Malleus Maleficarum*. Trans. Montague Summers. New York: Dover.

La Fontaine, Jean S. 1963. "Witchcraft in Bugisu." In Middleton and Winter 1963, 187–220.

———. 1992. "Concepts of Evil, Witchcraft, and the Sexual Abuse of Children in Modern England." *Etnofoor* 5: 6–20.

———. 1998. *Speak of the Devil: Tales of Satanic Abuse in Contemporary England*. Cambridge: Cambridge University Press.

———. 1999. "Satanism and Satanic Mythology." In Ankarloo and Clark 1999c, 81–140.

Langmuir, Gavin I. 1984. "Thomas of Monmouth: Detector of Ritual Murder." *Speculum* 59, no. 4: 820–46.

———. 1990. "Ritual Cannibalism." In Langmuir, *Toward a Definition of Antisemitism*. Berkeley: University of California Press, 263–81.

Langone, Michael D., and Linda O. Blood. 1990. *Satanism and Occult-Related Violence: What You Should Know*. Weston, Mass.: American Family Foundation.

Lanning, Kenneth V. 1991. "Ritual Abuse: A Law Enforcement View or Perspective." *Child Abuse and Neglect* 15: 171–73.

———. 1992. *Investigator's Guide to Allegations of "Ritual" Child Abuse*. Quantico, Va.: Federal Bureau of Investigation.

Larner, Christina. 1984. *Witchcraft and Religion: The Politics of Popular Belief*. Oxford: Blackwell.

Lesourd, Dominique. 1973. "Culture savante et culture populaire dans la mythologie de la sorcellerie." *Anagrom* 3–4: 63–79.

Lestringant, Frank. 1997. *Cannibals: The Discovery and Representation of the Cannibal from Columbus to Jules Verne*. Trans. Rosemary Morris. Berkeley: University of California Press.

Levack, Brian P. 1995. *The Witch-Hunt in Early Modern Europe*. 2nd ed. Harlow: Pearson.

Lévi-Strauss, Claude. 1963. "The Sorcerer and His Magic." In Lévi-Strauss, *Structural Anthropology*. New York: Basic Books, 167–85.

Levine, Harold G., and Steven H. Stumpf. 1983. "Statements of Fear through Cultural Symbols: Punk Rock as a Reflective Subculture." *Youth and Society* 14, no. 4: 417–35.

Lewis, I. M. 1986. "The Cannibal's Cauldron." In Lewis, *Religion in Context: Cults and Charisma*, Cambridge: Cambridge University Press, 63–77.

———. 1989. *Ecstatic Religion: A Study of Shamanism and Spirit Possession*. 2nd ed. London and New York: Routledge.

Lewis, James R. 2001. "Who Serves Satan? A Demographic and Ideological Profile." *Marburg Journal of Religion* 6, no. 2.

———. 2002. "Diabolical Authority: Anton LaVey, *The Satanic Bible*, and the Satanist 'Tradition.'" *Marburg Journal of Religion* 7, no. 1.

Loftus, Elizabeth F. 1993. "The Reality of Repressed Memories." *American Psychologist* 48: 518–37.

Lowney, Kathleen S. 1995. "Teenage Satanism as Oppositional Youth Subculture." *Journal of Contemporary Ethnography* 23, no. 4: 453–84.

———. 1997. "Speak of the Devil: Talk Shows and the Social Construction of Satanism." In *Social Problems in Everyday Life: Studies of Social Problems Work*. Ed. Gale Miller and James A. Holstein. Perspectives on Social Problems 6. Greenwich, Conn.: JAI Press, 99–128.

Luhrmann, Tanya. 2004. "Trauma, Trance, and God: How the new style in American religion might be changing the psychiatric symptoms of trauma." *Criterion* 43, no. 2 (spring): 2–11.

Lynn, Steven Jay, Judith Pintar, Jane Stafford, Lisa Marmelstein, and Timothy Lock. 1998. "Rendering the Implausible Plausible: Narrative Construction, Suggestion, and Memory." In de Rivera and Sarbin 1998, 123–43.

MacFarlane, Alan. 1985. "The Root of all Evil." In Parkin 1985, 57–76.

———. 1999. *Witchcraft in Tudor and Stuart England: A Regional and Comparative Study*. 2nd ed. London: Routledge.

MacNutt, Francis. 1995. *Deliverance from Evil Spirits: A Practical Manual*. Grand Rapids, Mich.: Chosen Books.

Mair, Lucy. 1969. *Witchcraft*. London: Weidenfeld and Nicolson.

Malinowski, Bronislaw. [1961] 1984. *Argonauts of the Western Pacific*. New York: Dutton; repr. Prospect Heights, Ill.: Waveland.

Marcus, Joel. 1999. "The Beelzebul Controversy and the Eschatologies of Jesus." In *Authenticating the Activities of Jesus*. Ed. Bruce D. Chilton and Craig A. Evans. Leiden: Brill, 247–77.

Marwick, Max, ed. 1982. *Witchcraft and Sorcery: Selected Readings.* 2nd ed. Harmondsworth: Penguin.

McAlister, Melani. 2003. "Prophecy, Politics, and the Popular: The *Left Behind* Series and Christian Fundamentalism's New World Order." *South Atlantic Quarterly* 102: 773–98.

McClymond, Kathryn. 2002. "Death Be Not Proud: Reevaluating the Role of Killing in Sacrifice." *International Journal of Hindu Studies* 6, no. 3: 221–42.

———. 2004. "The Nature and Elements of Sacrificial Ritual." *Method and Theory in the Study of Religion* 16, no. 4: 337–67.

McGowan, Andrew. 1994. "Eating People: Accusations of Cannibalism against Christians in the Second Century." *Journal of Early Christian Studies* 2: 413–42.

McGowan, Margaret M. 1977. "Pierre de Lancre's *Tableau de l'Inconstance des Mauvais Anges et Démons*: The Sabbat Sensationalized." In Anglo 1977, 182–201.

Medway, Gareth J. 2001. *Lure of the Sinister: The Unnatural History of Satanism.* New York: New York University Press.

Meyer, Birgit. 1994. "Beyond Syncretism: Translation and Diabolization in the Appropriation of Protestantism in Africa." In *Syncretism/Anti-Syncretism: The Politics of Religious Synthesis,* Ed. Charles Stewart and Rosalind Shaw. London and New York: Routledge, 45–68.

———. 1995. "'Delivered from the Powers of Darkness': Confessions of Satanic Riches in Christian Ghana." *Africa* 65, no. 2: 236–55.

———. 1996. "Modernity and Enchantment: The Image of the Devil in Popular African Christianity." In *Conversion to Modernities: The Globalization of Christianity,* Ed. P. van der Veer. New York and London: Routledge, 199–230.

———. 1999. *Translating the Devil: Religion and Modernity among the Ewe in Ghana.* Trenton, N.J.: Africa World Press.

———. 2001. "'You Devil, Go Away From Me!' Pentecostalist African Christianity and the Powers of Good and Evil." In Clough and Mitchell 2001, 104–34.

———. 2002. "Occult Forces on Screen: Representation and the Danger of Mimesis in Popular Ghanaian Films." *Etnofoor* 15: 212–21.

———. 2003. "Visions of Blood, Sex and Money: Fantasy Spaces in Popular Ghanaian Cinema." *Visual Anthropology* 16: 15–42.

Meyer, Marvin, and Paul Mirecki, eds. 1995. *Ancient Magic and Ritual Power.* Leiden: Brill.

Middleton, John, and E. H. Winter, eds. 1963. *Witchcraft and Sorcery in East Africa.* New York: Praeger.

Mollon, Phil. 1994. "The Impact of Evil." In Sinason 1994, 136–47.

Monter, E. William. 1976. *Witchcraft in France and Switzerland: The Border-lands during the Reformation.* Ithaca: Cornell University Press.

————. 1993. "Les enfants au sabbat: bilan provisoire." In Jacques-Chaquin and Préaud 1993, 383–88.

Moody, Edward J. 1974. "Magical Therapy: An Anthropological Investigation of Contemporary Satanism." In *Religious Movements in Contemporary America.* Ed. Irving I. Zaretsky and Mark P. Leone. Princeton: Princeton University Press, 355–82.

Moore, Henrietta L., and Todd Sanders, eds. 2001. *Magical Interpretations, Material Realities: Modernity, Witchcraft, and the Occult in Postcolonial Africa.* London and New York: Routledge.

Moore, R. I. 1987. *The Formation of a Persecuting Society.* Cambridge and Oxford: Blackwell.

Morin, Edgar. 1971. *Rumour in Orléans.* Trans. Peter Green. New York: Pantheon.

Moscovici, Serge. 1987. "The Conspiracy Mentality." In *Changing Conceptions of Conspiracy.* Ed. Carl F. Graumann and Serge Moscovici. New York: Springer-Verlag, 151–69.

Muchembled, Robert. 1990. "Satanic Myths and Cultural Reality." In Ankarloo and Henningsen 1990, 139–60.

Mulhern, Sherill. 1991. "Satanism and Psychotherapy: A Rumor in Search of an Inquisition." In Richardson, Best, and Bromley 1991, 145–72.

————. 1993. "Souvenirs de sabbats au XXè siècle." In Jacques-Chaquin and Préaud 1993, 127–52.

————. 1994. "Satanism, Ritual Abuse, and Multiple Personality Disorder: A Sociological Perspective." *International Journal of Clinical and Experimental Hypnosis* 42: 265–88.

Murray, Margaret Alice. 1921. *The Witch-Cult in Western Europe.* Oxford: Clarendon.

Nagy, Àgnes A. 2002. "*Superstitio* et *Coniuratio.*" *Numen* 49: 178–92.

Nathan, Debbie. 1991. "Satanism and Child Molestation: Constructing the Ritual Abuse Scare." In Richardson, Best, and Bromley 1991, 75–94.

Nathan, Debbie, and Michael Snedeker. 1995. *Satan's Silence: Ritual Abuse and the Making of a Modern American Witch Hunt.* New York: Basic Books.

Needham, Rodney. 1978. *Primordial Characters.* Charlottesville: University Press of Virginia.

Newall, Venetia, ed. 1973. *The Witch Figure.* London and Boston: Routledge & Kegan Paul.

Newton, Michael. 1996. "Written in Blood: A History of Human Sacrifice." *Journal of Psychohistory* 24, no. 2: 104–31.

Niehaus, Isak. 2002. "Perversion of Power: Witchcraft and the Sexuality of Evil in the South African Lowveld." *Journal of Religion in Africa* 32, no. 3: 269–99.

Nippel, Wilfried. 2002. "The Construction of the 'Other.'" Trans. Antonia Nevill. In *Greeks and Barbarians*. Ed. Thomas Harrison. New York: Routledge, 278–310.

Noblitt, James Randall, and Pamela Sue Perskin. 2000. *Cult and Ritual Abuse*. Rev. ed. Westport, Conn.: Praeger.

Nock, Arthur Darby. 1972. "Greek Novels and Egyptian Religion." In Nock, *Essays on Religion and the Ancient World*. Vol. 1. Ed. Zeph Stewart. Oxford: Clarendon, 169–75.

Norton, Mary Beth. 2002. *In the Devil's Snare: The Salem Witchcraft Crisis of 1692*. New York: Knopf.

Notestein, Wallace. [1911] 1968. *A History of Witchcraft in England from 1558 to 1718*. Washington, D.C.: American Historical Association; repr. New York: Crowell.

O'Brien, Donal B. Cruise. 2000. "Satan Steps Out from the Shadows: Religion and Politics in Africa." *Africa* 70, no. 3: 520–25.

Ofshe, Richard J. 1992. "Inadvertent Hypnosis during Interrogation: False Confession due to Dissociative State; Mis-Identified Multiple Personality and the Satanic Cult Hypothesis." *International Journal of Clinical and Experimental Hypnosis* 40, no. 3: 125–56.

Ofshe, Richard, and Ethan Watters. 1994. *Making Monsters: False Memories, Psychotherapy, and Sexual Hysteria*. Berkeley: University of California Press.

Ogembo, Justus M. 2001. "Cultural Narratives, Violence, and Mother-Son Loyalty: An Exploration into Gusii Personification of Evil." *Ethos* 29: 3–29.

Ostorero, Martine, Agostino Paravicini: Bagliania, and Kathrin Utz Tremp, eds. 1999. *L'imaginaire du sabbat. Édition critique des textes les plus anciens*. Lausanne: University of Lausanne.

Overholt, Thomas W., ed. 1986. *Prophecy in Cross-Cultural Perspective*. Atlanta: Scholars Press.

Pagels, Elaine. "The Social History of Satan, the 'Intimate Enemy': A Preliminary Sketch." *Harvard Theological Review* 84, no. 2 (1991): 105–28.

Pailler, Jean-Marie. 1988. *Bacchanalia: La répression de 186 av. J.-C. à Rome et en Italie: vestiges, images, tradition*. Rome: École Française.

Parish, Jane. 1999. "The Dynamics of Witchcraft and Indigenous Shrines among the Akan." *Africa* 69, no. 3: 426–47.

Parkin, David, ed. 1985. *The Anthropology of Evil*. Cambridge and Oxford: Blackwell.

Parsons, Elsie Clews. 1982. "Witchcraft among the Pueblos: Indian or Spanish?" In Marwick 1982, 235–39.

Partridge, Christopher. 2004. "Alien Demonology: The Christian Roots of the Malevolent Extraterrestrial in UFO Religions and Abduction Spiritualities." *Religion* 34: 163–89.

Passantino, Bob, and Gretchen Passantino. 1992. "Satanic Ritual Abuse in Popular Christian Literature: Why Christians Fall for a Lie Searching for the Truth." *Journal for Theology and the Church* 20, no. 3: 299–305.

Pearlman, Laurie Anne, and Karen W. Saakvitne. 1995. *Trauma and the Therapist: Countertransference and Vicarious Traumatization in Psychotherapy with Incest Survivors*. New York: Norton.

Pocock, David. 1985. "Unruly Evil." In Parkin 1985, 42–56.

Pócs, Éva. 1999. *Between the Living and the Dead: A Perspective on Witches and Seers in the Early Modern Age*. Trans. Szilvia Rédey and Michael Webb. Budapest: Central European University Press.

Pope, Kenneth S. 1996. "Memory, abuse and science: Questioning claims about the false memory syndrome epidemic." *American Psychologist* 51: 957–74.

Praz, Mario. 1970. *The Romantic Agony*. Trans. Angus Davidson. 2nd ed. Oxford: Oxford University Press.

Pressley, Michael, and Lisa R. Grossman, eds. 1994. *Recovery of Memories of Childhood Sexual Abuse*. Applied Cognitive Psychology 8, no. 4.

Putnam, Frank W. 1991. "The Satanic Ritual Abuse Controversy." *Child Abuse and Neglect* 15: 175–79.

Raschke, Carl. 1990. *Painted Black: From Drug Killings to Heavy Metal—The Alarming True Story of How Satanism is Terrorizing Our Communities*. San Francisco: Harper and Row.

Redmayne, Alison. 1970. "Chikanga: An African Diviner with an International Reputation." In Douglas 1970, 103–28.

Remy, Nicolas. [1595] 1974. *Demonolatry*. Ed. Montague Summers. Trans. E. A. Ashwin. Secaucus, N.J.: University Books.

Richards, Audrey. 1982. "A Modern Movement of Witch-Finders." In Marwick 1982, 201–12.

Richardson, James T., Joel Best, and David G. Bromley, eds. 1991. *The Satanism Scare*. New York: De Gruyter.

Rives, James B. 1995. "Human Sacrifice Among Pagans and Christians." *Journal of Roman Studies* 85: 65–85.

Robinson, B. A. 2000. "Geraldo Rivera: Satanic Ritual Abuse and Recovered Memories." <http://www.religioustolerance.org/geraldo.htm>

Rockwell, Robert B. 1994. "One Psychiatrist's View of Satanic Ritual Abuse." *Journal of Psychohistory* 21, no. 4: 443–60.

Romm, James S. 1992. *The Edges of the Earth in Ancient Thought: Geography, Exploration, and Fiction*. Princeton: Princeton University Press.

Roper, Lyndal. 1994. *Oedipus and the Devil: Witchcraft, Sexuality, and Religion in Early Modern Europe.* London and New York: Routledge.

———. 2000. "'Evil Imaginings and Fantasies': Child-Witches and the End of the Witch Craze." *Past and Present* 167: 107–39.

Rose, Emilie P. [pseud.] 1996. *Reaching for the Light: A Guide for Ritual Abuse Survivors and Their Therapists.* Cleveland: Pilgrim.

Rowland, Robert. 1990. "'Fantasticall and Devilishe Persons': European Witch-Beliefs in Comparative Perspective." In Ankarloo and Henningsen 1990, 161–90.

Rowlands, Alison. 2001. "Witchcraft and Old Women in Early Modern Germany." *Past and Present* 173: 50–89.

Rubin, Miri. 1999. *Gentile Tales: The Narrative Assault on Late Medieval Jews.* New Haven: Yale University Press.

Sakheim, David K., and Susan E. Devine, eds. 1992. *Out of Darkness: Exploring Satanism and Ritual Abuse.* New York: Lexington Books.

Saler, Benson. 1967. "Nagual, Witch, and Sorcerer in a Quiché Village." In *Magic, Witchcraft, and Curing.* Ed. John Middleton. Austin: University of Texas Press, 69–99.

Sanday, Peggy Reeves. 1986. *Divine Hunger: Cannibalism as a Cultural System.* Cambridge: Cambridge University Press.

Scheper-Hughes, Nancy. 1996. "Theft of Life: The Globalization of Organ Stealing Rumors." *Anthropology Today* 12, no. 3: 3–11.

———. 2000. "The Global Traffic in Human Organs." *Current Anthropology* 41, no. 2: 191–211.

Schiffman, Lawrence H., and Michael D. Swartz. 1992. *Hebrew and Aramaic Incantation Texts from the Cairo Genizah.* Semitic Texts and Studies 1. Sheffield: Sheffield Academic Press.

Shaffer, Ruth E., and Louis J. Cozolino. 1992. "Adults Who Report Childhood Ritualistic Abuse." *Journal of Psychology and Theology* 20, no. 3: 188–93.

Sharpe, Jim. 1996. "The Devil in East Anglia: The Matthew Hopkins Trials Reconsidered." In *Witchcraft in Early Modern Europe: Studies in Culture and Belief.* Ed. Jonathan Barry, Marianne Hester, and Gareth Roberts. Cambridge: Cambridge University Press, 237–54.

Shaw, Rosalind. 1996. "The Politician and the Diviner: Divination and the Consumption of Power in Sierra Leone." *Journal of Religion in Africa* 36, no. 1: 30–55.

Shupe, Anson, and David G. Bromley. 1995. "The Evolution of Modern American AntiCult Ideology: A Case Study in Frame Extension." In *America's Alternative Religions.* Ed. Timothy Miller. Albany: State University of New York Press.

Simpson, Jacqueline. 1996. "Witches and Witchbusters." *Folklore* 107: 5–18.

Sinason, Valerie, ed. 1994. *Treating Survivors of Satanist Abuse*. London and New York: Routledge.

Sluhovsky, Moshe. 1996. "A Divine Apparition or Demonic Possession? Female Agency and Church Authority in Demonic Possession in Sixteenth-Century France." *Sixteenth Century Journal* 27, no. 4: 1039–55.

———. 2002. "The Devil in the Convent." *American Historical Review* 107, no. 5: 1379–1411.

Smith, Jonathan Z. 1978. "Towards Interpreting Demonic Powers in Hellenistic and Roman Antiquity." In *Aufstieg und Niedergang der römischen Welt* 2.16.1, Berlin and New York: De Gruyter, 425–39.

———. 1987. "The Domestication of Sacrifice." In Hammerton-Kelley 1987, 191–205.

———. 2004. *Relating Religion: Essays in the Study of Religion*. Chicago: University of Chicago Press.

Smith, Michelle, and Lawrence Pazder. 1980. *Michelle Remembers: The True Story of a Year-Long Contest between Innocence and Evil*. New York: Congdon and Lattès.

Spanos, Nicholas P., Cheryl A. Burgess, and Melissa Faith Burgess. 1994. "Past-Life Identities, UFO Abductions, and Satanic Ritual Abuse: The Social Construction of Memories." *International Journal of Clinical and Experimental Hypnosis* 42: 433–46.

Stephens, Walter. 2002. *Demon Lovers: Witchcraft, Sex, and the Crisis of Belief*. Chicago: University of Chicago Press.

Stevens, Phillips, Jr. 1991. "The Demonology of Satanism: An Anthropological View." In Richardson, Best, and Bromley 1991, 21–39.

Stewart, Charles. 1991. *Demons and the Devil: Moral Imagination in Modern Greek Culture*. Princeton: Princeton University Press.

Stirrat, R. L. 1977. "Demonic Possession in Roman Catholic Sri Lanka." *Anthropological Research* 33, no. 2: 133–57.

———. 1992. *Power and Religiosity in a Post-Colonial Setting: Sinhala Catholics in Contemporary Sri Lanka*. Cambridge: Cambridge University Press.

Strack, Hermann L. [1909] 1971. *The Jew and Human Sacrifice: Human Blood and Jewish Ritual*. 8th ed. Trans. Henry Blanchamp. London: Cope and Fenwick; repr. New York: Benjamin Blom.

Strickland, Debra Higgs. 2003. *Saracens, Demons, Jews: Making Monsters in Medieval Art*. Princeton: Princeton University Press.

Stroup, Karen Leigh. 1996. "The Rediscovery of Evil: An Analysis of the Satanic Ritual Abuse Phenomenon." Ph.D. dissertation, Vanderbilt University.

Swartz, Marc J. 1982. "Modern Conditions and Witchcraft/Sorcery Accusations." In Marwick 1982, 391–400.

Taussig, Michael. 1987. *Shamanism, Colonialism, and the Wild Man: A Study in Terror and Healing.* Chicago: University of Chicago Press.

———. 1993. *Mimesis and Alterity: A Particular History of the Senses.* New York and London: Routledge.

Thigpen, Corbett H., and Hervey M. Cleckley. 1984. "On the Incidence of Multiple Personality Disorder: A Brief Communication." *International Journal of Clinical and Experimental Hypnosis* 32, no. 2: 63–66.

Thoden van Velzen, Bonno, and Imeka Van Wetering. 2001. "Dangerous Creatures and the Enchantment of Modern Life." In Clough and Mitchell 2001, 17–42.

Thomas, Keith 1970. "The Relevance of Social Anthropology to the Historical Study of English Witchcraft." In Douglas 1970, 47–79.

———. 1971. *Religion and the Decline of Magic.* New York: Scribner's.

Trachtenberg, Joshua. 1943. *The Devil and the Jews: The Medieval Conception of the Jew and Its Relation to Modern Anti-Semitism.* Philadelphia: Jewish Publication Society.

Trevor-Roper, H. R. 1969. *The European Witch-Craze of the Sixteenth and Seventeenth Centuries and Other Essays.* New York: Harper and Row.

Twitchell, James B. 1985. *Dreadful Pleasures: An Anatomy of Modern Horror.* New York: Oxford University Press.

Urban, Hugh B. 2003. "The Power of the Impure: Transgression, Violence and Secrecy in Bengali Śākta Tantra and Modern Western Magic." *Numen* 50: 269–308.

Van Beek, Walter E. A. 1994. "The Innocent Sorcerer: Coping with Evil in Two African Societies." In *Religion in Africa: Experience and Expression*, Ed. Thomas D. Blakely, Walter E. A. van Beek, and Dennis L. Thomson. London: Currey.

Victor, Jeffrey S. 1993. *Satanic Panic: The Creation of a Contemporary Legend.* Chicago and LaSalle Ill.: Open Court.

———. 1998. "Social Construction of Satanic Ritual Abuse and the Creation of False Memories." In De Rivera and Sarbin 1998, 191–216.

Wakefield, Walter L., and Austin P. Evans. 1991. *Heresies of the High Middle Ages.* New York: Columbia University Press.

Walker, Anita M., and Edmund H. Dickerman. 2001. "A Notorious Woman: Possession, Witchcraft, and Sexuality in Seventeenth-Century Provence." *Historical Reflections* 27, no. 1: 1–26.

West, Harry G., and Todd Sanders, eds. 2003. *Transparency and Conspiracy: Ethnographies of Suspicion in the New World Order.* Durham, N.C.: Duke University Press.

Westerlund, David. 2003. "Spiritual Beings as Agents of Illness." In *African Spirituality: Forms, Meanings, and Expressions*. Ed. Jacob K. Olupona. New York: Crossroad, 152–75.

Whitehead, Neil L., 2002. *Dark Shamans: Kanaimà and the Poetics of Violent Death*. Durham, N.C.: Duke University Press.

Whitmore, John 1995. "Religious Dimensions of the UFO Abductee Experience." In *The Gods Have Landed: New Religions from Other Worlds*, 65–84. Ed. by James R. Lewis. Albany: State University of New York Press.

Widdowson, John. 1973. "The Witch as Frightening and Threatening Figure." In Newall 1973, 200–20.

Wilken, Robert L. 1984. *The Christians as the Romans Saw Them*. New Haven: Yale University Press.

Williams, Michael Allen. 1996. *Rethinking "Gnosticism": An Argument for Dismantling a Dubious Category*. Princeton: Princeton University Press.

Willis, R. G. 1968. "Kamcape: An Anti-Sorcery Movement in South-West Tanzania." *Africa* 38: 1–15.

———. 1970. "Instant Millennium: The Sociology of African Witch-cleansing Cults." In Douglas 1970, 129–39.

Wilson, K. B. 1992. "Cults of Violence and Counter-Violence in Mozambique." *Journal of Southern African Studies* 18: 527–84.

Winkler, Jack. 1980. "Lollianos and the Desperadoes." *Journal of Hellenic Studies* 100: 155–81.

Winter, E. H. 1963. "The Enemy Within: Amba Witchcraft and Sociological Theory." In Middleton and Winter 1963, 277–99.

Wright, Lawrence. 1994. *Remembering Satan: A Case of Recovered Memory and the Shattering of an American Family*. New York: Knopf.

Yamba, C. Bawa. 1997. "Cosmologies in Turmoil: Witchfinding and AIDS in Chiawa, Zambia." *Africa* 67, no. 2: 200–223.

Young, Walter C., Roberta G. Sachs, Bennett G. Braun, and Ruth T. Watkins. 1991. "Patients Reporting Ritual Abuse in Childhood: A Clinical Syndrome. Report of 37 Cases." *Child Abuse and Neglect* 15: 181–89.

Youngson, Sheila C. 1994. "Ritual Abuse: The Personal and Professional Cost for Workers." In Sinason 1994, 292–302.

Zika, Charles. 2003. *Exorcising our Demons: Magic, Witchcraft and Visual Culture in Early Modern Europe*. Studies in Medieval and Reformation Thought 91. Leiden: Brill.

Index